AF506061

Censoring Translation

Censoring Translation

Censorship, Theatre, and the Politics of Translation

Michelle Woods

continuum

Continuum International Publishing Group

The Tower Building   80 Maiden Lane
11 York Road   Suite 704
London SE1 7NX   New York NY 10038

www.continuumbooks.com

© Michelle Woods, 2012

All rights reserved. No part of this book may be reproduced, stored in a retrieval system, or transmitted, in any form or by any means, electronic, mechanical, photocopying, recording, or otherwise, without the permission of the publishers.

British Library Cataloguing-in-Publication Data
A catalogue record for this book is available from the British Library.

ISBN: 978-1-4411-8585-3 (hardcover)
978-1-4411-0057-3 (paperback)

Library of Congress Cataloging-in-Publication Data
Woods, Michelle, 1972–
Censoring Translation: Censorship, Theatre, and the Politics of
Translation / Michelle Woods.
p. cm.
Summary: "Looks at the explicit and implicit forms of censorship to which literature in translation is vulnerable"– Provided by publisher.
Includes bibliographical references and index.
ISBN 978-1-4411-8585-3 (hardcover) – ISBN 1-4411-8585-2 (hardcover) –
ISBN 978-1-4411-0057-3 (paperback) – ISBN 1-4411-0057-1 (paperback)
1. Theatre–Censorship. 2. Drama–Translating–Political aspects.
3. Drama–Censorship. 4. Havel, Václav–Translations.
5. Havel, Václav–Censorship. I. Title.
PN2042.W66 2012
418'.042–dc23
2011043969

Typeset by Newgen Imaging Systems Pvt Ltd, Chennai, India
Printed in the United States of America

For
Michael David Reisman
and
Liam Woods,
both of them

CONTENTS

ACKNOWLEDGMENTS

Many people have been incredibly kind to lend their time, thoughts, expertise, and support. The book would not have been possible without them. I'd like to thank Haaris Naqvi, who was interested from the start. And the Irish Fulbright Commission and Tanya Chebotarev at the Bakhmeteff Archive, Columbia University, where much of the initial research for the book was conducted. I'd also like to thank the Ústav pro českou literaturu, especially Professors Pavel Janáček, Michael Wögerbauer, and Petr Šámal. Also, with much gratitude, Zuzana Malá. Elaine and Charles Hallett were very helpful in supplying a personal picture of Vera Blackwell, and a wonderful conversation with Marie Winn gave invaluable background to the translation experience. My department at New Paltz was unwaveringly supportive and generous; I would particularly like to thank Professors Tom Olsen and Vicki Tromanhauser. Also, my three intrepid research assistants, and inspiring students: Krista Feichtinger, Ricky Harnden, and Leslie Green. Some material included here first appeared in a slightly different version as "Václav Havel and the Expedient Politics of Translation." *New Theatre Quarterly* 26.1 (2010): 3–15. My thanks to Gwen Orel for her expertise on the theatre and on Havel, and her friendship.

Writing this book brought me back continually to a spontaneous drive across Europe in December 1989 with my mother and brother, Yvonna Woods and Martin Woods, that ended in Prague, ringing in the new year, the new decade, and the new President on Wenceslas Square. And my father, Liam Woods, predicting a year earlier that it would happen. For them, Alma Mora, Liam Woods Mora, Monika, and Klara Homolová. And most of all, for my husband, Michael Reisman, who makes everything possible.

PREFACE

I think theatre should always be somewhat suspect.

VÁCLAV HAVEL

Asked about sexual censorship on the British stage, Kenneth Tynan uttered the word "fuck" for the first time on British television. Three years later, in 1968, official government censorship of the theatre in Britain ended. The following year, Tynan produced a revue, *Oh! Calcutta!* with contributions from Samuel Beckett, Sam Shepard, and John Lennon that involved long stretches of nudity from the cast and that ran for 20 years off-Broadway. Tynan claimed that "We are not trying to make a revolution" with the play, but it was a challenge to the prevailing tastes and morals of the British and American theatre world (Rich 1989). A few years later John Lennon questioned the revolutionary nature of Tynan's provocations, arguing that "the whole bullshit bourgeois scene is exactly the same . . . Kenneth Tynan's making a fortune out of the word 'fuck' " (Sandbrook 2006: xxiii).

The incidents are revealing about censorship and the theatre, most obviously that until recent times overt censorship existed in British and American theatres and that this censorship was effectively challenged and overturned by strong voices in the theatre community, such as Tynan's. But the "fuck" episode and *Oh! Calcutta!* also reveal that the fight against censorship can also be a profitable enterprise both in financial terms and in those of notoriety, in which the redemptive narrative against censorship is co-opted for financial gain.

Tynan came to regret that he would be remembered only for saying "fuck" on TV (Kathleen Tynan 1988: 236) and for the play which he felt was transformed into "a flesh show" (p. 283), perhaps realizing that his instincts for transgression and challenging the "Establishment" were serving to uphold it, providing a titillating safety valve rather than revolution. The provocation lay not in the content, but in the initially conceived aesthetics of the play, a sharp erotic revue collaborated on by avant-garde artists and directed by Harold Pinter. It became "a rousing celebration of the body beautiful" (p. 285), which fed into the zeitgeist of the sexual revolution, thereby not challenging what was quickly becoming the norm. The NYPD vice squad "agreed not to prosecute" (p. 284) and the play, over the years, made $360 million (p. 285).

In a less extravagant gesture, but potentially more upsetting to cultural norms, Tynan's championing of avant-garde and European theatre for the English stage was then at its height in both his work as dramaturg at the English National Theatre and as the influential reviewer for *The Observer* newspaper. In 1965, he traveled to Prague having heard rumours of a burgeoning theatre scene there, an "exhilarating" trip he would repeat the following year; his wife Kathleen wrote that here "was the model for the revolutionary future in Western Europe, or so Ken believed, until hindsight made a fool of him" (p. 247). But it was more than politics that attracted Tynan to Czechoslovakia; in a theatre and film scene that was subject to totalitarian censorship, he discovered a place of aesthetic experiment where "this is emphatically the age of the art house" (Tynan 1967: 102).

In a long article on the Czech theatre and film scene for *The New Yorker*, published in early 1967, Tynan seemed intrigued by the artistic possibilities opening up in Prague due to an easing on censorship and the positive effect of state subsidies (which were also used as a tool of censorship). "Temporarily uninhibited by economic and ideological pressures," Tynan wrote, "the performing arts have had time to consider why they exist and what human purpose they should serve" (p. 102). Tynan, who was involved in the setting up of a state-subsidized English National Theatre and in the repeal of the Lord Chamberlain's Act at this time, was surveying something of a utopian possibility in Prague where artists had figured out how to work with overt censorship and totalitarianism; "they know how to rebel," he writes admiringly, "while seeming to conform, so that dumb insolence would pass for obedience" (p. 99).

The impact of political repression and censorship gave theatre relevance to the society in which it functioned: "It is virtually impossible for a Czech artist to make a statement that has no political resonance," he wrote. "In Prague, even a Surrealist extravaganza like Jarry's "Ubu Roi" can be interpreted as an assault on the dictatorship of the *Lumpenproleteriat.* "No matter how remote a playwright's symbols and metaphors may be, the audience translates them into terms of practical politics and current events" (p. 102). Small theatres like the Theatre on the Balustrade, Tynan notes, were playing to 100 percent capacity.

Nevertheless, Tynan was aware of the dangers of romanticizing and misinterpreting what the importance of these plays was, as well as the reductive readings that might tempt a Western visitor. Of reading only political messages in the Czech plays, he writes: "This is a game that outsiders should play with some care; the natives tend to get nettled when tourists insist on finding parabolical significance in trapeze acts or revivals of 'Charley's Aunt' " (p. 102). His subversive self-identification as a colonial "tourist" telling the "natives" what their plays are about serves as a warning to his readers: that there is something perhaps exotic and attractive about this artistic world as a politically charged one, but this is not the entire story. A need to find political dissidence in theatre behind the Iron Curtain may say as much about what the "tourist" desires as what the "natives" are saying.

Tynan, all through the article, is viewing his own world as well as Prague, thinking about how politics, economics, and censorship affects aesthetics at home and abroad, rather than presenting Prague as the photographic negative of the free West. Surprised when he asks a Czech actor visiting London whether it was his first time abroad, the actor gives him "a sharp lesson in comparative political semantics" and replies "Oh no, this is my first time behind the Iron Curtain" (p. 102); in mentioning this in his article, Tynan seems to be turning the spotlight back on England from the vantage-point of Prague. And not only England, but also his readership in the United States—in relating the plot of Jan Němec's film, *A Report on the Party and the Guests*, often read as an allegory of the political situation in Czechoslovakia, he writes:

> The relevance of the message extends far beyond Czech audiences. Would you, despite the fact you disapprove of American policy in Vietnam, nevertheless accept an invitation to dinner at the White House or No. 10 Downing Street? If so, Němec is looking in your direction, and you may very well be the first to blink. (p. 122)

Tynan's article was published in *The New Yorker* days before Martin Luther King gave a famous antiwar speech in New York in which he explicitly connected questions of race, poverty, and colonialism with American actions in Vietnam. He argued that the American system needed to prove itself as better than it was in order to truly defeat any Communist threat. King would be murdered a year later, followed by the assassination of Bobby Kennedy. As a magazine, *The New Yorker* had become increasingly political in the upheavals of the sixties, publishing its first articles on race by James Baldwin (Yagoda 2001: 316) and on Vietnam where its "fire-and-brimstone fervor on the issue" stood out among media outlets (p. 360). Between 1966 and 1971, ad pages in the magazine fell by 40 percent and annual profits by 66 percent (p. 364). The "incongruity" behind the more radical "rhetoric and the advertisements sharing the *New Yorker*'s pages with it," Ben Yagoda writes, "had finally reached a level too great to sustain" (p. 362). One reader, irate at their attacks on "our great President, Mr. Nixon" wrote: "All of your format, and certainly your advertisements, are designed to appeal to the better class of decent people. If you subscribe to the liberalism which has done so much harm to our country, you should at least not allow it to show so obviously" (p. 363).

Tynan's article on Czech theatre, translating as it does another world from behind the Iron Curtain, is squeezed in between such ads for "the better class of decent people." These ads regale the contemporary reader with a narrative about the aspirational world being sold to the readers of the magazine: white, wealthy, traditional, and insular. This is a world of golf outings, cruises, country clubs, and weekends in the country, the "gracious," "smashing," "elegant" world of English Leather aftershave, and Keen's English chophouse, steak dinners and Martinis, Bobby Darin at the Copacabana, free parking at the Algonquin. If the contemporary world intrudes at all, it is in the new man-made fabrics: this is the new world of triacetate and nylon, polyester, Fortrel, rayon, and Dacron worn by lithe, white women who live in fictional towns: "Sportempos, Suburbia U.S.A." (Tynan 1967: 105). The only sign that there might be any other kind of racial demographic in New York is an advertisement for the famous Japanese restaurant, Benihana's, with a photograph of a Japanese man smiling. Just in case you're unnerved, the jaunty ad reassures the reader that however culturally different the sushi restaurant might be ("Ever heard of a fine restaurant without a kitchen? More chefs than waitresses?"), the "Japanese maitre d' is named Rocky" (p. 112). The domestication of the outside world is even more evident in an ad on the final page of Tynan's article. It shows a large American couple arriving at customs grasping trunks, and implausibly, a giraffe. "Why lose time with 'strange' customs?" the ad shouts, "With Percival Tours you can TRAVEL EVERYWHERE and be lazy about it" (p. 123).

This commercially imagined America, powerful enough to immunize and domesticate "strange customs" literally encroaches on the text of Tynan's thoughtful and nuanced cultural tourism, his attempt to smuggle in Prague for the *New Yorker* readership in a way that might, even slightly, challenge the norms of America, the product, which offers freedom of choice if not freedom of means. The blatant equation of consumerism with identity—the aspirational ability to buy into the WASP world that represents cultural and monetary power—sets the parameters of these norms, muscling the vision of the foreign into narrow columns. Tynan's worthy wares—his portraits of Czech theatre artists and filmmakers—are displayed because they are topical and, ultimately, because they serve to boost (despite Tynan's *caveat*) the notion of a dystopian negation of the world on offer in the margins of his text.

The "star turn" of one of the small theatres in Prague is Václav Havel, "a dapper, utterly assured man of thirty with straw-colored hair and the physical shape of a bullet. In a well-kempt way," Tynan adds, "he exudes integrity and moral resilience" (p. 114). Tynan lauds Havel's two hit plays, *The Garden Party* and *The Memorandum* as responses to "de-Stalinization" (p. 114) but Tynan, in his official capacity of dramaturg, had turned down Havel's plays for the English National Theatre: "*Memorandum* has been the rounds of this organisation," he wrote to Havel's translator Vera Blackwell in 1965, "and I'm afraid the general opinion is that—for English consumption—it doesn't quite work" (VBA Memo: 1, 10/11/65). Behind the scenes, Tynan had fought for at least a late-night reading of Havel's play (Kathleen Tynan 1988: 225), but Laurence Olivier overruled him.

Why lose time with strange customs? The problem with translated plays is twofold: they tend to be less commercially viable than English-language plays and they often do not fit into domestic traditions or expectations of the form. Translations only seemed to work if they bolstered the norms of the receiving culture, if "Sportempos, U.S.A" was somehow validated by the translated work. The story of translating Havel's plays into English is mainly a political one: the "dissident" playwright let the West peek through the Iron Curtain and confirmed what it suspected. But Havel's plays were "antipolitical" and never expressly dealt with the contemporary political situation; they were politicized in the West because of demands by theatres, reviewers, agents, and audiences to read them as such. It is only as political plays that these translations could reach the English-language stage and be commercially viable.

Havel, as Milan Kundera wrote, had a "life like a work of art" (Kundera 1990: 16), an intellectual playwright who led his country through a peaceful "Velvet Revolution" in 1989 and from Communist post-totalitarianism to democracy in the 1990s. He became a political figure, acting as President of Czechoslovakia and the Czech Republic from 1989 to 2003. But his plays have largely been forgotten or dismissed as political relics of the Cold War: "Don't give up your day job, Mr. President" one British paper cried, in their review of a 2008 revival of two of his plays (Letts 2008). But has the West misread Havel's plays by deeming them and producing them as political for its own ideological and economic ends? And does this constitute a form of censorship?

Havel became a poster-boy for free-speech in the Cold War era—literally: a 1980 "Havel Afternoon" produced by the British Writers' Guild shows a picture of Havel in its program with bars superimposed on his face that turn out to be, at closer glance, pens. Havel was in prison for cowriting the petition, Charter 77, which asked for free speech rights. But this portrayal of Havel as a saint or martyr was pure "kitsch" accompanying a translation of one of Havel's plays, *Protest*, that had been aesthetically disemboweled to leave in the play what the adaptor thought were the relevant political bits.[1] Banned in 1970 as a writer in his homeland, Havel and his main translator, Vera Blackwell, discovered a strange resistance to his plays in the United Kingdom and America, despite nominal support for his work against censorship. The redemptive narrative of the banned and imprisoned playwright gaining a voice on the stage in the West concealed a very complex relationship to his plays on the English-language stage. Western theatres required changes and adaptations—beyond inevitable acculturation—that even the Czech censors had not required in the 1960s.

The history behind the censorship of Havel's plays in Communist Czechoslovakia and the constraints on the English-language translations in Britain and America challenges the "David-and-Goliath" (Coetzee 1996:

---

[1] "My enemy is kitsch, not Communism!" Milan Kundera's character Sabina replies "infuriated" at a German exhibition of her paintings where "she saw a picture of herself with a drawing of barbed wire superimposed on it" (Kundera 1985, 254).

118) notion of censorship and the notion that censorship inevitably happens somewhere else, often in societies that seem ideological negatives of our own. The history of the translations also questions why we translate plays and how we translate them, whether in these translations we search for succor rather than strangeness. And, whether in searching for the familiar we are subject to a commodified cultural tourism of the mind, a tourism that requires an abdication of choice and curiosity, where we can travel everywhere and be lazy about it because it just looks and sounds like here.

Tynan rocked the quiet censorship of the British establishment by using the word "fuck," on TV, a linguistic challenge to moral norms (norms and a censorship still followed today by American network television). But John Lennon succinctly questioned the "bullshit" moral and intellectual seriousness of the motivation behind this challenge, with the sense that Tynan didn't want to change the establishment as much as he wanted to be part of it. The translations Tynan commissioned and reviewed, on the other hand, contained more potential threat to cultural, if not moral, norms. Much less obvious than the live TV expletive, these plays offered new forms of expression and thinking that tended to differ from the social realism of British theatre.

Like his hero, Samual Beckett, Havel's mainly abstract plays are predicated on his obsession with language and its failure to adequately convey human experience, its imprecision. But Havel is interested in how humans use language and how inhuman language uses us. Language can be a prison, one that seems like power, forcing us to censor experience rather than sense it. The general resistance to Havel's plays when they were translated into English failed to acknowledge this central element. This failure suggests two things: first, that producers, directors, critics, and audiences had already decided that the plays were about dissident Cold War politics and therefore were viable products, didactically and commercially, for the English-language stage; and, secondly, that these readers failed to see that the plays had censorship wrought into their very fundaments, not simply as textual protests against the conditions of censorship they were written in, but as meditations on where censorship also resides: in us.

Introduction: Contexts

On translation, censorship, theatre, Václav Havel, and Vera Blackwell

It is obvious that while so much attention has been given to the "loss of poetics" in translation, it should in future be directed to the politics of it.

SIRKKU AALTONEN

Surrounded by a delighted audience, John Roberts, the director of the Royal Shakespeare Company, sat watching a performance of Václav Havel's *The Garden Party/Zahradni slavnost* at the small Prague theatre, Divadlo na zábradli, in April 1964. The play, an absurdist investigation of "language as a barrier to knowing and realizing anything at all" (Goetz-Stankiewicz 1979: 48), was a sensation in Prague because the audience recognized that the play's humorous critique of language as an existential trap described the world they lived in, where language was "the weapon of the totalitarian system" (Rocamora 2004: 46). As all plays were subject to official censorship, an outright satire of the neo-Stalinist regime would never have reached the stage; Havel took another route, examining the mechanics of language and power in a decontextualized setting, injecting it with enough hermeneutical ambiguity to satisfy and provoke. Roberts, who spoke not a word of Czech, was struck by the infectious atmosphere: "[J]udging by the audience reaction, it is extremely funny" he wrote a week later (2/22/64), and commissioned a Czech émigré in London, Vera Blackwell, to translate the play into English for possible production with the Royal Shakespeare Company (RSC). She translated the play, her translation was adapted by an English playwright, NF Simpson, and the RSC never performed it. It wouldn't receive its premiere on the professional English stage for another 13 years, by which time Havel was more famous in the West as a dissident than a playwright.

For what motivated the interest in Havel's plays has also resulted in a resistance to them, namely the political context. This political interest in, and reading of, the plays is also tied to commercial impact and commercialized decision making surrounding the translations and productions of the plays. After all, censorship sells. Western interest in Czechoslovak literature and film of the 1960s was predicated on the narrative of resistance to neo-Stalinism, to the prospect of a cultural thaw motoring a political thaw behind the Iron Curtain, and ultimately, to the validation of Western democracy. In this schema, John Roberts, sitting in the Divadlo na zábradlí, needs no Czech to understand the relevance of the laughter around him; it signals to him that it will be relevant to a Western audience because it signals dissent. It is only when he actually understands the words, after reading the translation, that he regards it to be a "tricky play" and one that needed to be "adapted for an English audience." So, *The Garden Party* survives any cuts in the Czech censor's office but must somehow be changed once it crosses through the Iron Curtain. Roberts' discomfort with the plays, as we shall see, would reflect a general discomfort with them that moved between thinking the plays too locally contextualized in the politics of the time, but, at the same time, too abstract in form and content, and, thus, not overtly political enough to satisfy expectations of dissident literature. In other words, Havel's plays were only relevant when they filled a particular domestic need rather than being sought out for their artistic merit. As early as 1979, Marketa Goetz-Stankiewicz wrote that:

> It is fair to say that most critics and scholars, eager to point out Havel's incontestable political relevance have tended to shortchange the wider implications of his plays and pay insufficient attention to his artistic qualities [. . .] they have spent their energies on the political (though Havel might call it antipolitical) aspects of his writings [. . .] none has really tried to formulate the relevance of Havel's work for a Western democracy. (Goetz-Stankiewicz 1979: 39)

Why not? Sending her test translation of *The Garden Party* to Roberts, Blackwell wrote that a literal translation of the play was impossible because "the many verbal inventions [. . .] are in themselves the main force that moves the play, and thus (as the program says) are really not only a character in the play but its protagonist, its 'Villain' " (4/16/64). As such, she adds, "it was necessary, therefore, to try to adapt them a great deal so as to preserve some of that motive force and flavour of the original Czech 'Newspeak' " (Blackwell 4/16/64). There are several points of interest here: Blackwell emphasizes the importance of language as an area of investigation in the play—rather than local politics or the political context; she touches on the notion of the "antipolitical"—that if this is a protest play, it is a protest against the dangers of language; she notes, then, that the only way to deal with this radical investigation of language is to "adapt [the phrases] a great deal." Blackwell knows that a literal translation is impossible and doubly impossible because Havel, in the play, explores the ambiguity of language and meaning, deliberately using and misusing Czech sayings, aphorisms, and quotes from Czech poets such as Vítězslav Nezval and Jaroslav Seifert. These, Blackwell knows, have to be translated on a cultural plane. Finally, and in acknowledgment of this cultural translation, she frames Havel's games with language into an English cultural lexicon by referring to George Orwell's "Newspeak," the invented, government-controlled language in his novel, 1984. Blackwell, here, is highly aware of her role in mediating the translation linguistically, culturally, and also hermeneutically, in attempting to explain to Roberts what the play is about. Her strong agency in the process is not necessarily emblematic of the expected translatorial role of the time, but it stems from a fear that the play might only be read as a dissident text and not for its artistic credibility. It seems a paradoxical position, Blackwell aware that she must necessarily change the text (in culturally adapting it) while trying to prevent it from being fundamentally changed because of the prior expectations of what the play might represent in the target culture.

Havel is an intriguing case study for analyzing the relationship between censorship and translation because of the different forms of censorships in action, both in the domestic and foreign spheres. Often when we think of censorship and literature we think of overt forms of state-imposed censorship, a kind that certainly Havel was subject to in Czechoslovakia from his first plays in the early 1960s, through to the complete ban on his work during the period of normalization in Czechoslovakia, from the Soviet invasion in 1968 to the Velvet Revolution in 1989. But other kinds of less overt censorship are at work: self-censorship (the playwright's awareness of the parameters of censoring authorities); translatorial self-censorship (domesticating the text to target language tastes); market censorship (the adaptation of the text to prevailing taste ultimately for economic reasons by publishers, producers, theatres, etc); and gendered censorship (the relegation of female translators and translations themselves to a submissive, nonessential role). Though it would be facile to blindly label all sorts of extratextual "constraints" on the plays as censorship, it is important to understand that these constraints do have an effect in presenting politicized and reductive readings of other cultures, as well as in insulating the given identity of a particular domestic culture. If "censorship acts against [. . .] what disturbs identity, system and order" (Billiani 2007: 22), translations are clearly in the firing-line because they tend to challenge the "natural" or normative order of things: in the English-speaking world, they tend to be excluded or consumed—turned into sellable artifacts and absorbed painlessly. Havel's plays were overtly censored under the Czechoslovak Communist regime, but it is also worth investigating what happened to them as they were produced in the West. Specifically in the United Kingdom and the United States, for what that might tell us about the constraints undergone by the translations there and whether we should question any normalizing tendencies that might serve ideological, political, and economic ends. Havel as a case study allows us to question why we translate, when we translate, and how we translate.

Censorship and translation

*The study of censorship has always tended to involve translations,
if only because the foreign often attracts the censor's hostility.*

NÍ CHUILLEANÁIN, Ó CUILLEANÁIN, PARRIS

Censorship, as Michaela Wolf points out, is "a term overloaded with historical memory" often identified with "repressive regimes," but she argues, "the
range of meanings of the term censorship is so complex that its meaning
cannot be restricted to the oppressive practices of autocratic government"
(Wolf 2002: 45). Wolf articulates a growing strand in Translation Studies
that is interested in overt censorship and its effect on translation but also in
the more subtle censoring of texts in "the freest of nations" (Merkle 2002:
9). Denise Merkle argues that:

> censorship is not limited to oppressive autocracies . . . [it is] not the exclu-
> sive purview of explicitly autocratic regimes [. . .] the covert censorship at
> work in the free democracies of late modernity characterized by expand-
> ing globalization, though at time more difficult to detect, is nonetheless,
> at times insidiously, pervasive. (Merkle 2002: 9–10)

Merkle and others have built on Pierre Bourdieu's notion of structural
censorship that posits an "implicit social control" (Billiani 2007: 8) linking "censorship and norms in discourse" (Merkle 2002: 15). It is the social
structure of a given field that "repress[es] transgressions of the linguistic
code, controls discourse by controlling both the access to the means of
expression and the form that expression takes" (Merkle 2002: 15). Maria
Tymoczko explains these controls as:

> external constraints, a partial list might include institutions (for
> example, the government, laws related to censorship, media stan-
> dards and educational standards); the patron and the patronage sys-
> tem (for example, the boss, the publisher and so forth), as well as the
> definition of an assigned task; material conditions, including economic
> resources (which constrain the number and range of translations, the
> dissemination of translations and so forth, and, hence, acts as a form of
> censorship); social norms, linguistic norms, textual norms, and trans-
> lation norms; structures of language, including category formations,
> that constitute reality for ourselves and our audiences; the conceptual
> metaphors we live by; discourses; ideologies; and cultural practices.
> (Tymoczko 2008: 38)

In linking censorship with imposition of norms in expression and discourse,
Tymoczko identifies the translator as one of the nodes of potential censorship,

subject not only to these "external constraints" but also to "internal" ones too, having internalized the codes of dominant discourse, the:

> structures of language and metaphors that we accept without question; discourses and ideologies that we buy into and approve of; and the extent to which we accept and acquiesce in dominant views either because of our subject positions or a perception that such acceptance brings benefits of various types. (p. 38)

Thus, the translator can be regarded to be a "tacit censor" (Gibbels 2008: 74) or subject, in Tymoczko's terms to "self-censorship" (Tymoczko 2008). Having internalized the norms of the dominant group of a given culture, and working in a profession with little symbolic or material power, translators tend to stick to the "domain of the sayable" (Gibbels 2008: 73). Gibbels uses the example of four German translations of Mary Wollstonecraft's seminal feminist text, *A Vindication of the Rights of Women*, two of which were produced under conditions of overt censorship and two of which were not. She discovered that the two translations undertaken during periods of no state censorship made significant tonal changes to Wollstonecraft's text, because of internalized dominant social norms. In late nineteenth-century Germany, this affected the translator because of her female and Jewish identity. And in late twentieth-century Germany, "market dictates" affected the translation: the "[p]ressure of time, lack of careful editing and proofreading and the wishes of the publishing house for a fresh and modern text all imposed" on the text (Gibbels 2008: 61). Gibbels argues that these norms, in effect, inoculated the target culture from an "heretical" text, one that might challenge those exact dominant norms. The heresy of a given text may not be limited to ideological content, but also to different cultural, linguistic, or aesthetic norms. As Tymoczko writes, "translation is how newness enters the world. It is this newness that so often gets suppressed by censorship and self-censorship" (Tymoczko 2008: 45).

Tymoczko makes a case for the positive side of "self-censorship" in arguing that it is an indicator of the translator's agency. Traditionally seen as an "invisible" figure (Venuti 2008), whose work is elided from literary discourse, the translator has also been seen as something of a victim figure, underappreciated, badly paid, and without power. This "lack of legitimate competence and authority," argues Gibbels, "inclines translators [. . .] to make concessions" (Gibbels 2008: 73). However, as Tymoczko argues, the case is less black and white as the asymmetrical power relationship between author/translator, publisher/translator, and reviewer/translator might suggest. She uses the example of Lady Augusta Gregory, W. B. Yeats's partner in the Abbey Theatre, a particularly visible and "mobilized" (Tymoczko 2008: 36) translator, who recognized that translation was a political tool that could enhance Irish nationhood in providing a visible cultural heritage. At the same time Gregory and other Irish translators censored the overtly sexual and scatological nature of the early Irish material "because they confirmed nineteenth-century English stereotypes of and prejudices about the Irish that had been used to justify English rule and exploitation of Ireland" (p. 34). Tymoczko suggests that this is a "strategic self-censorship" (p. 36) under which "translators must prioritize and pick a strategy to deal with oppressive or coercive cultural constraints" (p. 36). As translation is necessarily a metonymic activity, it coalesces with a metonymy of resistance. In other words, translation necessarily changes a text, with the translator interpreting signification; as such, they can actively prioritize certain aspects of the translation.

But, of course, Gregory was also independently wealthy; translators often do not have such a blatant choice in the tone or ideology of a translation and have to acquiesce to market demands. As Gibbels writes:

> The only way to resist is to produce heretical discourse themselves, which, however, does not seem to be generally honoured by the market [. . .] until [translators] get the pay and the status of authorized speakers, they will be inclined to accede to the order of what is sayable in the given fields—and continue to be tacit censors. (Gibbels 2008: 74)

Tymoczko does suggest something of a strategy for translators, asking them not to be entirely submissive and to "develop a habit of self-reflexivity about how and why and for whom they translate, and to be aware of the choices they are making" (p. 38). Such a call for active agency may acknowledge that compromises necessarily have to be made, but that a translator can decide to choose the extent to which their beliefs, ideologies and identity might have an impact on the interpretive decisions they make.

Along with translators, other agents in the process have an effect on what is or is not permitted in a translation—editors, publishers, directors, producers, funders etc.—based on particular agendas or tastes. Instead of a "normative and abstract top–down formula" (Billiani 2007: 9) for translation and the static "notions of norms" (p. 8), Francesca Billiani argues that this network of agents can effect a performative and fluid form of "polymorphous" censorship practices, which may differ from culture to culture and era to era, in dictatorships and also "seemingly 'neutral' scenarios" (p. 3). Institutional and individual censorship can coexist and often serve to determine or uphold a national narrative or national tastes. "Censorship of foreign texts," she writes, "cannot help but act according to the wide national patterns of taste, or in other words to what is perceived as the sought after national textuality" (p. 15). This "active" censorship determines "dominant and subordinate discourses" in a given society at a given time, and determines the cultural, symbolic, and commercial capital of texts (p. 22). Foreign texts may not, in themselves, conform to the cultural, political, moral, or ideological tastes of an individual or a state at a particular time and are often rewritten to conform to them (Lefevere 1992: 14). Forms of "market censorship" (Jansen 1991; Keane 1991) apply to translations also, because of their lack of commercial value; either they must be made to conform to commercial norms, be subsidized, or not be translated at all (Venuti 1998).

The relationship between the different agents in the translation process, and the fluidity of censorship practices therein are productively studied via archives, because: "correspondence between [. . .] diverse cultural agents [. . .] sheds light on the process by which a certain aesthetic, ideological and cultural understanding of reality is shaped and, more importantly, shared" (Billiani 2007: 5). In "analyzing the narratives" in archives "we can understand how a community negotiates its own identity and textuality as well as its cultural and aesthetic paradigms" (ibid). Anna Bogic provides a strong example in her study of Howard M. Parshley's 1953 translation of Simone de Beauvoir's *Le deuxième sexe*. The long-standing translation omitted huge amounts of the original text and Parshley, a professor of zoology, has been maligned because of perceived sexist editing of the text (Bogic 2011: 154–5). But letters between Parshley and his publishers, Knopf, detail a different narrative "about 'behind closed doors' decision-making" (p. 158); one in which the editors expected "clarity and simplicity, condensing and 'packaging' the book for the 'average American reader' to achieve the best possible sales" (Bogic 2011: 160) without a real interest or understanding of the book (p. 162). The translator, Bogic points out, is "far from being a lone *translating agent*" (pp. 160–1); he was "one of many [. . .] an executor of many other demands and impositions" (p. 161). The Knopf archives produced a similar story of editorial pressure for more commercial editing in the case of Milan Kundera's novels (Woods 2006: 27–41). Translators are often at the front line of blame for problems with translations, but archives can reveal a censorial pressure—often to do with market demands—from others in the translation network.

Finally, another group central to the question of censorship and translation are the consumers themselves: the readers and audiences of translated work. Lawrence Venuti argues that the marginalization of translations in the English-language literary market is because of their "tenuous economic value" as the "domestic reader" tends to be "narcissistic" and "self-referential" (Venuti 1998: 124); publishers point to the lack of a market for translations as a reason not to publish or to severely limit the publication of translations, thus enforcing market constraints on translations. Voting with their feet (or their wallets), readers bear some responsibility for the small amount and conservative form of the translations they consume. Venuti argues that they look for a mirror of their own beliefs and ideologies, thereby feeling somewhat threatened by anything different or strange. But, it also means that consumers have an ability to read and consume at a more active level, whether through coming to an understanding of reading as a more complex and dialogic interpretation, as J. M. Coetzee has suggested (Coetzee 1996: 147–62), or whether through a "productive censorship"—a model Brian Baer suggests in terms of understanding Soviet readers of translations in which readers decode domestic narratives in the subtexts of translations (Baer 2011: 21).

Theatre and translation

First-rate writers from abroad are now more frequently heard than they were in the past, but are all too often asked to keep their voices down.

JOSEPH FARREL

While translated literature makes up only about 3 percent of published books in the Anglo-American market, Terry Hale and Carole-Anne Upton argue that about one-eighth of reviewed theatre productions in the United Kingdom are translated works, suggesting that "the theatre is the most receptive of all the various art forms in Britain as far as translation is concerned" (Hale and Upton 2000: 1). In the United States, the figure has been about 10 percent (Zaitlin 2005: 12). The surprisingly high number reflects the important role translation plays in the identity of English-language theatre, including the formation of the English-language tradition—Hale and Upton highlight the importance of translated works for Shakespeare and the theatre tradition since then (pp. 2–3).

However, the majority of translated theatre on the English stage now, they point out, is a form of canonical foreign theatre: retranslations of the Greek classics and a form of modern canon, such as Ibsen and Chekhov (p. 5). The situation is similar in the United States, where "most" of the translated plays were "of 'classic' authors, such as Molière, Chekhov and Ibsen [. . .] only 2.25% of the total productions [were] works by still-living, foreign-language authors" (Zaitlin 2005: 12). Hale and Upton note that the few foreign plays reviewed that do not fit into this canon have often been far more transformed textually, rewritten, and clearly domesticated for the English audience (p. 6). In addition, plays are often chosen because they "are seen as capable of being brought in line with the pragmatics, and [. . .] with the social discourse, of the target society" (Aaltonen 2000: 94).

While theatre translation appears to be the most active form of literary translation, in fact what constitutes a theatre translation is the least defined in literary terms. As Joseph Farrel argues, what is defined as a translation can often be one or a mixture of three things: a literal translation, a performance version, and an adaptation (Farrel 1996: 47). Often, theatres commission a literal translation of a foreign play, or use one already existent, which is then adapted by a playwright, and then subsequently changed during rehearsals for reasons of "speakability" or "performability" (Espasa 2000: 49). Language, which may seem adequate on the page, might seem wooden when spoken, and, thus, is changed to fit into the cadence of the actor or overall play. But, as Sirkku Aaltonen points out, there is some theoretical and practical confusion about what all these terms actually refer to—"adaptation" can involve relatively tiny changes or a complete rewriting of the text (Aaltonen 2000: 45), and "the vagueness of concepts such as speakability and performability" (p. 42) can conceal deliberate rewriting of plays. This rewriting has little to do with making the language simpler, but can be related to ethnocentric assumptions about the plays and egocentric translation practices on the part of the target culture (p. 51). Cultural hegemony and asymmetry between cultures can often mean that more liberties are taken with plays that are perceived as coming from "weaker" cultures.

The play text is regarded to be much more fluid than other forms of literary work (i.e. a novel or a poem that tends to retain its textual form once published). Along with the acceptance of page to stage changes as part of the norm, the collaborative nature of theatre—with input not only from the director, but also often the writer, the actors, stage-manager, dramaturg etc., who all "construct their own readings" (Aaltonen 2000: 6)—has meant that the alteration of translations has been much more acceptable in the theatre than in other literary forms. As Laurence Boswell argues, "everyone [. . .] combines to recreate the totality of the play [. . .] The translation is a voice among voices" (Boswell 1996: 146). For the translation, just as for the play text, there is a difference, David Johnston argues, between a published text and a performance text; the "playable translation is a dramaturgical remoulding [. . .] translation for the stage is about giving form to a potential for performance. It is about writing for actors" (Johnston 1996: 58). However, though rewriting is much more acceptable in the theatre than with "printed literature" it can conceal hegemonic assumptions, so while "it is usually taken for granted that the pragmatics of the theatre should outweigh the constraints of the source text" this can serve to attenuate the foreignness of the text: "the Foreign is not of primary interest" but it is "one's own culture, one's own society and one's own theatre" that prevails (Aaltonen 2000: 75).

But, what results can be—and has been—a fruitful reimagining of source plays for a domestic audience, a version of the source play that is an imaginative act itself that speaks to a given moment in the culture the play is coming into. This has been particularly evident in, for instance, postcolonial Anglo-Irish translations of classic theatre texts (from Yeats, to Brian Friel and Seamus Heaney), in which the translations are critiques of a hegemonic idea of "Englishness"—both linguistically and culturally—and in which the translations become, in some sense, part of the Irish canon. Yeats was and Heaney is particularly attuned to the idea that translations are central to the conception of a national canon, that a sense of the "through-otherness" (Heaney 2002: 364) permeates any literature and that translations serve to open up the inherent transnationality of language and literary texts.

Heaney is an example of the star translator in the theatre field; the "new figure" of the "surrogate 'translator' " (Farrel 1996: 54), who often works from a literal translation, or crib, to produce their own version of a play. Noel Clark argues that this new fashion for "translations" by "established playwrights, more or less known to the public" (or, of course, poets and writers) is partly due to "compelling box-office reasons" (Clark 1996: 25). The "performability" of plays is often connected to "the use of the name of a well-known, often monolingual, playwright to sell the translation of a lesser-known bilingual translator" (Aaltonen 2000: 44). If it is harder to persuade an English or an American audience to go and see a translated noncanonical foreign play, the name of a star translator, often a playwright, may help to soften the blow of foreignness and act as a commercial brand.

Playwrights often also argue that they have the theatrical *nous* and knowledge to produce a sufficiently artistic version (as opposed to the literal translation from which they often work). As Brian Friel maintained in an interview: "I think it's better for the translator to be a dramatist. There are bigger truths beyond that of the literal translation" (Friel 1999: 100). David Hare also argues for the primacy of the playwright-translator because of the necessity of changes to the original source language text in theatre. If the text is inevitably going to be changed for performability on an English-language stage, then a playwright has the sense of what is needed, he has an hermeneutical understanding that gives a "tilt on the play" (Hare 1996: 137). He gives the example of his "translation" of Brecht's *Galileo*, which he cut and changed; the notoriously protective Brecht estate allowed these changes "because I am a playwright, they trusted me not to be riding a hobby-horse; they knew that I didn't *need* to do this" (p. 139). Hare, who isn't fluent in German or Italian, worked from a literal translation for both *Galileo* and Luigi Pirandello's *The Rules of the Game*, and actually produced adaptations of both.

David Johnston, interviewing Hare, points out that the published version of Hare's Pirandello translation, "you have 'translated and adapted by' on the cover, and on the inside 'version by' " (p. 143), to which Hare answers:

> I didn't use those descriptions. They stuck them on. It really made me queasy when they said "translation" because I said "I don't speak Italian, how can you say I translated it?" I asked them if they could credit the person who did the literal translation but they told me that I was better known. I know there's some commercial pressure, but I don't think that's right. But if you believe that theatre basically is created out of rhythm, then why not get a rhythm expert in to make a version of the play? (p. 143)

Hare's reply is revealing on several levels. First, his uneasiness—it made him "queasy"—in the knowledge that he wasn't actually the translator. He then apportions blame on an unnamed "they" (presumably the publishers) but passively accepts the position. He is unable to credit the original translator even in a part of the interview where he is underlining the role of the literal translator (in a book about stage translation). This reflects his realization of why the star translator necessarily eclipses the literal translator, that is, the "commercial pressure," even if he doesn't think it's "right." And, finally, he justifies his acceptance of this situation—that, after all, he should be credited with the translation, because he is the "rhythm expert" (something, presumably, to which the actual translator, is deaf).

The argument is not that Hare shouldn't adapt Brecht and Pirandello, but that, as Jonhston hints, the distinction should perhaps be made in selling these versions as versions and not as translations. Secondly, the role of the "literal" translations should be given their due. Hare assumes that it is his work in adapting the play, that is, after the translation has been made, that involves the hermeneutical decision making, the "critique of the play" (p. 137), but that assumes that the actual translation did not involve a process of interpretation, that it is not a "decision-making process [. . .] a teleological activity, whereby the translator actively intervenes and appropriates the foreign text" (Heylen 1993: 24).

As Hale and Upton point out, "there is no such thing as a 'literal' translation" (Hale and Upton 2000: 10). While the nameless "literal" translator is making a translation from one language to another, they are involved in reading and interpreting the play. As Anthony Vivis points out:

> In the process of translation, essential decisions are made during the immediate, in this case the so-called literal, translation [. . .] Interpretation also has its place in translation. If a writer has deliberately broken the grammatical rules [. . .] the translator must first work out what rules are being broken and why. Only then can he or she create an equivalent effect, or at least attempt to, in English. (Vivis 1996: 37)

The problem, Vivis argues, is that in general the English-language theatre world believes that the literal translation is just that, a simple movement of one foreign word into English, which can then be "handed over to a writer to be made speakable" (p. 37). "Literal" translators are seen as "linguistics or academics" who hide themselves in "a kind of library life" and who can "chart a course through a dictionary but are all at sea with actors" (p. 37). In other words, there is no art or interpretation attributed to a "literal" translation, perhaps willfully, because it then allows a playwright or writer to institute changes in the name of art, as opposed to recognizing the act of translation as an art in itself.

It also sets up a hegemony of writing over translation; though in some senses it elevates translation to the position of a creative act, it only does so if it is done by someone who is not a translator and implies that translators are neither creative nor able to read and interpret on any profound level. As Farrel writes, the

> well-established writer [. . .] will justify his activity with a claim for sharper intuition and deeper empathy. Some unfortunate drudge will be

> commissioned to provide that most mysterious thing—a literal transla-
> tion—to which a star name will add the glitter of lilied phrases and wit-
> tily turned dialogue. (Farrel 1996: 54)

But, as Farrel argues, the question is not just the diminished status of the poor "unfortunate drudge," "the translator in the attic" (Aaltonen 2000: 97), unnamed and unaccounted for, but it is also that of actual knowledge of the source culture and language. Declan Donellan, for instance, states that "[y]ou don't need to understand the language to understand the sense of the original" (Donellan 1996: 78) and the general sense, among writers, is that a writer has no obligation to understand either the language or the theatrical culture from which the source play text springs. What this means, practically, is that the emphasis in commissioning star translations is on the domestic culture because "the surrogate owes real allegiance to only one [master]—his own language and culture" (p. 54). But because of the "inequalities of cultural interaction" (Aaltonen 2000: 51):

> interaction tends to use the values of dominant cultures as tools for con-
> structing images of the Other. Translations thus provide mirrors in which
> we can see ourselves rather than windows through which we can see
> the rest of the world. Moreover, the generalising of economic and cul-
> tural exchanges on a global scale may mislead us into thinking that a
> "one-world culture" is in the process of emerging, although it is rather
> a standardisation of social practices dominated by the capitalist West.
> (Aaltonen 2000: 52–3).

There is both anxiety and promise, then, in translation. A star name at least allows a version of a foreign-language work to get on the stage, and it is a new creative work that speaks probably to the theatrical canon and tradition it is entering, but the question is whether the version really is a cultural encounter that can challenge the norms and assumptions of the target, domestic culture, "the challenge of the new and unfamiliar" (p. 52). An example can be seen in Seamus Heaney's "translation" of Leoš Janáček's song cycle, *Zápisník zmizelého/Diary of One Who Vanished*, staged by Deborah Warner in 1999 (the same year of Heaney's much more famous translation of *Beowulf*). Based on "literal" English and French translations, the song cycle clearly fits into Heaney's *oeuvre* in its evocation of the local Derry life and language of Heaney's past. The cycle tells the story of the love affair between a Moravian farmhand and a gypsy girl and their forced exile because of racist attitudes. Heaney's version connects the Roma girl with a romanticized picture of Irish Travellers from his youth, and the evocation would seem to fit in with the thin edge of nostalgia and violence inherent in his poetry. The song cycle would likely never have got on the stage, and certainly not received the attention it did, were it not for Heaney's name. The published version reflects this: Heaney's name in large type on the front cover with the tiny addendum of Janáček's. There is no mention of the "literal" translators (Heaney 2000).

Heaney's version is important and vital on many levels that connect, perhaps politically, with *his* wider work: the postcolonial "translation" into Hiberno-English, the highlighting of a minority within Irish national identity (Traveller and Derry) as well as within Czech identity (Moravian and Roma), the European transnational connection between the use of dialect in Czech and Irish work, and the questioning of national identity. What it does not do is connect with Janáček's aesthetic project with language (using Jozef Kalda's libretto), the stripped-down modernist aesthetic that tightly poeticized everyday speech. *Zápisník zmizelého* has none of the romance or nostalgia of Heaney's version; it is breathtaking in the brutal, bare language that exposes the racism of the community. In other words, while Heaney creates something that is part of his aesthetic, it does not challenge it; he fails to translate the newness, the strangeness, and the unfamiliarity in Janáček's work.

Now, this is not to say that a "literal" translator who spoke Czech and English (and was conversant with Moravian dialect) would necessarily achieve anything better, and the likelihood of a production getting off the ground with an unknown translator would be small. But it is important to recognize that a theatrical version like Heaney's is about his language and his aesthetic—about Hiberno-English, Heaney's work and the Irish/English stage tradition. In itself, this is wonderful, but it is vital to recognize that the version does not engage with the newness or profound foreignness of Janáček's work, and is one that eschews the shockingly bare rhythms and cadence of the Kalda libretto.

"This is the strategy of the dramatist," Johnston writes:

> the violence that he chooses to commit on language in order to create a language that is qualitatively new, and it must be the strategy of the translator as dramaturge if that play is to enjoy the same impact in performance. Equivalence, in short, is based on theatrical re-enactment rather than simple linguistic accuracy. (Johnston 1996: 63)

Johnston is right; the translator's job is to interpret the "violence" or newness of the original and, part of this, as Hare suggested, is being a "rhythm expert" but, ideally, this requires expertise in the source language and tradition, so that the translator can effectively read what is different, new, and "violent" about the playwright's work. It is also necessary not to wholly succumb to the needs of the target culture over the possible newness that can be brought from the source culture.

The temptation—and sometimes the pressure—is to smooth over or domesticate the translation: "how do we put across the idiosyncrasies of a foreign author?" Eivor Martinus asks, "Should we try and give the text a foreign flavour or should we set it firmly in this country with regional and social accents and English—or British—metaphors?" (Martinus 1996: 113).

Often, the choice is not in the theatre translator's hands; if a sample translation has to be "dramaturg-friendly" (Vivis 1996: 42), knowing that "few theatres read a foreign text in the original language" (p. 42), the chances of a textually adventurous play being chosen lessen. Martinus gives the example of translating Strindberg whose "metaphors take huge leaps and are frequently shocking and original," and thus, "it is tempting to tone them down, to 'translate' them into something more digestable" (Martinus 1996: 113). In the case of metaphors or figurative language, this often occurs because of the danger of incomprehensibility, but sometimes the newness of the figurative language in the source text—it may sound strange in its own language—is neutralized to make it palatable on the domestic stage. Some see this as particularly true of England, certainly in the recent past; Steve Gooch writes of the "largely insular and culturally xenophobic British public" (Gooch 1996: 16) of the 1970s; Vivis of "insular" Britain (Vivis 1996: 36). British "cosy provincialism" assumes "that the audience can only cope with what is already familiar, and is incapable of facing the challenge of the foreign" (Farrel 1996: 49).

But others argue that some domestication is inevitable, even desirable, and that plays have to be translated into a domestic mindset. Dominic Donellan, speaking about Racine and Corneille, argues that their alexandrine verse cannot be translated as verse into English because of the different cultural impact; in English, he argues, "rhyme sound[s] anything other than clever and slightly hollow in that clever way" (Donellan 1996: 80) and that, thus, the English tradition of blank verse should be used. "[Y]ou have to re-conceive the whole thing in an *English* way," he argues, and not only in form but also in content, as the French playwrights are too "intellectual and cerebral" and you "need much more concrete Anglo-Saxon images in order for people to understand speech" (p. 80). Acculturation is inevitable in translation (Bassnett 1998: 93) and there is something to be said for the new creative work that arises from an English or anglicized (or Americanized) Corneille, or an Irish Chekhov; this form of adaptation is integral to furthering the arc of the adapting playwright or tradition, but there is also an entropic or hermetic comfort in looking for what is familiar in the foreign, or what can be rendered familiar.

As Susan Bassnett argues, the Chekhov seen in England is an "honorary Englishman" (p. 92), "an English middle-class Chekhov" (p. 94) who is a different playwright to the Russian Chekhov, one "invented through the translation process" (p. 94). She quotes the English playwright, Michael Frayn, as saying that no knowledge of Russian was necessary to translate Chekhov because of his universality (p. 93) and Brian Friel agrees; his translation of *The Three Sisters* was made from "five standard English translations" and though conceived politically as a postcolonial translation (Friel 1999: 84), the adaptation speaks to the Irish and English traditions rather than a respect for the newness of the language in the original.

Donellan sets up the problem between a knowledge of the original and a desire to adapt and anglicize it as a problem between the academy and the theatre; he suggests that by emphasizing the impossibility of translation, the academy effectively censors the playwrights such as Racine or Corneille, giving no support or impetus to theatrical productions. But it is something of a false dichotomy; what is actually at issue is the role and status of the translator—the unnamed, bypassed "literal" translator. The role, itself, is problematic as are the expectations: the translator is the person ideally aware of both source and domestic languages; even more ideally they are aware of the source and domestic theatre traditions (to an extent that the domestic directors or actors may not be) but, as Bassnett argues, the translator is not one of the physical producers of the play. Their role, she argues, is limited to the text; they should

> engage specifically with the signs of the text: to wrestle with the deictic units, the speech rhythms, the pauses and silences, the shifts of tone or of register, the problems of intonation patterns: in short, the linguistic and paralinguistic aspects of the written text that are decodable and reencodable. (Bassnett 1998: 107)

Then, she argues, it is up to the director, actors, and others to interpret the text in their own tradition. But the "translator's survival as a translator depends on how willingly she or he follows the conventions or system" (Aaltonen 2000: 31); if the translator experiments or does not want to overly domesticate the play text, their translation may not be used and they may not get work.

Practicing theatre translators underline the desirability of the translator's voice during production, "keeping a hotline open to a director or producer" (p. 39) or acting "in loco parentis" (p. 31) for the foreign playwright, not only to "protect the original," but "also to help when required" (p. 31). Noel Clark points out that the translator can aid a production when lines are not working on stage, because of their knowledge of the original, a knowledge that the actors might not have, in order to prevent the core of a play from too much alteration or adaptation. Clarke adds that the play is not "an infinitely negotiable commodity" (Clark 1996: 31), and that perceived flaws could and should be addressed before production. Translators, as primary readers and interpreters of the text, are aware of the rhythms, cadences, and silences of the text, but also of the limits and possibilities of their own interpretations as they translate. As such, they are potentially powerful collaborators in developing a play text as it makes inevitable changes in production: aware both of the central core of the author's style, and of the possibilities of interpretation and decoding. As Patrice Pavis suggests, the translator is capable of making a translation that is "not so much the *mise en scène à l'avance*, but a preparation for this *mise en scène* [. . .] leaving aside certain zones of indeterminacy" (Pavis 1989: 32). In other words, the translator, with their knowledge and skills can set up an hermeneutically sound basis for future interpretation.

But theatre translators retain a low status in the hierarchy: "Translating is the invisible art," Farrel writes, "in the sense that the good translator, like the trusty butler, must accept being ignored as proof of a job well done. He is expected to be heard, but not seen" (Farrel 1996: 46). Badly paid and rarely credited, the theatre translator is often doing it for interest and love rather than as part of a professional or professionalized career; it is, one translator writes, "a miserable business" (p. 81). Translators' work is sometimes reworked and rewritten without permission (p. 132). Much of this attitude is based on the mistaken reading of the "literal" translation and "literal" translator being an interlingual transliteration and a workhorse, rather than realizing that this transference from one language to another involves a reading by a living person with their own preferences, attitudes, and ideologies. While the translator's view should not necessarily be privileged, theirs is a "voice among voices" in the production (p. 146), their input should be acknowledged and effectively used. They, too, are the "rhythm experts"; Laurence Boswell writes: "if the translator is aware of the foreign rhythms of what he's translating, then no matter how that play is staged or adapted, its otherness will be communicated" (1996: 147).

Reading Farrel and Boswell's defence of the translator, another power dynamic is clear: the assumption of the translator's sex: "*He* is expected"; "what *he*'s translating." What of the role of the female theatre translator? Very little has been written about female translators in the theatre; it is a lacuna in feminist translation theory and this perhaps speaks to the real invisibility of women in translatorial and decisive positions in the theatre world, and, I suspect, to their more traditional role as forgotten "literal" translators. Their history in the theatre has effectively been censored through disinterest—what Michael Cronin has called a "censorship of indifference" (Cronin 2003: 100) to the work of the translator.

As feminist translation theory has argued (Chamberlain 1992; Simon 1996; von Flotow 1997, 2011), the position of the translator is a feminized one, both through the metaphorics of translation and in legal, commercial, and cultural standing. Aaltonen's formulation of the theatre translator as the "translator in the attic" knowingly refers to Sandra Gilbert and Susan Gubar's seminal feminist book, *The Madwoman in the Attic*, and she suggests that the theatre translator is feminized because of their legal standing, that is, the lack of copyright control in a "typically male" legal hierarchy (Aaltonen 2000: 98). She argues, though, that if all theatre is necessarily adapted for the target culture stage, then "a theatre translator's work does not differ so much from that of the playwright" (p. 98) and they should be recognized (and paid) equitably.

Translation in the theatre and in general is not a transparent activity; studying the process makes visible the nodes of negotiation, decision making, relationships between different agents in the process, and reveals elements of possibilities and constraints. Most importantly, analyzing the way in which translation happens (or does not happen), tells us about how we view other cultures and how we construct our own. It is not necessarily a comfortable experience as the "process of translation leaves gaps and interstices between our world and the image of the world created within us by what is read or viewed" (Shaked 1989: 7).

Theatre, translation, censorship: Britain, United States, Czechoslovakia

There is a world elsewhere.

KEN TYNAN

According to Herodotus, one of the first Greek tragedies, Phrynicus' *The Capture of Miletus* reduced its audience to tears, was fined 1,000 drachma, and plays on the subject of the city's sack were banned. "And that," Zygmunt Hubner writes, "is how it started" (Hubner 1992: 7). Thirteen hundred years later, Ken Tynan spent most of his career as a critic, then as literary manager of the English National Theatre fuming and fighting against British censorship of the theatre, embodied and controlled by the Lord Chamberlain's Office (1737–1968). His struggle culminated in his appearance in front of the Joint Committee on the Censorship of the Theatre in 1967, one of only nine witnesses called (Shellard and Nicholson 2004: 172). The Joint Committee voted to abolish the Lord Chamberlain's Office arguing that no one man "should possess unqualified dictatorship" (p. 172) over what plays could be performed on the British stage, and theatre censorship was formally ended in Britain in 1968.

As Katja Krebs has shown, the Lord Chamberlain's Office mostly displayed a patronizing attitude toward translations, exhibiting "xenophobic" tendencies that showed it "believed in the superiority of British culture" (Krebs 2007: 179), and often deliberately targeted translated "foreign" plays for censorship. At the same time, in some instances, the Office allowed translations with controversial sexual or religious content a license to be performed "because of the very fact that they were non-British" as it would "demonstrate the Other's cultural inferiority" (p. 179). Other means of dealing with foreign plays was to license the original, but not the translation, as happened initially with Pirandello's *Six Characters in Search of an Author* and Beckett's *Endgame*, one of the reasons being that "the class of audience the censorship was striving to protect (or control) was not thought likely to speak a foreign language" (Shellard and Nicholson 2004: 85). The avant-garde nature of some of the new European plays helped them get a license—when the Lord Chamberlain, Lord Cromer, himself snuck in to see Pirandello's play in a "private club" performance in 1928 (one means of evading the censor was setting up invited performances in club theatres), he changed his mind. "I do not think it is likely to appeal to a wide audience," he wrote, "or to have a long run" (p. 86). A similar undercover visit saved *Waiting for Godot*. After Lady Howitt made a complaint of sordidness, Charles Heriot, from the Office, went to see for himself. He wrote in his report that he "endured two hours of acute boredom" and that by the all too brief interval, "many empty seats gaped" (p. 150). The perception was that translated avant-garde plays would only appeal to a limited audience, would not be commercial, and therefore, would not significantly affect social and moral norms for the general class of person.

But, as Krebs points out, "the censorial power of the Lord Chamberlain's office" was not limited to the "government agency" or the "individual occupying this office" (Krebs 2007: 169), but was a network of "complicity and collusion" (p. 170) which involved theatre practitioners themselves, such as directors, producers, playwrights, reviewers and, of course, translators. Tynan, too, argued that it was not just the actual Lord Chamberlain who was a repressive top–down censor but that the idea and presence of theatre censorship made his shadow "a baleful deterrent on the threshold of creativity" (Tynan 2008: 249). Thus, playwrights and theatres conducted their business expecting censorship and thus "playing it safe" (p. 53), that is, self-censoring themselves.

For Tynan, this self-censorship was a disaster for British theatre in the 1950s and 1960s, leading to a "ghastly norm" (p. 126) of farces, melodramas (p. 133), and country-house dramas (p. 77), stripped of anything radical either in form or content, especially in terms of what was going on in Europe with the likes of Brecht and Beckett. He castigated the insularism of British theatre, arguing that the perceived "national taste" (p. 77) was a construct arising out of censorship and fear, not only of and in theatre practitioners, but also the audience. The expectations that British audiences had of plays was cited, wrongly in Tynan's eyes, as the consumer basis for the kind of middlebrow, class-ridden theatre on stage. But Tynan felt that this was simply what they were fed, and thus, what they were used to. His outspoken support for a National Theatre was partially based on an idea of "re-educating" the audience as well as playwrights (p. 242), of presenting audiences with something new and foreign to given precepts of theatre. Once the English National Theatre was founded, Tynan was expressly employed because of his exposure to foreign theatre (from trips abroad) with the remit to include translated works on the new National Theatre stages. For Tynan this was paramount, not only as a means to introduce new life into British plays, but also into the English language: "When Shakespeare was born," he wrote, "language was being pelted with imports, from France, from Italy, from classical translations [...] A stock-pot was bubbling, which everyone tasted and tried out in speech; and drama evolved out of an epidemic of logorrhoea" (p. 41).

The idea of a subsidized National Theater released plays from "box-office tyranny," from "a dictatorship ruled by economic pressures" (p. 133).

Because of commercial constraints, theatre had become "a short-term art, dependent on quick financial returns" that supported "easily digestible, uncontroversial, ego-massaging, audience-ingratiating trifles" (p. 238) and effectively censored anything deemed too strange, radical, subversive, or foreign. He called the absence of subsidies a form of censorship, "enslaving the artist to the box-office and forcing him, unless he is a genius, to turn out lovable, undisturbing after-dinner entertainments" (p. 239). Tynan compared the British situation to Europe where for many countries—in Scandinavia, France, Germany, and in Eastern Europe—the "very idea that good theatre should be required to turn a profit would seem indecent" (p. 238). He connected a nonreliance on profit to open attitudes to translation. Comparing British theatre to a "pet patient, starved and racked" he said at last in 1955 "we pump in our printed transfusions" (p. 50) of three translated plays (Pirandello, Anouilh, and Ibsen) whereas in Sweden, in what was seen as a mediocre year, there were "four Shakespeares, three Chekhovs, three Pirandellos, two Molieres, two Shaws, two Ibsens, two Giradoux" as well as "Vanbrugh, Wycherley, Lorca, Kafka, Brecht, Ugo Betti, Arthur Miller, Anouilh, Eliot, Beranos and Samuel Beckett" (p. 52). British insularism, arising out of overt and internalized censorship, presided over by the Lord Chamberlain, and out of "box-office tyranny" made British theatre the "laughing-stock of the Continent" (p. 90).

Tynan's idealism about the birth of the National Theatre did not overly focus on the effect of patronage even with public subsidies, which, as Krebs warns, still contain protective interests and possibilities of censorship. For Krebs, the end of official censorship only led to a diffuse range of censorships and censoring bodies who "took upon themselves the role of the now unofficial censor" (Krebs 2007: 170–1). These "multiple locations of censorship" (p. 170) include corporate sponsors, board members, charitable foundations, controllers of state subsidies, local governments, that is, bodies responsible for paying for theatre, who might be unlikely to offend social or moral norms. Thus, censorship functions as a network of censorships rather than a "binary structure" or top–down repressive instrument (p. 170). Richard Burt, however, warns against misuse of the word "censorship." Using it to cover practices as wide as:

> institutional regulation of free expression, market censorship, cutbacks in government funding for controversial art, boycotts, lawsuits, and marginalization and exclusion of artists based on their gender and race to "political correctness" in the university and the media [means] that the term is overwhelmed even trivialized [. . .] one implicitly discounts the rather significant difference between going to a gulag for saying something subversive and not getting an NEA grant. (Burt 1994: xiii)

What he proposes instead is thinking about "discourse[s] of legitimation" and "delegitimation" (p. xv) that pervade societies and are related to questions of power. He is right to question any blanket criticism of various funding or administrative bodies as censors, but I think it is worth at least considering these bodies under the rubric of censorship even to discount it, in order to question how theatre functions within sociopolitical discourses of given periods of time, and especially how translated plays often challenge domestic social, moral, and political norms because they come from other sociopolitical contexts, different traditions, and theatrical norms.

Translated plays undergo a number of rewritings, from the translator onwards, and looking at the network of "control factors" (Lefevere 1992: 14) or "external constraints" (Tymoczko 2008: 38) opens up questions of why and when certain plays are performed, and, more generally, what the social purpose of literature beyond entertainment might be in openly repressive *and* democratic societies. It also reveals questions of what cultures—especially, here, the dominant English-language cultures of the United States and Britain—are prepared to accept and comprehend when it comes to translated theatre.

Theatre translators, as we have seen, are both at the center of the linguistic and cultural transformation of translated plays and at its margins. Translators, who are not famous writers or playwrights, tend to be overlooked and seen as a necessity but are not given their professional due, either through recognition or through payment. In many cases, especially when their translation has been adapted by a more famous name, they are not given due credit for their work (this is especially true of female "literal" translators). Michael Cronin dubs this a "censorship of indifference" (Cronin 2003: 100) toward the translator and the process of translation. Because the translated play text is regarded as a simple "literal" linguistic transfer rather than an exegetical interpretation, the translator often is not regarded as a central figure in the play's production or performance.

The translator can also act as a censor, as Krebs argues, sometimes in anticipation of overt censorship; before the repeal of official censorship in Britain, she argues that translators "were very much aware of the censor" (Krebs 2007: 178), making them a "translator/censor hybrid who acts as a censor towards the source text and at the same time is censored by the existing institution of censorship" (p. 178). As with playwrights, the atmosphere of censorship led to self-censorship in the act of translation—often of plays that had been written abroad in societies with no formal censorship—and these translations, read by the Lord Chamberlain's office, were often censored.

The translation of Pirandello's *Six Characters in Search of an Author* was turned down, but the reader at the Lord Chamberlain's office, G. S. Street, recommended the second translation "Put into English by H. K. Ayliff" because this translation "reads more naturally and vigorously [. . .] it is also an improvement from the censorship point of view" (Shellard and Nicholson 2004: 85). The comment reveals that the office or someone involved in the potential production had advised the new translator of the objections to the first translation and cuts were made, but also, tellingly, that the "naturalness" of the translation recommends it also. This suggests a less overt censorship at work, that is, the requirement of a fluent translation. Often commissioned by the target culture theatre, producer, or director, the translator's subsequent loyalty is to that culture and language. Loyalty means an emphasis on speakability and fluency in the target language. This might not be problematic if the director and actors are conversant with the tradition, context, and artistic style of the source play text, but problems can arise when decisions to smooth out and "English" the play text are made without a coherent sense of the playwright's aesthetics. It can, in some circumstances, lead to basic misreadings and censorship of the source text, via cuts or transpositions that do not speak to repetitions or rhythms, or what Johnston calls the "ideotext" in the source text. Smoothness and fluency also serves to hide the work of the translator and the translator's identity and "translator-effect" (von Flotow 1997: 35) on the text, thus negating their contribution and adding to the sense of a "censorship of indifference" to their work.

Translators also bring their own agendas to the translation, whether political, ideological, or moral, and can either be significant agents policing the norms of a given culture, or deliberately subverting them. Both J. Michael Walton and Matthew Reynolds consider translators' censorship of the bawdiness in classic Greek theatre; Walton arguing that via the translator "each age recreates the ancient world in its own image, finding reasons, where possible, to account for what is uncomfortable, or ignoring it altogether" (Walton 2007: 150–1); and Reynolds suggesting there was a tradition of "semi-censorship" (Reynolds 2007: 188) in Britain where the educated classes read the full originals in Greek, but translators often removed troubling moral material when translating the plays into English. Again, class and education were an issue in translation censorship with an "underlying assumption, that the wealthy and the skilled in languages were less prone to corruption than anyone else" (p. 188). Walton argues that censorship, whether by the Lord Chamberlain's office or by the translator, "in stage translation into English has usually been an issue of taste and morals rather than political message" (Walton 2007: 153); but, as Hubner points out, the "moral censorship" of theatre, too, "has a political basis and serves to consolidate the moral norms of the social groupings actually in power at a given time" (Hubner 1992: 27).

Historically in America, though there was no official federal censorship body for theatre, the question of morals led influential bodies into protesting plays, sometimes driven by the audience, made up of "pressure groups, self-appointed vigilantes, vice crusaders, and drama critics who protested against permissiveness in the theater" (Laufe 1978: 48). It was also driven by institutions, such as the Church, the police, and city License Commissioners. In the politically charged atmosphere of the pre-WWII era, the question of morality was intimately tied into the question of politics;

because of a "fear of revolution," conservative forces demanded a "return to traditional values" (Houchin 2003: 127). Eugene O'Neill's *Desire under the Elms* was investigated by the New York District Attorney for vulgarity making it hugely successful at the box office, leading one of the jurors after they'd seen the play to comment that the "audience needed more censorship than the play" (Laufe 1978: 54–5). Lillian Hellman's classic *The Children's Hour*, which touched on lesbianism, was denounced and prevented from opening in Boston by the Commissioner of Licenses, Herbert L. McNary, who said it was not a "proper presentation" for Boston. When it went to trial, the Judge agreed that the play "was not acceptable for Boston" but "reminded the court that he had not legally 'banned' the production" (Houchin 2003: 125). Yet, Judge Sweeny had effectively banned the production, showing that "officials in Boston used their power to shield conventional morality and religion from any questions that might be generated by theater" (p. 125). In New York, the Catholic Church got involved with Cardinal Hayes denouncing the theatre in New York as "an outrage of public decency" (p. 119), leading the police to raid some productions on grounds of immorality (p. 120).

The moral scare was linked to a radical moment in American theatre when the theatre seemed to be a platform to discuss the conditions of the Depression, revolution, and workers' needs. This "politically aggressive theatre was not universally welcomed and often triggered violent response from those conservative forces it assailed" (p. 131). The Works Progress Administration's Federal Theater Project, set up in 1935 by Harry Hopkins and run by Hallie Flanagan, as a " 'free, adult, uncensored' theater that would not blindly follow the New York commercial model" (p. 132) quickly became controversial in Congress, with attacks beginning in 1936 against the Federal Theater Project (FTP) "spreading its radical theories through its stage productions" (p. 146). In 1938, Martin Dies headed the new House Committee on Un-American Activities (HUAC) and called dozens of those involved in the FTP to testify; by 1940, Congress withdrew funding from the FTP, signaling its end. American theatre was not legally protected by First Amendment rights until 1970, in a judicial decision involving a Boston production of *Hair* (Houchin 2000: 32), and, finally, until the Supreme Court endorsed this right in 1975, following a ban on *Hair* in Chattanooga (p. 35).

If Congress exhibited "a palpable fear that foreign subversives were bent on destroying American democratic institutions" (Houchin 2003: 144), the arrival of Bertolt Brecht did nothing to assuage fears. His first trip to the United States in 1935, however, was initiated by his outrage over the Theater Union's (one of the left-wing theatre groups) translation of *Mother* (Brecht's adaptation of Gorky's novel). His reaction, once he arrived, to the translation and production "required no translation": "Das ist Sheisse! Das ist Dreck!" (Lyon 1980: 9). Brecht was ejected from the production and the emendations and cuts were reinstituted in the translation by Paul Peters (p. 9), leading Brecht to accuse the theatre of doing so for commercial gain (p. 10). When Brecht emigrated to the United States over the war-time period, he became very choosy about his translators, finally getting W. H. Auden to adapt a literal translation of *Caucasian Chalk Circle*, written in the United States, to be produced on Broadway; but it was not performed for 20 years because it "was hopelessly at odds with the American theater of the day" (p. 129), perhaps deliberately so, as James Lyon argues, a protest against Broadway conventions. But translation would also ease the path for Brecht; he denied that his work advocated Marxist principles in front of the HUAC in 1947 by challenging the translations of his work offered by the Committee (p. 332).

Brecht's experiences revealed the uneasy relationship between translations and Broadway; that translations were not seen as commercial enough to succeed, that they had to be adapted and rewritten for an American audience, and that a certain aesthetic ruled in commercial theatre. In New York to survey the Broadway scene in 1956, Tynan saw two translations, one of the successfully "Englished" by Lillian Hellman, that is, adapted by a now fashionable American playwright, and the other, the first Broadway production of *Waiting for Godot*. Godot's producer, Michael Myerberg, had first produced the translation in Miami where it had been a "stupendous flop" (Gelb 1956) and decided that, in order to generate publicity for the obscure translation, he would provide an interview with *The New York Times* in which he took "the precaution of publicly warning theatergoers in search of casual entertainment not to buy tickets" for the play (Gelb 1956). "Wanted: 70, 000 Playgoing Intellectuals" the headline ran, "to Support Plotless Play." Myerberg was savvy in recognizing that he could turn the fear of the translated play into a marketing tool that people might want to be recognized as intellectuals and thus be game enough to brave the play. The audience in Miami had walked out, he said, because they found "themselves on a level with the two tramps" and realized that "life has no meaning, no purpose despite wealth and position." "And that's why," he added, "we aren't aiming any more for popular appeal" (Gelb 1956). One of his mistakes in Miami, he said, was casting comic stars, like Bert Lahr, giving the audience expectations that the play would speak more closely to domestic forms of mainstream humor; he kept Lahr in for the Broadway run and it was, perhaps because of the *New York Times* dare, a huge success.

The commercial demands for Broadway productions were an inhibitor for translations, especially of avant-garde plays. Brecht (albeit with a Swiss passport and exalted position) returned to East Germany feeling that he had, paradoxically, more freedom than in America because of the financial resistance to staging avant-garde plays (Lefevere 1998: 119). Tynan, too, had something of an idealistic picture of East Berlin and the theatre behind the Iron Curtain seeing it as a model for the West; when he arrived in Prague in the late 1960s, he felt that the new atmosphere of post-Stalinist censorship had created an "age of the art house" (Tynan 1967: 102), because playwrights and filmmakers were no longer inhibited "by economic and ideological pressures" (p. 102). But this was not quite true; interviewed in May 1968 during his trip to New York, Václav Havel said that "at the moment censorship exists on paper, but not in practice," and that, "in theory, the censor can clamp down tomorrow." That was why he and some in the Czechoslovak writer's union were moving to "get a law today to remove censorship and guarantee freedom of speech and freedom of assembly" (Klaidman 1968). The Central Publishing Agency, one of the main bodies responsible for censoring plays had ceased censorship activities in February 1968; in June 1968 a new Press Law dissolved the Agency (Neumann 1994: 41). Two months later, the Soviets invaded Czechoslovakia; Havel would not have another official performance of his plays until 1990, by which time he was President.

The Prague Spring—associated with the tumultuous year of 1968— actually began in the early 1960s and the thawing over translations had something to do with it. Foreign writers banned in the post-Communist coup neo-Stalinist years (1948 onwards), were suddenly acceptable, following a "de-Stalinization drive" (Beneš 1972: 99), including Franz Kafka in 1963 (an important influence on Havel). Translations of avant-garde playwrights and authors, banned under the repressive hegemony of Party-endorsed socialist realism (Špirk 2008: 219–20), led to a flowering of Czech theatre: "Increased literary activity was accompanied by the re-establishment of connections with the Western world," Hana Beneš writes, "This was most evident in the enormous increase in translations from Western literatures and in the staging of a great number of Western plays" (Beneš 1972: 101). In 1964, the theatre Havel worked for, Divadlo na zábradli/Theater on the Balustrade, produced *Waiting for Godot* and Ionesco's *Chairs*, as well as theatrical version of Kafka's *The Trial*. These new translations—of the likes of Beckett, Ionesco, and Pinter—would have an effect on the young generation's rejection of the previous enforced norm of socialist realist political theatre (Holý 2010: 61). The "little theatres," where these new translations and new plays, influenced by the translations, became one of the cornerstones of the Prague Spring. The cross-fertilization—famous innovative Czech productions would travel abroad—led to an opening of discussions about power, freedom of expression, language, and the social role of theatre.

Translation was a means by which some writers in the 1950s had been allowed to publish at all, their work otherwise censored (pp. 60–1). New translations of classic authors such as Shakespeare allowed some "camouflaged" freedom of expression—in Zdeněk Urbánek's late 1950s translation of *Hamlet*, for instance, instead of Hamlet declaring "there's something rotten in state of Denmark," he announced that "there is something rotten in our country," an electric statement to the audience for the time (p. 61). Translators were respected figures in Czech society and most writers were also translators: Milan Kundera was first published as a translator of Ukrainian and Russian verse, Josef Škvorecký was famed as a translator of American literature. Unlike the English-speaking world, a healthy flow of translations was seen as vital to the health of Czech literature, and a means by which Czech writers could throw off the yoke of repressive artistic policies. Milan Kundera's famous 1967 speech to the Writer's Union explicitly connected translation with the struggle against censorship (Hamšík 1971: 167–77). Following the Soviet invasion, and harsh crackdowns on hundreds of writers, translators were also targeted: Havel's translator, Vera Blackwell, was placed on the Index of banned authors and declared an enemy of the state. Other translators had their names removed from translations; Ludvík Kundera's (Milan Kundera's cousin) translations of Brecht, for instance, were republished without Kundera's name (Špirk 2008: 221).

Censorship in Czechoslovakia under Communism has often been read in the West as a top–down form of censorship, with the totalitarian regime enforcing its power over victimized functionaries, as well as victimized writers. Jiřina Šmejkalová-Strickland challenges this model, arguing that this was not quite the whole story, that censorship was also performative, made up a series of agents (publishers, booksellers, paper manufacturers) who were never "quite certain about the extent of his or her decision-making power" (Šmejkalová-Strickland 1994: 202), leading to a contradiction between the actual "internal weakness of the official domain of literary production" and "its *performed* stability and consistency" (p. 202). In other words, those involved in literary production assumed censorship practices, that is, self-censoring themselves, thereby becoming part of a network of censorship. Using Judith Butler's notion of performativity to expand on Havel's own notion of the performance of false identity as a pillar of the "post-totalitarian" regime in his essay, "The Power of the Powerless," Šmejkalová-Strickland argues that censorship conditions were constructed by the repetition of censorship practices by individuals. "Not only did people perform what they considered to be their own roles," she continues, "but they also acted in anticipation of the possible reaction of an imagined audience, taking into account the expectations and constraints on other actors" (p. 204). Thus, editors might ask authors to remove "rebellious" chapters, the author "might avoid writing certain passages" and translators might choose not to translate certain material in anticipation of other censors. The positive side of this—what Havel addressed in "The Power of the Powerless"—is that "actors" could decide not to participate in such self-censorship and take part in the nonofficial literary sphere. But, she argues, dissident literature itself became the norm, the canon, post-1989 and itself began to exclude others, along with the market and commercial literature. In thinking about censorship as a network of "actors," she argues that the "post-totalitarian" model of performative censorship is instructive to any socioliterary system.

Julek Neumann makes a similar argument in terms of Czechoslovak theatre in the 1970s and 1980s, that it was not simply a story of an "autonomous censor, a victimized author, and a deprived reader in the seductive 'oppression-domination' explanatory dichotomy" (Šmejkalova-Strickland 1994: 211). Neumann argues, first, that there were different kinds of censorship at different points during this period of "normalization," that a variety of "actors" were involved in "self-censorship or self-mutilation" (Neumann 1994: 40), and that "individuals, rather than dark unknown forces, were responsible for the particular acts of censorship" (p. 42). Neumann splits the era into three distinct periods: 1969–72, 1972–77, and 1977 onwards. In the first period, Neumann writes that a "culture pogrom" occurred (p. 45), with the expulsion or demotion of the major theatre figures of the 1960s, and the banning of leading playwrights of that era such as Havel, Pavel Kohout, Josef Topol, Ivan Klíma, and Milan Uhde (p. 51). "The actual task," Neumann writes, "of stopping these people from being performed was the work of the theatre management" (p. 51) and the regime installed directors and dramaturges who would be loyal to the regime and who were the frontline individuals or "preliminary censor" (p. 51) making the decisions about whether to perform certain plays and in what form, "often using 'higher authority' as an excuse" (p. 64), as no one was quite sure of the limits of censorship. Local authorities instituted a "pre-view" (p. 48) of plays to make sure they were ideologically correct, but the changes demanded often were subjective and "irrational." Some of the language in one production of Brecht's *Mother Courage* was censored because one of the negative characters had the same first name of the new, postinvasion President, Gustav Husák. In protest, the actors performed the script with silences in the places where the censored material had been removed.

However, the pre-1968 censorship laws had not been reimplemented, so that theatre censorship "was never officially restored" in such form, but "the indirect pressures which replaced it in the end proved much more effective than the old system of direct censorship" (p. 48). The regime saw the theatre as "one of the most dangerous activities" because it blamed "directors and playwrights for the tumultuous social changes of the late sixties" (p. 44) and did close down some theatres, but did not want to be seen internationally as cracking down on all of theatre. Thus, the "indirect pressures" were applied to keep a (rather transparent) veneer of legitimacy.

DILIA, the state, and sole, literary, and theatrical agency (the name derives from a partial acronym: *Divadelní, literární, audovizuální agentura*) in Communist Czechoslovakia, tightened its grip after 1972, disallowing contracts for banned authors, translators, and plays, effectively then censoring them. Some confusion reigned over who exactly was banned as different authorities had different names on their lists, but because of this, the director of DILIA decided, on his own volition, to collate all the separate lists and ban all the names on them: "When asked who was on it, he claimed that it would be quicker to name those who were not" (p. 52). According to Neumann this meant that "most playwrights, and almost all translators, were affected"; it meant as a result that there were no acceptable French translators, "only a handful of second-rate translators from English" and only one woman at Communist Party HQ was allowed to translate Russian plays (p. 52). The Theater Institute (Divadelní ústav) was, however, still commissioning plays from banned translators, though paying a tiny wage and none of the plays were ever produced.

The hardline director of DILIA did not necessarily speak for others in the organization. It is evident from the correspondence between DILIA and Vera Blackwell, as well as Havel's comments about his meetings with DILIA, that some in the organization actively went against official policy in their advice to Havel. Indeed, after Havel's plays were officially banned, some at DILIA were still trying to work with him (at least in terms of translation contracts), they advised him how to get around the ban of Blackwell as his translator and, finally, advised him to jettison their own organization when it was clear that others at DILIA would never allow a foreign contract for his plays. They suggested he work solely with a Western agent and bypass official Czech contracts.

There were also ways and means of getting past—or at least trying to get past—the network of censors (theatre management, dramaturges, DILIA, the Theater Institute). One means of which was a "front"; Milan Kundera's *Jakub a jeho pán/Jacques and His Master* was performed under the director's name, even after Kundera had been banned. One of Havel's plays, *The Beggar's Opera* (a rewriting of John Gay's eighteenth-century play that had provoked the English Prime Minister, Robert Walpole, into tightening censorship laws against the theatre in England), was performed in a tiny, provincial hall because the local "inspector of culture" did not recognize his name (as it had been banned). Some new, small theatres deliberately worked without text so that they could get past the censor, thus producing vibrant, experimental, work. Others deliberately put in flagrant material they knew would attract the dramaturg's or director's eye and act as a decoy for other material in the text (p. 59).

Ironically, Charter 77 brought many banned practitioners back into the theatre. Havel, already banned, was eventually imprisoned for the second time in 1979, and all of the signatories of the Charter were affected personally and professionally. But the government, in response to the Charter, offered a "general amnesty for theatre people" if they signed what the government called the "Anti-Charter" (p. 63). "In most theatres," Neumann writes, "the signing was massive" and it allowed those who had been banned or sidelined to return to work (p. 63); because "the extremely violent repression concentrated on the signatories, the years 1977 to 1989 ironically brought further liberalization to the theatres" (p. 63). But after 1977, the Theatre Institute gained new powers in being asked to send an "expert" to shows to decide whether or not they were acceptable, adding another layer of "informal pressure" (p. 64).

Both Šmejkalová-Strickland and Neumann emphasize that there was repressive government-backed censorship in Czechoslovakia under the Communist regime, but also argue that, in the case of Czechoslovakia, censorship was also a more fluid and individually administered process than usually assumed, based often on fear, power, and self-censorship. The importance of this understanding is that while experiences of censorship can differ from regime to regime or government to government, it may be possible to think about censorship as a network functioning via the choices and decisions of various individuals, thereby also enabling us to think about resistance to censorship as a performative and, perhaps, fluid act (one thinks perhaps here of current Belorussian street resistance, reacting to the banning of marches, resulting in ingenious forms of nonviolent protest such as the setting of simultaneous cell phone alarms in public spaces).

In terms of the theatre and translation, the sense of individual choice as collusiveness in censoring play texts or performances, whether for political, religious, ideological, or commercial reasons should not simply be a damning indictment of power structures in given societies, but should suggest a pathway for empowerment and resistance, especially for the readers, audiences, and consumers of plays, at the vanguard of which is the translator. In focusing on the reader (the first of whom, in a target culture, is often the translator), we can begin looking at what Brian Baer calls "productive censorship," that is, practices of evading censorship and the "(re)production of alternative (sub)cultures and of a moral if not overtly political opposition" (Baer 2011: 21). Baer argues that the "reader is typically construed as a passive victim" (p. 22) under repressive censorship but that in a "productive model functions as an active participant decoding the Aesopian language and baroque forms of the censored text and in reconstructing the "original" source text that has been deformed or altered through censorship" (pp. 22–3). This "generates alternative interpretative communities" (p. 24) that challenge "established hermeneutic practices" (p. 25). The reader-translator or audience even in nonrepressive circumstances (i.e. in conditions of more covert forms of censorship) can also move beyond the language of victimhood (i.e. badly paid, marginalized translators in a field resistant to producing translated plays, or audiences without access to translated plays or simply resistant to them because of their cultural "strangeness") to being finally seen as or becoming "active participant[s]" in searching out, being self-aware, and demanding translated theatre that is not yoked to commercial demands.

Havel's notion of appellative theatre—deliberately ambiguous theatre that demands the audience to be active interpreters—was often misconstrued as simply Aesopian, encoded theatre that once decoded spoke about given conditions of repression at a given time. But it moves beyond that: while certainly inspired by conditions of censorship where certain things could not be said, Havel's theatre took that censorship as a starting point for exploring the openings and ambiguities of hermeneutics, giving the audience responsibility for their own reactions rather than trying to manufacture those reactions. It is why considering Havel's plays is so important to the question of censorship and translation, because first, it is one of the most difficult elements of the plays to translate without falling into reductive readings (i.e. that they are only allegories of Communist rule and, therefore, simplistic and outdated) and secondly, because the plays invoke the very process of translation (as an interpretive act) and censorship (what we don't want to hear) in the audience. Havel's plays did not and do not poke fun at or challenge a faceless censor; they challenge us. This has been a reason for their intermittent success, and their intermittent failure.

Václav Havel

Being has a memory. And thus even my insignificance—as a bourgeois child, a laboratory assistant, a soldier, a stagehand, a playwright, a dissident, a prisoner, a president, a pensioner, a public phenomenon, and a hermit, an alleged hero but secretly a bundle of nerves—will remain here forever, or rathr not here, but somewhere.

VÁCLAV HAVEL

Asked for his autograph in an elevator at the Library of Congress in Washington in 2005, Havel duly agreed; hesitant about his English he simply replied "Yes" until it dawned on him that the man had asked him whether he had written *The Unbearable Lightness of Being*. "I couldn't very well change my answer," he wrote, "and there was no escaping, so I had to remain in a state of embarrassment until the moment of liberation when our elevator arrived at the right floor. A truly Kunderian situation" (Havel 2007a: 122). Havel never replicated Kundera's bestselling success in the West; though the romance of the writer as ruler, a "fairy-tale, if not pure kitsch" (Havel 2007a: 24) captured the West, his plays did not. In a recent Untitled Theater Company #61 production of a play based on a Havel essay (by Havel and Vladimír Morávek), *The Pig, or Václav Havel's Hunt for a Pig*, the screen crawl on TVs set up along the walls of the theatre space (for a CNN-alike station), ran, among other news, some about Havel: "Avant-garde Czech playwright still basically unknown in the US."

Why? Since his involvement with Charter 77, the 1977 petition for freedom of speech and recognition of human rights, Havel has been an "international media celebrity" (Keane 2000: 247). His "life like a work of art" (Kundera 1990: 16) catapulted him from prison in May 1989 to the Czechoslovak Presidency in December 1989, from his country cottage, Hradeček ("Little Castle") to the Hrad (Prague Castle); he was the Czech "star in the theater of opposition" (Havel 2007a: 55) who led a peaceful, Velvet Revolution in 1989 to oust a 40-year-old Communist regime. For a time, he was one of the most famous political and human rights figures in the world, "a man who achieved fame as the political figure who taught the world much more about power, the powerful and the powerless than most of his twentieth-century rivals" (Keane 2000: 505).

By 2006 all of his nearly 20 plays[1] had been performed in English and from the first professional stage production of one of his plays in English translation, *The Memorandum*, in 1968 (Public Theater, New York), Havel's plays have been reviewed and written about in national and international publications. There are biographies, good (though not too manifold) academic criticism, and a recent book about his plays, Carol Rocamora's *Acts of Courage* (2004). There were recent extensive off-Broadway and fringe festivals of his work in New York and London (Untitled Theater Company #61's Havel Festival in 2006 and the Orange Tree Theatre's Havel Season in 2008). Havel found "home[s] away from home" (Rocamora 2004: 350) in the Public Theater, New York, and the Orange Tree Theatre, London, both of which, Rocamora argues, "had the courage and commitment to give their stages to Havel's plays" (p. 350). Although neither were Broadway or West End theatres, for a playwright translated into English, Havel had some

---

[1] Havel (b.1936) has written 18 plays *Rodinný večer/An Evening with the Family* (1960), *Zahradní slavnost/The Garden Party* (1963), *Vyrozumění/The Memorandum* (1965), *Anděl strážný/Guardian Angel* (1968), *Motýl na anténě/Butterfly on the Antenna* (1968), *Ztížená možnost soustředění/The Increased Difficulty of Concentration* (1968), *Spiklenci/ The Conspirators* (1971), *Žebrácká opera/The Beggar's Opera* (1972), *Audience/Audience* (1975), *Vernisáž/Private View* (1975), *Horský hotel/Mountain Hotel* (1976), *Protest/Protest* (1978), *Chyba/Mistake* (1983), *Largo desolato/Largo Desolato* (1984), *Pokoušení/Temptation* (1985), *Asanace/Redevelopment* (1987), *Zítra to spustíme/Tomorrow We'll Start it Up* (1988), *Odcházení/Leaving* (2007). The small and large spaces between the writing of plays reflect either Havel's time in prison (1977, 1979–83, 1989) or his Presidency (1989–2003). His plays were banned in Czechoslovakia between 1970 and 1989; apart from underground performances, his plays from *The Conspirators* onwards premiered abroad in translation (mostly in German). The Memorandum was Havel's first play to have a professional English-language stage production in 1968 (Public Theater, New York), followed by *The Increased Difficulty of Concentration* in 1969 (Lincoln Center, New York), both translated by Vera Blackwell. The next English-language professional stage productions were 8 years later: *Audience and Private View* and *The Memorandum* in 1977 (Orange Tree Theatre, London), translated by Blackwell. Protest was produced in 1980 (Orange Tree Theatre, London); *Mistake* in 1984 (RSC, London), both translated by Blackwell. In 1985 and 1986, *Largo Desolato* was produced in New York and London in two different translations (Marie Winn's translation at the Public Theater and Tom Stoppard's at the New Vic, Bristol). *Temptation* was also performed in separate American and English translations in 1987 (Marie Winn's translation at the Public Theater and George Theiner's by the RSC in Stratford). After the Velvet Revolution, the Orange Tree produced the English-language premieres of *Redevelopment* in 1990 in James Saunder's adaptation of Marie Winn's translation, the *Beggar's Opera* in 2003, and *Leaving* in 2008 both in Paul Wilson's translation. In 2006, the Untitled Theater Company #61 produced an off-Broadway Havel festival, comprising 18 plays including several English-language stage premieres and new translations: *Butterfly on the Antenna, The Conspirators, An Evening with the Family, Motomorphosis,* and *Mistake* translated by Carol Rocamora and Tomas Rychetsky; *The Memo, Guardian Angel,* and *The Beggar's Opera* translated by Paul Wilson; *Mountain Hotel* translated by Jitka Martinova; *Tomorrow* translated by Barbara Day; *The Increased Difficulty of Concentration* translated by Stepan Simek; *Audience, The Garden Party, Protest,* and *Unveiling* translated by Jan Novák; *Largo Desolato* translated by Tom Stoppard; and *Temptation* and *Redevelopment* by Marie Winn.

good exposure and, during the time his work was banned in Czechoslovakia (1970–89), an audience.

David Remnick, in a *New Yorker* profile of Havel at the end of his presidency in 2003, wrote that Havel's plays:

> were all understood by their audiences as implicit critiques of the regime: its stifling "automatism" (a favorite term of Havel's), its inhuman language. Those plays, which were produced abroad as specimens of the cultural thaw, became emblems of the Prague Spring [. . .] After the Soviet Union invaded Prague [. . .] he veered increasingly toward a position of full-time dissent. Thrilling as *The Garden Party* was for young audiences in Prague, this next phase was even more important—and, perhaps, even more appropriate to Havel's real talents [. . .] Far more ambitious, and more lasting, were Havel's dissident essays. (Remnick 2006: 147)

Remnick astutely observes that Western interest in the plays was tied to political interest, that they "were produced abroad as specimens of the cultural thaw," and were "emblems" of the 1968 Prague Spring; they gave a picture of life under Communism and reinforced the West's notion of itself as the very opposite. But Remnick also suggests that they were, anyway, political plays, "implicit critiques of the regime" that, as such, were less "lasting" than Havel's "dissident essays." So while Havel's first major play, *The Garden Party*, was "the right play written at the right time" (Rocamora 2004: 49), the sense is that the sell-by-date of these plays as "implicit critiques" has come and gone. Reviews of Havel's plays in the last 4 or 5 years have tended to read the plays within these terms—as historical curiosities revived because of who Havel is on the political stage. So, Quentin Letts, writing a review of two of Havel's one-act plays, *Protest* and *Private View*, fulminates that the plays are "less entertaining" than Havel's political career and that it is "unlikely they would be revived had he not gone on to become President" (Letts 2008). "The best excuse that I can think of for Mr. Havel," he adds, "is that his plays have lost something in translation" (Letts 2008).

Indeed they have, but generally not because of Havel's translators. Havel, from the beginning, was vehement that his plays were not political, and yet, they have consistently been read as such. Often staged because of the contemporary political context—it is no coincidence that the majority of productions of Havel's plays centered around political changes: 1968 (the Soviet invasion of Czechoslovakia), 1977 (the Charter 77 petition), 1989 (the Velvet Revolution), and the end of his Presidency in 2003—the plays were fundamentally read through a political lens by those staging them, audiences, and those reviewing them. The central problem was that his poetics made little sense or seemed to be superfluous to the political meaning perceived in the plays. Havel's prolix style, his repetitions, and particular punctuation, his concentration on language as the momentum of the play seemed alien to what was seen as their purpose, that is, political critique. At best, the style seemed a pretension to absurdist theatre, itself somewhat outmoded by the late 1970s when his plays were more frequently produced. Yet it is at the level of language that Havel's theatre carries its potency and its real existential inquiry. What was actually dangerous and unsettling and new in Havel's work was read as irrelevant and even faulty. Fortunate with his translators on the whole, who acted as responsible and even activist readers, those staging his plays, on the other hand, have often done so without a real sense of what Havel tried to achieve and with an emphasis on a political reading that seemed to be undermined by those poetics. He never became a commercially viable playwright, and the fact that theatres like the Public and the Orange Tree *had* to show "courage and commitment" in producing his plays indicates that he was never a box office or even necessarily a critical boon even to those theatres.

"Understanding Havel's plays," James Pontuso writes, "is a little like learning a language" because, in Havel's concept of theatre, there "must be something indeterminate about the plays, and the audience ought to share some of the work in uncovering each play's meaning" (Pontuso 2004: 75). The epistemological burden that Havel places on the audience at its heart runs contrary to the aims of censorship, a practice that always betrays "the monologic terror of indeterminacy" (Holquist 1994: 21). Havel's concept and praxis of theatre arose from conditions of censorship in Czechoslovakia yet were not an ideological but an exegetical and epistemological response to it. That the plays were, and are, read reductively in the West as political served to curb the "indeterminacy" of meaning, thus enacting the mechanisms of censorship that the plays attempted to subvert.

Was Havel really censored in the West? It seems a ridiculous question, given the actual hardships and punishments he underwent under the Communist regime where his fight for free speech ensured his imprisonment and near death. It seems a strange, enforced moral equivalency to suggest that just because some people fundamentally did not comprehend his plays or because some theatres produced his plays for their political worth, that this is also censorship. But it is a question worth asking because something fundamental is at stake and it is something that is central to and overlooked in Havel's plays: what role do *we* play in making and suppressing meaning? How do our choices of legitimacy affect those around us and the society in which we live? What responsibilities do we, as an audience, have in subverting or opposing censorship practices?

The intricacy of Havel's poetics enacts and performs legitimization and delegitimization on stage—of the self and others—of which the audience is part. In opening up ambiguities and uncertainties, feigns, and embattlements, Havel involves the audience in the mechanics of censorship, at its root, existential levels. In not posing a political position, Havel leaves it up to the audience to interpret for themselves and to understand that any interpretation inevitably involves some form of extirpation of other meanings, if only temporarily. We see ourselves, performing censorship, in dealing with the indeterminacies of the play and of life.

The humor of Havel's plays, sewn into the heart of this exchange, acknowledges the fallibility of the human, the predominance of desires over moral duties. The seduction of language is as strong in his plays as the seduction of others. The lack of anger in the humor points away from political satire to a more profound tragic-comic worldview that, nonetheless, is inherently optimistic about our miscommunications and self-delusions in the very act of recognizing them. Since censorship is inherently human, it too is fallible: whatever forgetting is going on, *someone* remembers.

The archive at the heart of this book—that of Havel's translator for 20 years, Vera Blackwell—tells a surprising story of resistance in the English-speaking world to Havel's plays. They were consistently rejected, adapted, or cut because their authorial style made no sense to theatres expecting political plays and where artistic norms and tastes leant more toward realism in the theatre. The covert ideological demands in England and America, the need for them to see a comprehendable, and thus marketable, version of Eastern Europe, excised translatable elements of Havel's plays that actually were performative dialogues with the activity of censorship.

Being mistaken for Kundera in a Washington elevator was perhaps not as surprising at it seemed; Kundera has been outspoken about the market-driven demands behind Western editorial decisions and the reductive political readings of Czech and East European literature (Woods 2006: 27–41). The cultural hegemony of the West (over its internal East) resulted in "inequalities of cultural interaction" (Aaltonen 2000: 51) and "reified worldviews" (Gentzler and Tymoczko 2002: xvi) that determined the shape of texts in the "mirror" (Aaltonen 2000: 52) of their own cultures and interests. While a certain amount of domestication is inevitable—there are certainly untranslatable elements of Havel's language and idiom—changes and omissions for reasons of speakability or performability often concealed hegemonic ideological practices, perhaps unwittingly, but certainly because of a lack of hermeneutic understanding of the plays. Unlike Havel, Kundera became a bestseller; only then could he "control" the aesthetics of his work in the West (Woods 2006: 186).

In itself, the archive is an important picture of the working life of a translator that is often elided in literary discourse. It also provides an insight into the process of translation as a negotiation between agents in a network of needs, agendas, requirements, and ideologies. The redemptive Cold War narrative of a banned writer gaining free speech in the West is only superficial: the complex requirements and expectations both in East and West paint a much more fluid and ambiguous picture about legitimization through the translation process, about what is allowed and what is not. Theatres, producers, directors, dramaturgs, and translators all have a stake in such decisions. In analyzing how individuals react in different situations and at different times, the question of constraints and censorship on both sides of the Cold War divide is at the heart of the archive. The Blackwell archive suggests that censorship does not provide a "neat narrative" and is "an unstable concept" (Hyland and Sammells 1992: 13), not necessarily imposed socially in a faceless normative guise but something that emanates from and is supported by individuals. Understanding censorship in such a way reveals possibilities for resistance, and as Havel's plays suggest, for the potential performative action of someone remembering.

The three chapters in *Censoring Translation* focus on different but interconnected forms of censorship: in Chapter 1, "Censorships and constraints," the relationship between overt and covert forms of censorship is explored on both sides of the Iron Curtain; Chapter 2, "Gender censorship," focuses on the plight and activism of the female translator in a male-dominated literary and theatre world; and Chapter 3, "Market censorship" explores the effect of the market on determining the place and aesthetics of translated literature and Havel plays in particular.

Vera Blackwell

Blackwell, neé Věra Jakešová, translated Havel's plays over a period of 20 years, from 1963 to 1985. A Czech émigré and graduate student, married to an American television producer, Blackwell began translating Czech plays for BBC radio in the early 1960s at the behest of Martin Esslin. Esslin, author of *The Theatre of the Absurd*, was an Hungarian émigré who worked for British intelligence during WWII and then for the BBC Theatre division, and who was central in bringing continental theatre to postwar England, at least in radio versions. Blackwell had worked for Radio Free Europe in Munich, following her escape (by foot) from Czechoslovakia in 1953 and met her husband there.

Blackwell, who had translated for American troops in Plzeň as the war ended, and who then worked for the British Council (with Kafka's translators Edwin and Willa Muir), worked on a PhD dissertation on theatre with the prominent literary critic Václav Černy at Charles University. She received a Masters in literature from Radcliffe College and wrote plays and poetry throughout her life. Though she began her translating career keen to translate various Czech writers, through the 1960s, 1970s, and 1980s, she solely translated Havel's work. Her archive attests to her incessant activity in promoting Havel's work, writing to agents, producers, directors, and publishers to persuade them to produce his play. Following the Soviet invasion, Havel gave her power of attorney over his work in the English-language world in case of persecution or imprisonment and, from the beginning, offered her a 50/50 split in fees. After the Soviet invasion in 1968, Blackwell was deported from Czechoslovakia and denounced as a spy on Czech television.

Blackwell's translatorial relationship with Havel ended in 1985 when she was blamed by Havel's central foreign agent Klaus Juncker for the lack of success and productions of Havel's plays in the United Kingdom and the United States. Juncker regarded her to be at fault in a number of ways: her translations were linguistically inadequate; she was intransigent in allowing changes to her translations in production (a usual demand in theatre for reasons of local "speakability" issues); and she demanded too much recompense for her work (Juncker disagreeing with the validity of a 50/50 split between author and translator).

Juncker's discomfort with Blackwell opens up a series of issues regarding the role of the translator in theatre translation: is the play being translated for stage or for publication? Should translations be open to change during the production process? What does this mean for the translator in terms of intellectual property and in terms of status? What kind of percentage should a translator receive in recompense for their work? But it also raises wider contextual issues. Is it the translator's fault when foreign plays don't achieve wide audiences or success on a domestic stage? How can we judge? Are translators, as marginalized figures, easy targets? If Blackwell's translations are not wholly at fault for the lack of productions, then is there a larger cultural resistance at work?

Blackwell certainly believed so, several times noting the "Anglo-Saxon insularism" of British and American theatre. In her view, the rejection of the translations had little to do with the translations themselves but with a fundamental lack of understanding of what the plays attempted to frame. It was not, in other words, her language that was rejected, but Havel's investigation of language: the style and content of the plays. Throughout her career as Havel's translator, she felt that attempts to change her translations when productions were mounted were rooted in miscomprehensions and reductive, politicized readings of Havel's plays. She was not necessarily threatened by a sense of invasiveness on her text, but by a sense that she had to protect the misunderstood aesthetics of Havel's plays.

Reading Blackwell's translations of Havel's plays today, it is evident that Blackwell was primarily a literary, rather than a theatrical, translator. Her translations are not geared toward speakability or "nowness" and they are made in the very fluent and very correct British English she spoke. The literariness of the translations are, perhaps, due to not only her scholarly background, but also due to the fact that most of her translations were performed by BBC radio (when received pronunciation was the norm) and published (by Cape and Grove) before they were performed on stage. It is understandable why productions (especially in the United States) might have demanded traction in the text for reasons of playability.

Having said this, the translations demonstrate that Blackwell clearly understood what Havel's aesthetics were and she attempted to be faithful to the style of the plays, to their inner logic—for instance, retaining the repetitions and circularity of phrasing, or retaining the punctuation (important

for pauses and effect). Her intransigence toward changes to her translations were sometimes very justified; for instance, with a 1980 production
of *Protest* whose director randomly cut and edited the text, removing repetitions and punctuation that changed the style of the play making it seem
more politically direct than it was. Thus, the issue of speakability is thornier
than it might appear; while it might make sense to localize a play or update
it to modern parlance, the updater needs to do so with a knowledge of the
source language and with a knowledge of the playwright's aesthetics.

Havel made it clear in his letters that he respected her translations even
when they were being criticized—not because he could judge linguistically whether she had made the right word choice for a particular word or
because he expected an absolutely faithful translation (knowing that this is
not possible given cultural transference), but because he felt she understood
what his "narrowly defined poetics" were (Havel 2007a: 335). Throughout
their correspondence, he treated her and her work with respect.

Blackwell, by all accounts, was strong-willed, something that comes
across vividly in her letters. What also comes across from her varied correspondence is that the worlds she moved in—theatre, radio, television—
was male-dominated. Acting as a promoter for Havel's work, she writes to
central figures in the theatre world: Esslin, Tynan, Papp, Peter Brooks, Tom
Stoppard, etc., and the only real business connection she has with a woman
is with the agent she chooses to be Havel's UK theatrical agent, Peggy
Ramsay. Ramsay—Ionesco's agent (and lover) as well as Beckett's—was no
wilting violet either (as witnessed in Simon Callow's wonderful memoir of
his friendship with her), and the archive paints a world (the business end
of the theatre world) where, to be taken seriously, a woman needs to be
thick-skinned and where she will always be questioned. Blackwell, herself,
does not make any reference to a sense of gender inequity but as a woman,
a foreign woman, and a foreign female translator, her work was constantly
treated with suspicion.

From 1984 onwards, Blackwell did not translate any more literature or
plays. She became increasingly involved with the Catholic Church, specifically with Opus Dei. She did live to see Havel become President and her
homeland freed of the Communist rule that exiled her. Blackwell died in
1995 in New York; her executrix sent President Havel a rough draft of a
sketch Blackwell had written about her first impressions of him. These were
her last, posthumous words to Havel:

All the time I've known Václav—I mean the time I was able to meet with
him—that is, between 1964 and 1969—the year I was last in Prague—his
face was quite angellic [sic]—it radiated angellic innocence—and since
he's also rather short and chubby—I always thought if you gilded him,
you could hang him over one of the sumptuous baroque altars in which
Prague is so rich—and you wouldn't know him from the other chubby,
cheerful, innocent, golden baroque angels.

I saw some photographs taken after his first imprisonment in 1977—and it seems his face has changed almost beyond recognition.—Now it seems to match more closely his razor-sharp intellect and wit—the previous face was so utterly different from his writing.—It may be because he lost a lot of weight in prison—he seems to have rounded up again since then. That is, before he was arrested again last May—heaven knows what he looks like now!

He's always tended to be chubby—he loves good food, he loves to cook—and he is a magnificent cook—he'd very gregarious, friendly, loves to have people around, loves to talk—can go on for hours—his talk is always witty, beautifully phrased—enviably so—his mind is incredibly well-organized, totally logical—his arguments are watertight—so much so that it is almost impossible to pierce them—even when one sometimes knows he's wrong. To argue against Václav can be a very frustrating experience. Sometimes I think what hell his interrogators in prison must be going through. Not that I had much opportunity to be thus frustrated—mostly—though not always—I agreed with him—we always seemed to think along the same lines. (Vera Blackwell Archive or VBA 2:8)

1
Censorships and constraints

Ballas: Friends! We are all guilty.

THE MEMORANDUM

"Havel was a playwright and essayist who wrote as if censorship did not exist" (Remnick 2006: 145), David Remnick writes, but, when he began his career as a playwright in the 1960s, Havel was aware of the censorship conditions under which he wrote, conditions that were not, however, as "David-and-Goliath" (Coetzee 1996: 118) as the West supposed, that is, just the victimized writer repressed by a faceless censor. Havel, in the 1960s, seemed to have one available option: to write what Jarka Burian has called "camouflaged" (Burian 2000: 101) plays, plays that used allegory and subtexts to convey to a literate and hungry audience truths about the specific society in which they lived—truths that could not be said out loud. "To the Czech audience on opening night," Carol Rocamora writes of *The Garden Party*'s premiere, "that wasn't an absurd world, that was Czech realism" (Rocamora 2004: 48).

It was the Czech audience's reaction, their act of reading between the lines and laughing, that attracted the first foreign interest in the Havel's first major play. But translation posed a problem: if this was a "camouflaged" play, pointedly using Czech reality as a subtext, then how could that "local" subtext be translated successfully? The attraction of Havel's plays abroad was linked to the perceived subtext; he was a writer challenging the regime with absurdist theatre and was, therefore, important on a cultural level (making theatre socially vital) and on a political level (criticizing neo-Stalinist Communism). The fear was that a foreign audience might understand the totality of the message of the subtext, that is, that they were watching a play critiquing Communist Czechoslovakia, but not understand the complexities and nuances of the localized critique, thereby making the play lose its force. In other words, what attracted Western producers to Havel's plays was also crucially an obstacle: to make the plays more relevant to Western audiences they had to be altered to try and regain some of the effect while at the same time consolidating the source effect of the initial critique. For such a critique of Communism, of course, also consolidated the freedoms of the West.

But were Havel's plays "camouflaged"? If so, we may be right to dismiss them as now redundant "emblems of the Prague Spring" because the effect they had would speak only to a given historical context, when audiences deciphered the plays like they were news. Similarly, reading correspondence about and reviews of the plays in England and the United States in the 1960s, the translations were also read like news, relevant to an understanding of the post-Stalinist cultural thaw and then the Soviet invasion and crushing of the Prague Spring. Why, then, perform them now, except as acts of appreciation or as historical artifacts? But Havel did in fact have a second option against Czech censorship in the 1960s and that was to write plays that took censorship and its mechanisms and explored them. In this way, his plays were not culturally bound to a particular culture or context, but suggested ways to interrogate an experience we all share—not overt totalitarian censorship, but our own propensity to be seduced by language and to use it to gain or cede power. His plays are also, fundamentally, about reading, about the audience actively interpreting what is going on, and questioning their interpretations; Havel and his director, Jan Grossman, called this "appellative theatre," theatre designed to provoke questions, to unsettle the audience, rather than to provide didactic answers.

"What is the genuine?" J. M. Coetzee asks, "Is it possible to write the genuine in a regime of overreading?" (Coetzee 1996: 151). Writing about Zbigniew Herbert's poetry, Coetzee questions the "Aesopian" (p. 153) method of writing and reading under censorship, "to propose that uncloaking the allegory constitutes a reading does far less than justice to it" because such readings arise out of the "paranoia of censorship [. . .] which, constitutionally opposed to innocent readings, spreads its habits of overreading through the whole of the reading community" (p. 151). If the writer writes for this overreading then they too are part of the game, producing a reductive, utterly contextualized piece of writing. For Coetzee, such writing works within a parallel system (to censorship) of a utopian ideal populated by:

> absolutists who believe that the universe we presently have is an imperfect form of another, ideal order [. . .] Interpretation is therefore the road absolutists take to the truth behind poetry. The censor is a figure of the absolutist reader: he reads the poem in order to know what it *really* means, to know its truth. (p. 160)

The censor, in this model, looks for a "second-order writing (metaphor, allegory) that will open itself to interpretation" (p. 160), indeed expects it. The writer writing under censorship, if he or she works on the "between-the-lines" (p. 152) method, may be susceptible to writing in this "second-order." This may work as a strategy because the censor has to prove "the presence of a something where there seems to be a nothing, a blank" and thus "risks ridicule," but it also means that the censor "is quite as capable of reading between the lines as the writer is of writing between them" (p. 152). Playing chicken with the censor might be a necessity, but it means that the writer is involved in the game and deliberately self-censoring her/himself not only to evade the censor but also to convey an interpretable, and thereby reductive, "between-the-lines" message to the reader or audience.

Coetzee argues that the best—and not all—of Herbert's poetry does something different in the face of censorship and that is in thinking about interpretation, interrogating, and evading, interpretation. In making the reader think, in challenging them, the poetry resists the kind of "second-order" reading of the censor and, for Coetzee, resists the "language of the ideal order," that is, language abstracted from real life that fits a perfect interpretable form, for "human language, which is an imperfect medium born of an imperfect world" (p. 160). The tricky element for art—that necessarily abstracts human language into artistic forms—is to preserve the messiness, the unaccountable elements, the ambiguities that constitute the languages in which we live, "the imperfect, this-worldly language of the flesh" (p. 160).

What was ingenious about Havel's plays in the 1960s (and beyond) was the mixture of architectonic form—order above all else—and content that dealt with the idea of utopian language or language pushed to the boundaries of rational possibilities and order, and, finally, a subversion of that order in the way that he used that language as it fell apart under its own idealism. Havel does not despair of language, it is not presented as meaningless, even though it may inherently, as an entity or tool, be so—what makes language meaningful are humans themselves. It is the mechanism of those constructions of meaning that interest Havel as a playwright, as do the agendas and interests behind such constructions. Havel's plays were not enlightening to Czech audiences because they presented an allegorical "between-the-lines" picture of life in Communist Czechoslovakia where the pseudorationalistic language of Marxism-Leninism shaped public discourse. They made people laugh because they saw their own collusion in the game; it made them think about language and how it shaped reality—certainly under Communism— but also in a more general and existential way. To interpret the plays as just Aesopian vehicles would allow an audience to escape their small portion of the blame.

Coetzee's notion of the reader as a censor is important because it applies beyond totalitarian borders and gets to something universal: the need for overarching and hermetic interpretation and the utopian and idealist bent behind it. Readers and audiences want the satisfaction of knowing what a poem or book or play is about, such interpretation cradles the mind, but it can also lead to entropy and damaging misreading. Havel's plays came with

Western preconceptions about what their subtext and their message was; in part this made them interesting, newsworthy, and thus produceable; but it also defined them in and confined them to a particular reading that served sociopolitical and commercial interests in the West. In Coetzee's sense, we can see some of these "external constraints"—producers, directors, theatres, dramaturgs, reviewers—on the plays in Britain and the United States as reader-censors, coming with predetermined expectations and readings of the plays that attenuated Havel's aesthetic and philosophic aims that were, in essence, translatable.

In this chapter, then, I want to explore different forms of censorship and constraints that applied simultaneously to Havel's work, both at home and abroad, in the 1960s. First, it is important to understand Havel's theory of appellative theatre as his response to censorship conditions—as an artistic rather than a political response. In some senses, this is a domestic, intralingual translation, what I and Mandana Taban have called "analogical translation," a mode that is not an encoding of secret political messages as subtext but that actively translates the conditions of censorship into an artistic text in order to investigate and explore the modality of censorship. Havel's own theories of playwriting challenge the notion of him as just a political, dissident playwright; these theories can elucidate a reading of his plays that tell us something about the mechanism of censorship and its practices, especially as it relates to language and the individual.

The conditions of censorship in Czechoslovakia in the 1960s are central to Havel's response and central to understanding totalitarian censorship as more covert and invasive, as well as more flexible than has previously been assumed (previous to work by translation studies scholars such as Kate Sturge). This flexibility and invasiveness is important to understand, not only in the Czech case, but also in thinking about strategies to resist and overcome overt and covert censorship practices in closed and open societies.

Havel's case elucidates what can happen under conditions of source-language censorship when translation enters the equation. Surprisingly, the authority with the ability to censor translations of his work, the state literary agency, DILIA, moved between obfuscation and keen support of the translations. In this case, a totalitarian regime saw advantages in translating ideologically suspect plays for two reasons: money and prestige and, in doing this, curiously reflected producers and agencies in the Western market economies. In addition, DILIA showed little interest in textual interference, using extratextual tactics (withholding contracts, bureaucratic delays, pressure on the translator, withholding income) for censorship purposes; in essence, applying contractual constraints on Havel, sometimes to prevent or delay foreign productions, but also often to leverage better or more prestigious contracts.

Finally, I want to question the redemptive narrative about Havel's plays, one that suggests that they moved from total censorship to a free-speech stage because of the agendas and misreadings behind the English-language productions of his plays in the 1960s. Left untouched textually under censorship conditions at home, Havel and his translator were under constant pressure to adapt and cut his plays in English. Havel was fully aware that there would be necessary changes to the translations because of cultural and target language differences, but the changes demanded by theatres and producers went beyond necessity and reflected an ideological motive in rewriting the plays for cultural taste and norms. As Denise Merkle, Francesca Billiani, and Maria Tymoczko have suggested, such reductive readings of translated texts exhibit features of covert censorship. Coetzee's notion of the "absolutist reader"—the reader searching for interpretable texts—opens up questions of why Havel was read in the West as a political playwright mired in his local context and time and whether this case can inform how English-language cultures inculcate the meaning and message of translated plays for their own ends, thereby ridding the plays of their actual "newness."

Appellative theatre and analogical translation

Havel's director and collaborator in the 1960s, Jan Grossman, argued as an introduction to the first English publication of *The Memorandum* (in the *Tulane Drama Review*, 1967) that the ambiguity in the play was not a political expediency—a means of escaping the censor—but rather a means of making the play interactive so that "the audience should be considered not just as a production requirement, but as co-creator" (Grossman 1967: 118). Havel's plays, he writes, "create a specific dialogue between stage and audience, with ample room for complementary meanings and associations" (p. 119). Grossman and Havel called this the "appellative" theatre, one which posed questions in jarring juxtapositions for the audience to answer (Burian 2000: 120). Grossman did not regard this to be a revolutionary approach to drama:

> Both Shakespeare and Chekhov, in their vastly different ways, through mystery, fragmentation, ambiguity—the strange unspecified space which lures the audience and tempts it to fill the void—evoke a dialogue. A great theatre reveals not only itself and its story: it also reveals the viewer's story, and with it his urgent need to confront his own experience with the theme presented on stage. Such a play does not end with the performance; the curtain is only the beginning. (Grossman 1967: 118)

Although *The Memorandum* has been read politically as a critique of the nonsensical "communication in the totalitarian system in which Havel and his fellow Czechs live" (Rocamora 2004: 65), "satirizing the slogan-like phrases of the Communist Party and demonstrating how incomprehensible and meaningless they really are" (p. 66), or, as a critique of "the questionable nature of the post-Stalinist reforms" (Trensky 1978: 120), the play is neither polemic nor merely a political satire of a given situation. What interests Havel is the metaphysics of language as power and the mechanisms by which human control of language only exposes an ontological entrapment by language as a power force itself. In other words, censorship can originate with us, bottom up, as well as from above.

To get his play on the stage Havel could not be political—DILIA, the state literary, and theatrical agency would not have given permission for it to be produced. But Havel did not simply write a "camouflaged" satire of the official or bureaucratic language of the Communist state and state organs such as DILIA. He was, like Czech filmmakers of his generation:

> not interpreting meaning for the domestic audience or imposing a meaning—a loaded encoding—because the [plays] are not propagandistic or polemic, but they all allow, amongst other things, a space for interpretation under censorship that directly engages with the censorship practices themselves [. . .] the indirect, the unsaid expresses a modality of translation within the domestic languages the purpose of which was not simply to evade censorship but to engage with its practices, uniformity and unilingualism. (Taban and Woods 2006: 105)

Even in the domestic sphere, *The Memorandum* (as with Havel's other plays) directly asks for a translation—the "loaded encoding" of the play demands an intralingual translation (what does Havel *really* mean?), but at the same time, makes the audience aware that in imposing their own readings on the play they are enacting a translation, the dangers of which (given the content of the play) are apparent. In deliberately not imposing meaning—by placing the play in an abstract, dehistoricized context—Havel subverts the political reductiveness of censorship practices, but also questions how we, the audience, attribute meaning and the extent to which we have the potential of being censorial ourselves. In demanding that the audience participate in applying meaning, in translating, Havel demands that they think about the process itself.

In his prison letters to his wife (1979–82), Havel extrapolates on his theatrical philosophy (though denying that it is a philosophy, rather, a set of meditations on the theatre), emphasizing three important elements: first, the notion of openness of meaning; secondly, the danger of ideological playwriting as a threat to this first notion; and thirdly, the importance of structure and order in the play that allows openness of interpretation. Havel, of course, was formulating these thoughts under conditions of censorship; he was instructed only to write about himself and letters from the outside were frequently held back or doctored. What is remarkable about these meditations on the theatre, written under censorship, is how Havel formulated his thoughts about a theatre, that is, at its very basis, antithetical to conditions of censorship on a metaphysical rather than a political (i.e. dissident) level.

The problem with political theatre, in Havel's eyes, was its codification of reading and meaning, in that it presented a message for the audience to digest rather than provoking them to read the play as it was performed, to interpret, and translate the play into their own experience. He noted that "modern drama is so frequently thesis-ridden, so infected—either deliberately or voluntarily—with didacticism or ideology. Such an approach, it seems to me, throws the baby out with the bathwater" (Havel 1988: 285). Referring to his respect for Brecht, the poster-boy of political playwriting, he wrote "it's a cool and polite respect; frankly, I only like his non-Brechtian moments, when the thing, as it were, becomes bigger than his is" (p. 285). For Havel, the institution of a political message or raison d'etre in a play cut off the potential reverberations and multivalent meanings it might have for an audience, making them passive consumers of a thought or teachable moment. The problem, for Havel, was that good playwriting should transcend the efforts of the playwright: "the message of the play, because it has many levels of meaning, always transcends the playwright's intentions" (p. 285). In Karel Hvížd'ala's interviews with Havel in *Disturbing the Peace*, Havel underscored this:

> Even as a playwright, I've always believed that each member of the audience must sort the play out himself, because this is the only way his experience of it can be authentic; my job is not to offer him something ready-made. (Havel 1990: 8)

This lack of a didactic message in his plays extends to allegorical symbols or easy "translation" of some coded intent that "exhaust[s] the entire meaning of the play" (Havel 1988: 170). "On the contrary," he writes:

> I like it when a work can be interpreted in different ways, when it something of an enigma and when its meaning, though it may transcend the work itself, does so by radiating in all directions [. . .] the purpose of the play is not to have the viewer leave with this, or any other, exclusive conceptually clarified awareness of its "meaning"; if we can explain and name anything too well, we come to terms with it too quickly, our interpretation soothes us, the work ceases to tantalize and irritate us and we quickly forget it . . . I would rather the play disturbed them in some indeterminable way. (170–1)

"This kind of theatre," for Havel:

neither instructs us, nor attempts to acquaint us with theories or interpretations of the world, but by "probing" beneath the surface, it somehow inspires us to participate in an adventurous journey towards a deeper understanding, or rather to a new and deeper questioning, of ourselves and the world [. . .] It's as though the theater had carried us with it to a path leading along a dangerous mountain ridge—and to our astonishment, we can walk along it, though we'd never before suspected that such a path existed or that we were capable of negotiating it. The author of the play or the creators of the performance, of course, are no more clever or knowledgeable than anyone else. They are not taking us somewhere they are familiar with and we are not. Everyone goes through the adventure together, and it's equally surprising, tantalizing and disturbing for us all. (pp. 252–3)

Of course, Havel intimates that this "probing" and "living with the question" (p. 225) is something that the audience has to take upon themselves and involves their willingness to partake in a kind of *writerly* (in the Barthesian sense) interaction with the performance. In a profound way, this speaks to Havel's notion of personal responsibility as a mode of living ethically with ourselves and, thus, with the world around us: "vouching for ourselves in time, knowing everything we have ever done and why, what we are doing and why, and what we have decided to do" (p. 233). In being aware of our relationship to ourselves and our community, in consistently thinking about, or at least being aware of, existential questions, we are then "in constant touch with this mystery that ultimately makes us genuinely human" (p. 225). Havel used the notion of personal responsibility, or living in truth, in his seminal essay on nonviolent resistance, "The Power of the Powerless," in which he argued that the "post-totalitarian ideology" of the regime was being upheld by each individual and in resisting the outward requirements of the ideology, the act of each individual could combine to unmask the regime and render it powerless. In terms of an audience watching a play, this "living in truth" requires a genuine interaction with meaning and interpretation on an individual and community basis, a willingness to face the "mystery" and the "questions" the play probes. For Havel, this is an iteration of faith, which is "a state of persistent and productive openness, of persistent questioning, a need to 'experience the world' again and again" (Havel 1998: 190).

In contrast, ideological thinking is hermetic and entropic; when "a person falls for a ready-made ideological system or 'worldview', [. . .] he will bury all chances of thinking and freedom, of being clear about what he knows [. . .] he will deaden the adventure of the mind" (pp. 191–2). In sealing off multivalent interpretations, or the possibility of such, this kind of ideological thinking in plays had more in common with the hermeneutics of censorship than in a protest against it. Havel, entering the theatre scene as a stagehand in 1960, knew whereof he spoke. The established, or so-called "stone" theatres had offered ideological plays in the 1950s and the flowering of "small" theatres in Prague were a reaction to overtly political and politicized theatre. Watching a performance in one of these small theatres, the Semafor, was revelatory to Havel, where the "performances were not about anything" but seemed a series of songs, held together by "the delight in performance, the rhythm, the pure fun, that seemed to make all those learned ideological debates seem fundamentally inappropriate [. . .] It was a manifestation of uncensored life, life that spits on all ideology" (Havel 1990: 49). The plays in the small theatres of the 1960s were deliberately "nonideological" (p. 51).

But they were not an escape from engagement with the society around them, rather they were, in Havel's terms, an engagement with life in its mysteries and complexities rather than a prescriptive and proscriptive analysis of problems and solutions. The absurd seemed an appropriate form for this engagement even though it was considered apolitical, "nihilistic" (p. 53) and embracing of meaninglessness. Yet Havel argued that Beckett's and Ionesco's absurdist plays "are merely a warning. In a very shocking way, they throw us into the question of meaning by manifesting its absence" (p. 53). For Havel:

> absurdity is never—at least not as I understand it—the expression of a loss of faith in the meaning of life. Quite the opposite: only someone whose very being thirsts after meaning, for whom "meaning" is an integral part of his own existence, can experience the absence of meaning as something painful, or more precisely, can perceive it at all [. . .] this sensation and distance from the world, of having abandoned the conventional stereotypes of experience on which the superficial and mystified meaning of the world is based, that opens the door to genuinely fresh, sharp and penetrating vision. (Havel 1988: 177–8)

Rather than offering a message, the absurd theatre allows "'amplification' of an ordinary situation" (p. 285), probing the existential questions beneath it and demystifying them (p. 284). Havel connects his interest in the absurd with his feeling of alienation and outsiderness as a child, both as a wealthy boy and as a fat boy, a "piglet," as the "fundamental experience of not belonging" (Havel 1990: 6). But this feeling of "fitting in nowhere" (p. 6) puts him in a position of comprehending the "absurdity" of the quest for meaning becoming a meaning in itself. "I have the feeling" he wrote, "that, if absurd theatre had not existed before me, I would have had to invent it" (p. 54).

Martin Esslin included Havel's work in the second edition of his seminal book, *The Theatre of the Absurd*; Esslin saw absurd theatre as "expressing the tragic sense of loss at the disappearance of ultimate certainties," but that, paradoxically, "is also a symptom of what probably comes closest to being a genuine religious quest in our age [. . .] at least in search of a dimension of the Ineffable" (Esslin 2004: 400). Like Havel, he viewed it as "an effort to make man aware of the ultimate realities of his condition [. . .] to shock him out of an existence that has become trite, mechanical, complacent, and deprived of all the dignity that comes of awareness" (p. 400). At the same time, Esslin appended a political reading to Havel's choice of the absurd, calling his first major play a "mixture of hard-hitting political satire, Schweykian humour and Kafkaesque depths" (p. 324) and argued that the adoption of the absurd tradition in Eastern Europe in the 1960s demonstrated that the absurd was, in some dimensions, political or could be used for political means. Referring to a debate between Kenneth Tynan and Eugene Ionesco, in which Tynan called Ionesco's repudiation of politics and ideology an ideology itself, and in which Ionesco forcibly argued that it was not a playwright's place to offer "a didactic message" (p. 129), Esslin seemed to present the absurd in Eastern Europe as fundamentally political and, therefore, as vindication of Tynan's position. But Havel rejected the notion of "satire" as inherently caught into the same hermetic circle as ideological theatre which only presents "superficial critiques of abuses, shortcomings, human weaknesses [. . .] bureaucracy, and bribery" (Havel 1990: 41). The fact that Esslin might refrain from calling Beckett or Ionesco political but not any playwright from Eastern Europe in the same tradition (even though, of course, Esslin was East European himself), suggests an ideological reading of these playwrights as necessarily political because of preconceptions about their aims. For Havel, the absurd was a means of going beyond the political, of transcending it.

Esslin, too, suggests that the message of the absurd is a rather bleak one, portending of meaninglessness and, ultimately, an artistic consequence of the horrors of WWII. Havel's notion of the absurd differs; while it may plunge us into uncertainty, discomfort, shock, the awareness, or touching on, the "Ineffable" ultimately is a hopeful condition. Thus, a good work of art "sets our drowsy souls and our lazy hearts 'moving'!" he writes, "And can we separate the awakening human soul from what it always, already is—an awakening human community?" (Havel 1989: 135). In other words, the absurd—though apparently a form centered on alienation (and chosen by Havel because of his own childhood alienation)—can, in its affect, effect a movement toward a better understanding of our search for meaning as individuals and as a community.

Havel also diverged from Esslin in believing in some "Order of Being" or "absolute horizon" by which our actions are measured, remembered. Although not expressly religious, in some senses, he did not work in Esslin's Lukácsian worldview, that is, in a world devoid of meaning because of God's absence. Although Havel expressly eschewed theological dogma, he argued that the sense of an absolute might come from a personal search for it. While the "Order of Being" was "veiled in mystery" (Havel 1988: 185), Havel argued that the "order of life"—of which art was a part—was a means of searching for meaning, and thereby giving meaning to life (p. 186). Havel's strong sense of a kind of universal order, he argued, was reflected in his attention to structure in his plays—often, in translation, the most misunderstood element of Havel's plays.

What Havel calls "my pedantic fondness for rational structures (obvious, for instance, in the architecture of my plays" (p. 184) is not an insistence on aesthetic form for form's sake, but an attempt to implement strict rules of structure in order to explore what those structures can reveal. "[I]f, for example," he writes:

> conventions and structures are characteristic of my plays (e.g., the mechanical and geometric patterns that occur in the dialogue), then this was only because I was attempting, through them and against the backdrop they

provided, to give dramatic shape to a particular question, surprise, mystery or shock—either, by developing those patterns ab absurdum or, on the contrary, by gradually breaking them down [. . .] Transcendence can only take place when there is something to transcend. (p. 198)

The mechanical architecture of Havel's plays, the verbal repetitions, scene repetitions, repeated entrances and exits, have often either been truncated in translation or, when performed in the complete translation, have often been seen as either naïve elements of the plays (glib and outdated comment on the mechanization of man, or the totalitarian mindset) or, simply, faults—the plays go on too long. The perceived bagginess of the plays often has something to do with the preconceived notions of what the plays are about, that is, that the point of the plays are to express satiric comment on a given political situation. Within these narrow terms, the plays do go on too long: if Hugo in *The Garden Party* or Gross in *The Memorandum* are read as entrapped and empowered functionaries in a barely concealed Communist system, then the audience might not need three long acts to get the message. The problem may be, however, in the simplistic reading of the plays and the failure to recognize that what Havel attempted was not to deliver a message, but to pull the audience in, frustrate them, wind them tight, get them involved in the constrictions of language, and to get them questioning their own relationship to language and to the everyday.

The first three major plays: *The Garden Party*, *The Memorandum*, and *The Increased Difficulty of Concentration* all probe the question of language and the dialectic relationships humans have with it, as masters and mastered. In *The Garden Party*, the young man going out into the world, Hugo Pludek, rises in the world because he learns not only to imitate the language and idioms of others, but manages to regenerate the clichéd language into an imprisoning poetry of its own. In *The Memorandum*, Gross is ousted from his position of power in an office because of the introduction of a new language, Ptydepe, that few speak but which promises to make language more scientifically efficient and denude it of redundancies (but in fact is far more complex); Balaš, who instituted the language, ends up a victim of it too, unable to speak it and therefore unable to see his end coming. In *The Increased Difficulty of Concentration*, Puzuk the computer is being used to extract the essence of individual humanity through a questioning of humans, most notably the play's protagonist, Huml, but in fact the hero's humanity comes out in his repeated clichés to lovers and wife. The "pedantic" order of Havel's plays is, as he puts it, an "order for disrupting order" (Havel 1988: 257), and it is a tightly equipoised order that pokes at the limits of language and identity, at an uncomfortable place of misunderstanding, miscomprehension where humanity might finally reside.

The tight composition of plays for Havel is "immensely important" (p. 286), but is also something at risk in translation, especially when those commissioning or producing the translation on stage are more intent on a "message" than on the aesthetic form of the play. English-language productions, as we shall see, wanted to cut the plays, adapt the plays, make them more "speakable"—on a certain level, of course, a desirable aim—but often the speakability was aimed toward a fuller understanding of the message rather than attempting to engage with the aesthetics, possibly achievable through a genuine rewriting of the play that engaged with the rhythms of the Czech original. "Even small errors in rhythm," Havel wrote:

> Timing or the distribution of motifs can turn a play that was otherwise wonderful into bad theater. I have even observed that small rhythmic differences in different performances of the same production can sometimes lead to success and sometimes to failure [. . .] The composition and development of motifs, the way they are arranged, repeated, reinvoked, combined, interwoven, connected, gradated and brought to a climax, their precise location—all these things—whether they be emphasized or disguised, whether they are more the result of a conscious effort or "merely" of a sensitivity to the matter—are what make a play a play. (p. 286)

On reading Vera Blackwell's translation of *The Garden Party*, Havel's director, Jan Grossman, complimented her on the precision of the translation, but said, in reference to the RSC's decision to adapt the play, that adaptation was perhaps inevitable because of the cultural specificity of some of the Czech language used in the play. However, he made the point that, while any adapter should be free to adapt a play, this "Freedom is the first condition of 'fidelity' in the deep sense of the word" (VBA 1:1, 30/7/64); in other words, though free to translate and adapt each word or phrase, there needed to be an assumption of fidelity to the spirit, rhythm, and aesthetics of the play. It needed to be a faithful rewriting of the play that allowed for multivalency in meaning (it was adapted, instead, and never performed, as a straightforward farce).

Havel's attention to language and to the question of meaning was a metaphysical response to the "entropic" language of ideology and political interpretation; in freeing language and meaning from politicized content, Havel was embracing a freedom from ideology and asking his audience to do so too. Only in this sense was Havel ever a "political" playwright, disdaining the didactically political theatre of the 1950s because it fell into the metaphysical territory of censorship when it told its audiences what to think.

Censorship

Although there were no official censorship laws regarding literature and the press in Czechoslovakia in the 1960s, Dušan Hamšík writes that after Kruschev's Twentieth Congress Speech in 1956 disclosing Stalin's crimes, Novotný's neo-Stalinist regime began sending out officials to publishers and newspapers, so by "such quiet, inconspicuous steps did censorship inveigle its way into our daily routine" (Hamšík 1971: 109). A Main Board of Press Control was set up under the aegis of the Ministry of the Interior but "stalinist socialism tried to conceal [the censors] existence altogether" and this censorship "was characterized not only by the bureaucratic brutality normal under stalinism, but also by a certain hypocritical slyness and calm pretence that nothing was amiss" (p. 110). Hamšík notes how certain types of literary texts evaded censorship because they were not seen as directly critiquing the regime:

> Our censors were in fact a great deal less interested in purely literary matters than the reader might think [. . .] The works of Franz Kafka, Albert Camus, Eugene Ionesco and their followers in Czechoslovakia, all representatives of "rotten, degenerate bourgeois pseudo-art", made little impression on the eagle-eyed guardians of socialist doctrine as long as there was no intrusion into current public affairs [. . .] Literature that either ignored current events or only passed obscure or indirect judgement on them was given a certain scope for development. (pp. 95–6)

The literalist approach to censorship had an immense and negative impact on reporting and realist assessments of Czechoslovak society and economics, but it meant that avant-garde literature and plays had a chance to be disseminated. Following the strict official adherence to socialist realism and didactic politicized texts in the 1950s, the 1960s saw translations of avant-garde plays and literature that would have an enormous impact on Czech literature (Beneš 1972: 101). The Theatre on the Balustrade was the scene for enormously successful productions of translated plays such as Beckett's *Waiting for Godot* and Alfred Jarry's *Ubu roi* that would have a direct impact on Havel's writing. The turn toward the absurdist tradition allowed for an aesthetic that would not confront the political context head-on but that could investigate and analyze the metaphysical fallout of totalitarian thought and methods.

The attraction of the avant-garde also lay in the proscription of so-called decadent texts in the Stalinist 1950s; writers began to shy away from overt political and polemical writing so that, as Paul Trensky argues, while absurd theatre was becoming more contextually concrete in the West:

> the Czech absurdists were writing increasingly more abstract and philosophically oriented plays. Their concept of relevance broadened; and in the peculiar cultural atmosphere, the preoccupation with existential questions became a form of a protest against the stereotyped, doctrinaire policies of the regime. An apolitical standpoint began to be understood as containing important ethical implications that might have a significant long-range impact on the country's political course as well. (Trensky 1978: 104)

In some ways, then, the narrow totalitarian concept of political literature and secretive censorship practices contributed to the Czech embrace of the absurd and the avant-garde during the thaw in the 1960s: it seemed an ideal form with which to engage issues in a "camouflaged" manner (Burian 1992: 410), but also to broaden out the local critique into more universal concerns. In his 1968 interview with the *New York Times*, then, Havel reportedly agrees that *The Memorandum* is a "political metaphor," but emphasizes that the artificial languages in the play "stand for all the political and ideological systems made to serve man, but which end by mastering him" (Klaidman 1968).

One of the major forces of sly censorship came via the state literary and theatre agency, DILIA, "another new mechanism of control" (Neumann 1994: 52). DILIA was the sole agent for all literary and theatrical work and, as an agency, could choose whether to issue contracts or not; "If a contract was not issued, the play could not be performed officially" (p. 52). DILIA at times prevented or delayed according to translation and performance rights to Havel's plays abroad in the 1960s and, following the Soviet invasion of Czechoslovakia in 1968, effectively banned any official representation of Havel's plays abroad, but the picture of totalitarian censorship is perhaps less cut and dried when we look at DILIA's correspondence with Havel's translator, Vera Blackwell, and interactions with Havel in the 1960s. While DILIA always had the power to clamp down on foreign rights to plays, they also appeared keen to promote Czech theatre abroad and to do so in prestigious foreign theatres. There was an ideological and commercial reason for their backing of ideologically suspect playwrights like Havel: presenting Czech culture abroad could promote the idea that the Communist regime provided a tolerant and creative crucible, and secondly, as DILIA received a percentage of foreign royalties, it was also a means to earn some hard currency (though in relatively small amounts). DILIA, in Havel's case, seemed concerned that he have a prestigious agent in the United Kingdom and United States and that his plays be performed in prestigious theatres or by well-known companies. Havel's plays, however uncomfortably they sat with the regime at home, provided the possibility of cultural and monetary capital abroad.

Havel's huge success with *The Garden Party* in Prague seemed to unnerve DILIA; when Blackwell initially asked for the rights to translate the play (the first English translation of any of Havel's work), DILIA refused without stating why. "[T]hey thanked me for my interest in Havel's *Garden Party* but they can't give permission for an English adaptation, but perhaps they might in the future," Blackwell wrote to the play's director Jan Grossman (VBA 1:1, 8/13/64). Blackwell questioned what they meant by "the future" as their permission was deliberately left as a vague possibility, indicating the ambiguous terms of the "sly" censorship. Worried that the RSC would lose interest in producing the play, she asked Grossman to relay to DILIA how important the timeliness of their permission would be:

> if they don't give permission now, it will kill interest in it in England. If they care about the prestige of their young Czech theatre in the world, then they must value it themselves, or else it's a joke. Can you explain it to them? As you know, I emphasized this from the start. It will be now or never. The play is very relevant because of the election, during which they are going to be talking about bureaucracy, conservatism, the absurdity of officialdom etc. Later, once it's over, then it won't be so relevant [. . .] Of course, it's also quite possible that this is all clear to them that they want to kill it and for a variety of reasons don't want to say so directly. Is it possible to get to the bottom of it? [. . .] I'm under the impression that Roberts and this Royal Shakespeare [sic] will lose interest in meeting with Prague about anything, if Prague is going to act so Maoist. (VBA 1:1, 8/13/64)

Blackwell was keenly aware that Havel's play might have a shelf life in terms of its relevance for an English audience, certainly because of the way in which Roberts envisaged the play, adapted, and domesticated for English tastes and political interests (following the Labour victory in the British General Election in October 1964). But she also realized the worth of the play to the regime in promoting itself abroad and aligning itself to prestigious foreign cultural institutions, and perhaps the space—albeit frustrating—for negotiation and pressure in a censorship system that is undefined and sly.

DILIA gave permission for English rights within the month and Havel, in a letter to the RSC, elucidated the reasoning behind the change:

> Your serious interest in the play gave an important help in this, because you are for all of us a guarantee that it will be properly understood and produced [. . .] The problems did originate in certain unusual circumstances—a great interest from western organizations for the first time, and certain doubts that followed regarding whether Czech art should be represented exactly by a play of this type. But after the Berlin premiere, it was approved. (VBA 1: 1, November 1964)

Underlining the hesitation of the authorities about "a play of this type," Havel also suggested that the regime comprehended the value of the "great interest from western organizations" especially following the success of the play in Germany. However, in the same letter in which Havel thanked the RSC for having "patience" with the Czech authorities and DILIA in particular, he also addressed his own concerns about the way his plays might be altered once they were translated abroad.

While he emphasized his gratitude for the RSC's interest and the guarantee that because of their reputation "it will be properly understood and produced" this carried a hint of Havel's concern about the adaptation, of the play being "properly understood." He expressed his faith in the adaptation as long as they listened to Blackwell because "we discover that we share our views about theatre and art, so I feel that in every way she can and does speak for me" (VBA 1:1, November 1964). In other words, Havel saw his translator's role as his eyes and ears in England, watching out for reductive changes to his text as it was domesticated. The RSC had expressed interest in his next play, *The Memorandum*, but Havel refused to send it as it was incomplete and also argued that it should be optioned as a translation rather than an adaptation: "When you see it," he wrote, "I hope you will agree with us that it is quite understandable in its original form for non-Czech theatre public, without adaptation" (VBA 1:1, November 1964). Havel was quite aware of the commercial and ideological "constraints" in the West that might fundamentally alter the aesthetics and meaning of his plays.

DILIA also caused problems with the rights to *The Memorandum*, going on hiatus and freezing English-language rights for a short period in 1965, but then became increasingly demanding in letters to Blackwell regarding the promotion of Havel's plays in the United Kingdom and United States. Blackwell had hired the Dina Lom Agency in London to represent her translations of Havel's plays (Lom was the Czech-born actor, Herbert Lom's, wife, a fact that Blackwell thought might help Havel and his plays), but DILIA began pressurizing Havel to leave the agency as they felt not enough work had been done to promote the plays. They suggested Blackwell contact Samuel Beckett's London agent, who was interested in representing Havel. Finally, Blackwell suggested Margaret Ramsay, a prominent theatrical agent.

Throughout the mid-1960s, DILIA kept trying to involve itself in the promotion and production of Havel's plays in the United Kingdom and United States and showed frustration in delays. Like Blackwell, they did not understand why options and promised interest did not always come to fruition. When they turned their blame from Dina Lom to Blackwell herself, she protested vigorously pointing out her role in contacting theatres and directors to promote the plays. DILIA backed down, emphasizing in two separate letters how much they supported Blackwell's work and their officially obsequious language indicates that they realized how useful she was and how valuable Havel's success could be for the regime:

We highly value your work and we know that in you we have a good helper in propagating our literature abroad. We are very grateful for your efforts and can only imagine with what difficulties you are meeting. We want to make clear to you that we don't want to overstep the boundaries of your work, but rather that we will try to support you as much as we can (VBA 2:6, 6/8/66) [. . .] We regard the English and American publications of Havel's plays as a great success for our literature. Let us take this opportunity to tell you again how much we value your effective help. (VBA 2:6, 8/18/66)

They also acknowledged her success in interesting the BBC who produced *The Garden Party* on radio and *The Memorandum* for television, thanks to the enthusiasm of Martin Esslin, and indicated that they valued his interest because of his status as a theatre scholar: "We know Mr. Martin Esslin well," they wrote, "from his series Book Programmes aired every Tuesday on the BBC and also from his well-known book on the theatre of the absurd. We are delighted that a specialist of his insight and erudition took an interest in Havel's plays" (VBA 2:6, 6/8/66). The admission from a state organ that they listened to the BBC, an organization *non grata* in Communist Czechoslovakia, was telling: indicating both a nod and a wink to the consumption of officially censored material but also a sense that they wanted to convey their comprehensive knowledge of what was going on in the West with a chilling undertone of censorial panopticonism.

In the 1960s DILIA did act in the manner of a censor, choosing when and where to give permission for Havel's plays to be produced abroad as well as at home, at times frustrating Havel's efforts and those of his translator to disseminate his plays. But something else interesting is at work: the officials at DILIA recognized Havel's plays as commodities, with the potential for commercial and cultural capital. It seems that they were not always against his plays being produced, even though they were aware that the plays were politically subversive. They were more concerned with the prestige of the theatres and theatrical figures involved and with the potential for commercial success than with any possible political fallout. What is striking about DILIA in the 1960s is how much they mirror any literary or theatrical agency, bound as they are to the question of commerce and cultural impact. In addition, the correspondence shows that the notion of state censorship in Czechoslovakia was more complex than an authoritarian denial of subversive texts because of the potential capital the plays might produce.

Kate Sturge, in her study of translated fiction in Nazi Germany, showed that censorship practices in the cases of translated work were much more complex than a blanket, authoritarian, and ideological banning or censorship of texts. Although "murderous state measures obliterated certain segments of translated literature" she writes, "the commercial core survived" (Sturge 2002: 165). In addition, she argues that the market might have been as responsible for reductive changes to popular texts or the choice of formulaic texts as the regime and its various censoring bodies: "can we claim that all the changes occurring in translation were politically enforced 'censorship?' " she asks, "Or did the market itself ask for satisfaction of a taste for moral simplicity, for formula?" (p. 165). Sturge's article challenges preconceptions of authoritarian or totalitarian censorship practices, often assumed to be monolithic and all-embracing in the case of translated texts, which often threaten to disrupt established cultural norms. It raises the question of the market and how it functions in such societies alongside ideological needs. In the case of DILIA and Havel's plays in the 1960s, the market potential (as commercial or cultural capital) of the plays served to mitigate ideological pressures to suppress them. However aware of it or not, DILIA was capitalizing on foreign interest in plays that challenged the political apparatus they served to uphold.

The back-and-forth of a tentative censorship by DILIA changed to a hardened form following the Soviet invasion of Czechoslovakia in 1968. A period of "normalizace" or "normalization" ensued as the Communist regime cracked down on those it deemed involved in the Prague Spring, including Havel. A huge majority of the members of the Writers' Union were ousted (thereby basically excluding them from being published or performed) and Havel was among the 130 of the members who were officially blacklisted (Rocamora 2004: 109). But even at the beginning of 1970, Havel was not clear about whether his plays could be produced or not. Writing to Blackwell in April 1970, he said that although he doubted his plays could be performed, there was no official censorship yet (VBA 3, 4/28/70) and he had offered a new play, *Spiklenci/The Conspirators*, to a Prague theatre, Cinoherni klub. However, he was fully aware that it was unlikely to be approved in Czechoslovakia and sent the play via a third person to Blackwell, asking her to give a copy to Klaus Juncker, his German agent at Rowohlt Verlag. Havel wanted to send his new play still to DILIA, writing "I want to play 'fair play' with them, even if they mainly don't play 'fair play' with me" (VBA 3, 4/28/70). Within a month "the situation was considerably worse" because one of the DILIA employees, Mr Kalaš, had been "criticized" for agreeing to a contract with Blackwell's name on it (VBA 3, 5/19/70). There was discord within DILIA; Kalaš told Havel that he had been ordered not to sell the foreign rights of any work of eight authors (including Havel) because of their "political orientation," but that he would try to make exceptions and help Havel. His colleague, Dr Pechold, however, Havel wrote, was more than happy to uphold the new edicts (VBA 3, 6/1270). Rather than being condemnatory of DILIA, Havel argued that the employees he dealt with were in a difficult situation themselves, "DILIA are being tossed between fulfilling various requests, directives and orders from their superiors," he wrote, "as well as complying to threats and pressures, and efforts to help authors even a little; many institutions are in this situation now" (VBA 3, 5/19/70). Through 1970 and 1971, Havel came to the realization, through a suggestion from Kalaš at DILIA, that he would have to bypass DILIA altogether and deal only directly with foreign agents, with Juncker as his main agent, his "new DILIA."

Not issuing foreign rights was one means of trying to censor Havel beyond the Czechoslovak border, another was attempting to disgrace and ban Havel's translator, Vera Blackwell, and to make it impossible for the two to work together. If, before the Soviet invasion, DILIA had "highly value[d]" Blackwell's work and known that she was "a good helper in propagating our literature abroad," now that role had become threatening. The act of translation suddenly became extremely visible and potent: while the regime could enact increasingly stringent censorship practices at home, translation offered a lifeline for Havel and his work, not only artistically, but also as a practical means of survival. Indeed, in the 1970s and 1980s as Havel was only allowed occasional menial work and spent 4 years in prison, foreign royalties from his translations would sustain him. The potency of the translator's position in disseminating censored work was recognized almost immediately by the regime: they applied pressure, as seen above, to DILIA to reject any contracts with Blackwell's name on it from 1970 onwards, they placed Blackwell on the censored index, and they vociferously attacked her personally in the media—on state television and in the newspapers (VBA 3, 4/28/70). Immediately Blackwell became a *persona non grata*, and Havel was warned, as mentioned above, that DILIA could not agree to contracts with Blackwell's name on it. This was a quite wily attempt at overt censorship beyond Czechoslovak borders via an attempt to muzzle the translator. The regime did not stop there: Blackwell was deported from Czechoslovakia in 1969 and prevented from traveling to Czechoslovakia (despite an elderly father). The official conferral of her PhD was withheld until the 1980s (Havel bravely confronted the regime about this). To side-step this attempt at censorship, Havel and Blackwell decided to make the translator invisible again by inventing an imaginary beard of a translator, a "Mr Just" whose name could go on contracts, but who would, of course, be Blackwell herself (VBA 3, 6/30/71).

The ploy worked and DILIA accepted contracts with the fake name on them, fully aware that it was nothing more than a ploy, but able, as an agency, to cover themselves against the ideological requirements of their superiors. It seems paradoxical that DILIA were allowing foreign contracts for Havel's plays but they demanded that they would be informed of them and of the payments—the Czech regime wanted to make money—hard foreign currency—from the plays even while issuing a blanket ban on Havel's plays at home. Their position would change over the next year, as they then intimated to Havel that in fact he could strike agreements with foreign producers irrespective of DILIA, but then hardening their stance in 1972, demanding 90–95 percent of foreign royalties from banned authors. In March 1972, DILIA told Havel that they were ceasing payment completely for previously contracted foreign royalties (VBA 3, 3/2/72). These decisions led Havel to decide to obviate DILIA and their control; from 1972 onwards, contracts for foreign productions were made without DILIA, with Havel being paid straight into his bank account or money being smuggled into Czechoslovakia.

The regime did try to exert control via other methods: Havel was under indictment for signing an anti-invasion petition in 1969, he was being monitored, as was his correspondence and, in 1972, this became pronounced; Havel was less forthcoming about some issues in his correspondence with Blackwell for safety reasons and suspected his mail was being tampered with or was not getting through. The regime tried to control personal access to Havel's German agent, Klaus Juncker, who they prevented from entering the country in 1971. Havel, dependent on his foreign royalties, was only allowed intermittent employment given to him by the regime—so, in 1972, he worked briefly as a manual laborer in a brewery (which would give him material for his 1977 one-act, *Audience*).

Rumors began circulating in England about Havel's dreadful "psychological" state and his addiction to drugs, rumors that he suspected originated from the regime. "This news really made me laugh, because right now—even though it might seem paradoxical—I'm living more peacefully than ever before and even more peacefully than the majority of my fellow citizens," he wrote to Blackwell in 1972. Forced into a kind of internal exile, banned from working, he paints a bucolic picture of his life at his country cottage:

> Untied from all my duties and business, uninterrupted by anyone, I'm doing what I want: I'm studying, sometimes I write something, other times I look after the cottage, making repairs to the surroundings, the garden etc, sometimes I cook various treats and other times I try to support my most afflicted friends [. . .] I don't have existential or financial worries, I don't have to look for work or anything like that [. . .] the fact is that I have had enough money up till now, and I've had enough that I could do up my house in the country, buy a new flat in Prague, buy a Mercedes and live for the past three years.

The regime would finally try and prevent income coming in officially, but Blackwell and others set up bank accounts abroad for Havel and money was sometimes smuggled in personally. Havel, banned from working in the theatre, now, however, had time to write, even if it was for the foreign stage and for productions he would not be allowed to attend. But he was still trying to crack the English market; it would take another few years for his plays to be produced professionally on the English stage. His first two successful English-language productions in America, in 1968 and 1969, gave him hope that it would happen, but after 1969, the next American production was in 1983. At the point when Havel was utterly dependent on translations to have his plays produced at all, there seemed to be some resistance to them. His translator and her translations were blamed, but, in fact, even in the 1960s it was clear that more was at stake.

Translations: *The Garden Party*

John Roberts, the Managing Director of the RSC, saw *The Garden Party* in Czech at Divadlo na zábradli in Prague: "judging by the audience reaction," he wrote to Blackwell in February 1964, "it is extremely funny" (VBA 1:1, 24/2/64). Not being able to speak Czech, Roberts was relying on instinct and on the atmosphere in the theatre. He worried though that this Czech reception of the play was only because of the given context, that it was

funny only "because it seems to be the first play that in any way criticizes
Authority and jokes themselves may be local" (ibid). He asked Blackwell
for one or two pages of a translation if she thought it "could be adapted for
English audiences" (ibid). From the start, there was an assumption that the
play could not be translated and performed as it was because it would be
too "local" for an English audience, based on what Roberts assumed to be
the in-jokes relating to the Czech political context.

Blackwell sent Roberts a short synopsis and a translated extract and his
suspicions were confirmed, writing that it was "a very tricky play and may
need special adaptation for London" (VBA 1:1, 3/3/64); but he asked for a
literal translation. After Blackwell sent him her translation, Roberts felt she
had done a "remarkable job," but that "there is a lot of work to be done on
it to adapt it for English audiences" (VBA 1:1, 4/27/64); he optioned it on
the proviso that "it should be given a universal meaning and not be either
a play about Czechoslovakia, or even to be set in that country" (VBA 1:1,
5/13/64). He asked her to write to Havel and explain that, "so long as local
references are left out, an English audience will find his tilts at bureaucracy
extremely funny and be able to identify them with our own administration"
(VBA 1:1, 5/13/64). There was a further proviso to the option: it needed to
be completely adapted and that Blackwell would collaborate on it with an
English playwright, Norman Frederick Simpson.

As with the reviews above, Roberts places emphasis on a need to mine the
"universal" in the play, which meant actually denuding the play of local reference and importing substitute target culture references ("our own administration"). So while on the surface, Roberts is not interested in what he sees
as the politics of Havel's play, because they were too local and would not
have meaning in an English context, there is an ideological undercurrent in
assuming that the play was about politics at a particular time and place and
that it needed to be "universalized," which actually meant "anglicized."

Roberts' reading is particularly striking with *The Garden Party* because
the play is not in fact set in any given historical or political context, let alone
being referentially local to Czechoslovakia in any political or geographical
terms. The play could not have been performed in Prague at that time if it
had been, due to censorship, but more importantly, Havel was explicitly
writing in the absurdist tradition of his heroes, Samuel Beckett and Eugene
Ionesco, not in a realist tradition, more familiar to an English audience. It
was the equivalent of asking Beckett to take out all of the Irish political references in *Waiting for Godot*, and suggesting it needed to be adapted, and
the text changed, because it was too local in its Irish jokes. That it would
not be asked of Beckett but would be of Havel may, of course, be a result of
Beckett's fame, but also perhaps because Havel was writing in Czech rather
than French and this was seen to be somehow more foreign, and, perhaps,
more irrelevant.

In *The Garden Party*, the Pludeks are sending their son, Hugo, into the
world—to the garden party—and he turns out to be a wild success. Hugo's

secret is that, consciously or not (we never know), he simply repeats a mish-mash of what he has been told by the other characters and this catapults him into the higher echelons of the world of the garden party—by the end of the play he is declared the head of liquidating the Liquidation Office and the Inauguration Office, then the head of reconstructing them. The play's Czech director, Jan Grossman, argued that they play is, above all, a critique of the power of language. Grossman upbraided an English journalist for his reading of the play as a polemical broadside against the Communist regime, pointing out how German audiences had responded to it aestheti-cally, rather than politically, by focusing on the critique of language in the play (VBA 1:2, 1/11/65). Blackwell, writing to Roberts, said that the "ver-bal inventions" were "themselves the main force that moves the play, and thus . . . are really not only a character in the play but its protagonist, its 'Villain' " (VBA 1:1, 4/16/64).

If language was the play's villain, it was also its joker: Roberts wanted a play of which he had not understood a word when watching it in Prague and it became clear to Blackwell that he had seen a different play. In watch-ing the audience laugh and the absurdist action on the stage, Roberts con-ceived of it as farce, and in choosing Simpson, a writer of fashionable farces, Roberts projected what he perceived to be English tastes on the potential play. In demanding a universalism in the translation, Roberts was blind to the universalism of the play, because he already read it as a political piece—even though he wanted something different.

Simpson, after three attempts, came up with a farce called *The Centre*. Full of nonsensical puns, Simpson plays lightly with language for the sake of humor rather than using the language to provide a critique of how language defines and imprisons us, how we can use language to control others and control the truth; Remnick rightly wrote of Havel's play that it dissected the "inhuman" in language. Simpson, however, showed no sense of understand-ing that Havel's use of repetition, a key to his dramatic poetics as a means to deconstruct meaning, has anything more than a nonsensical value. One example is Hugo's final speech in the play; the speech is a declamation from Hugo about the *bricolage* of his identity, built from sayings other characters have given to him. In Havel's play, the quicksand of his personality is built up in his use of repetition (this is also a speech repeating what he has heard from others) that at the same time deconstructs the notion of identity as a thing that is made up of the repetition of experience or memory; it is rather something fluid and mutable. Here is just less than half of the speech (in Blackwell's translation):

Me? You mean who I am? Now look here, I don't like this one-sided way of putting **questions,** I really don't! You think one can ask in this simpli-fied way? No matter how one answers this sort of **question,** one can never encompass the whole truth, but only one of its many limited parts. What a rich thing is **man,** how *complicated, changeable, and multiform*—there's

no word, **no** sentence, **no** book, **nothing** that could describe and contain him in his whole extent. In **man** there is nothing *permanent, eternal, absolute,* **man** is a continuous **change**—a **change** with a proud ring to it, of course! Today the time of static and un**change**able categories is past, the time when **A** was **only A**, and **B** always **only B** is gone; today we all know very well that **A may be** often **B as well as A; that B may just as well be A**; that **B may be B**, but equally it **may be A** and C; just as **C may be not only** C, but also A, B, and D; and in certain circumstances even F may become Q, Y, and perhaps also H. I'm sure you yourselves must **feel** that what you **feel** today you've not **felt** yesterday, and what you **felt** yesterday you don't **feel** today, but might perhaps again **feel** tomorrow; while what you might **feel** the day after tomorrow you may never have **felt** before. Do you **feel** that? (Havel 1993: 50, my emphasis)

Havel builds up the oppressive pressure in the speech through the repetition of terms and syntactical structure, while introducing the concept of change in the repetition of the word "change" but also the indeterminacy of the adjectives: man is "complicated, changeable, and multiform" and in him there is nothing '"permanent, eternal, absolute"; this is also underlined in the verbal game with the letters. The emphasis on "feel" at the end denies the primacy of rational thought, underscored by the emotional oppressiveness of the speech. Havel is, here, linguistically mirroring the existential basis of the speech, and these elements are translated well by Blackwell. Simpson, in his version of the speech (the Hugo character is called Bernard) attempts a tone of officiousness and bureaucracy:

Ah. Well now. That raises a thorny old question or two. Which we must strain every nerve to come frankly and fearlessly to grips with. Who am I? A question the formal brevity of which testifies to the careful thought which must clearly have gone into the framing of it. Would that the answer we shall with God's help arrive at were likely to achieve a matching simplicity. But many and varied are the countless facets of so complex an entity as is here presented for our scrutiny, and no one single answer could begin to encompass a significant fraction of the truth towards which we are groping. It is the truth which even to the experts must present in the manifold plurality of its labyrinthine convolutions a veritable Hydra's head of doubt and dismay through which in vain one looks for some clear path on which to set one's feet. (VBA, unpublished MSS, 74)

Simpson strives above all for the immediate humor of tone in Bernard's recognizable pomposity and pseudointellectual rationalizing of identity. He introduces the notion of mutability of meaning and signification, for instance, when Bernard talks of "many and varied are the countless facets" and the "manifold plurality of labyrinthine convolutions" of the truth. However, the humor only functions on the level of satire and the "truth" that Bernard talks of, is ridiculed by the pomposity of his tone. In Havel's play, we laugh at Hugo's officiousness, but at the same time, realize that he is conveying a truth; that truth itself is constructed, malleable, and scaffolded in language. Havel shows as he tells, the bedrock repetitions in his sentences building the wall of evidence. The humour is as tragic and true as it is simply funny.

Simpson sets the play, *The Centre*, in a holiday camp quintessential of its time and recognizable to English audiences; the place where the working- and middle-class English went for organized fun because they couldn't afford to go abroad. It could be a metaphor for the adaptation; the presumption that the play had to be retro-fitted with a perceived English humour (satirizing the pomposity of class) because they assumed the English audience would not understand a "foreign" play. In doing so, the nuance and the metaphysical importance of the piece—its actual universality—is lost. The RSC never used the adaptation, and let their option on the play drop.

The Garden Party was first staged in England by an amateur group at the Coulsdon Youth and Social Centre, Chipstead Valley in 1970; a staging of Blackwell's translation. Blackwell attended the performance:

> On Sunday night I was in some hole in Croydon, where your Garden Party was staged for the first time in English. They were amateurs and they did it badly and did not understand it at all, but the community rolled with laughter, mostly in the first two acts (for them it was like obviously absurd comedy of Edward Lear or Alice in Wonderland or like the contemporary—and not unknown to you, N.F. Simpson) and finally, when Hugo suddenly became Harold Wilson (the guy who played him imitated Wilson perfectly), the English audience figured out the totally incomprehensible closing monologue completely differently, if quite wittily, when you consider that Wilson just lost the election and that here he is generally thought of as a man of no less than three faces . . . To my surprise Plzak was played as Montgomery (including the uniform) which did quite bother me, but the audience applauded. (The director later told me that it was just for fun, and that some of Plzak's cliché's reminded him of Montgomery's manner, which I can't judge because I only know him as an old, pompous and honoured general.) They tried to caricature Ted Heath through the character of the Director, but I don't think anyone recognized the imitation. (VBA 3, 7/31/70)

Using voice imitations (apparently successfully and unsuccessfully) to mimic current English political and public figures—Prime Ministers Harold Wilson and Ted Heath, as well as the WWII general Viscount Montgomery—the actors attempted to locate the play in the contemporary English political sphere. The mimicry belies a surface reading, that *The Garden Party* would only be relevant to an English audience if its local political signification could be "translated" into the English political lexicon; the language of the play, its "nonsense," is irrelevant other than being an aural joke, playful and suggestive of politicians' windbaggery. Thus Hugo's final speech in the play, a coruscating and beautifully constructed monologue that creates a palimpsest of the clichés and folk sayings he has absorbed through the play for his own truth, interrogates how truth is constructed; here, according to Blackwell, in its first English production "the incomprehensible closing monologue" is turned into a pastiche of political jargon associated specifically with the outgoing Labour Prime Minister, Harold Wilson. Though this may have been "quite wittily" done, as Blackwell points out, and clearly spoke to the audience, it betrays both the aesthetics of the play (its critique of language) and suggests the play is simply a political critique and only worthwhile if it can be made relevant to local political sphere.

Translation II: The English *Memorandum*: Two memos

The Memorandum opens with Gross, the Managing Director of an unnamed office, opening a memo:

> Ra ko hutu d dekotu ely terbomu emusohe, vdegar yd, stro reny er gryk kendy, alyv zvyde dezu, kvyndal fer tekynu sely. Degto yl tre entvester kyleg gh: orka epyl y bodur depty-depe emete. Grojto af xedob yd, kyzem ner osonfterte ylem kho dent [d] de det detrym gynfer bro enomuz fechtal agni laj kys defyj rokuroch bazuk suhelen. Gakvom ch ch lopve rekto elkvestrete. Dyhap zuj bak dygalex [gydalox] ibem nyderix tovah gyp. Ykte juh geboj. Fyx [fys] dep butrop gh. (Havel 1993: 55)

Like you, he has no idea what this means; his secretary tells him that it is written in "Ptydepe," "A new office language which is being introduced into our organization" (p. 57). He discovers his Deputy, Balaš, has introduced this new language, one that is "designed to make office communications more accurate and introduced precision and order into their terminology" (p. 58), and has ordered everyone, except Gross, to take compulsory Ptydepe classes. Balaš has set up a Translation Center where the Accounts Department used to be. But the Translation Center deliberately uses bureaucratic methods not to translate anything, and when Balaš himself is presented with a Ptydepe memo (having ousted Gross at the end of Act One), they won't translate it. Balaš, like most of the workforce, has dropped out of Ptydepe classes. Finally, Gross, who had been demoted to "Staff Watcher" spying on all the offices from a small space in between all them, persuades a young woman to translate the original memo. The memo tells him that the "Ptydepe campaign" was "a profoundly harmful attempt to place office communications on a confused, unrealistic and anti-human basis" (pp. 114–15). It praises his courage and asks him to "liquidate" any "attempt to introduce Ptydepe into organization" and to punish those who propagated it" (p. 115).

In the end, language carries its own negation within its very message: Gross cannot interpret the memo and thinks he knows what it means without having to decipher the language, that is, that Balaš is trying to overthrow him. The physical memo embodies the semiotics of power—what it actually says is irrelevant for the majority of the play, and yet the deferred message is ultimately powerful and misunderstood by the messenger, Balaš, whose power is finally undermined when the language is translated. The signature at the bottom is "illegible" but toward the end of the play we discover that Ballas's sidekick, Kubš/Pillar (in Blackwell's translation), who has been silent all through the play, has been behind the plot all along. He runs out shouting: "Death to all artificial languages! Long live natural human speech! Long live Man!" (p. 123). Coetzee's notion of the reader-censor seems relevant here, with Havel considering the dark side of the "utopian" move toward an ideal, fully interpretable language, a language that signifies its own power just by being, with the characters colluding in its implementation—not by understanding its semantics but simply the meaning of its implementation and their indifferent agreement to it. Silent Kubš does not partake, remains silent and apart from the collusion (despite seeming to be at the very heart of it) until his outburst when he sides with "the imperfect, this-worldly language of the flesh" (Coetzee 1996: 160).

Over a decade later, Havel, in his essay "The Power of the Powerless," used the example of a greengrocer who places a sign among his goods "Workers of the world, unite!" but has no interest in its actual semantics; he is just putting it up because "[i]f he were to refuse there would be trouble" (Havel 1989: 41). What the slogan says is irrelevant, it is just "a *sign*" that means he does not have to put a placard up that says, "I am afraid and therefore unquestioningly obedient" (p. 42). Havel argued that in a "post-totalitarian system" (p. 44) ideology becomes "a world of appearances, a mere ritual, a formalized language deprived of semantic contact with reality" (p. 47); in presenting an "inner coherence," ideology has "appropriated power from power" (p. 47) and creates, rather than describes, reality. Once the greengrocer refuses to put up the placard, he then questions that irreal reality, and refuses to live the life of ideology by exposing its semiotic pillars. The idea that "individuals confirm the system, fulfill the system, make the system, *are* the system" (p. 45) is explored in *The Memorandum*, where the characters give life to the lie of this new language that purports to herald a new, more precise expression of reality, but which they know is all about power, despite and because of their apathy.

Translation and its perils are also at the heart of the play. Both intralingually—the notion of all communication as acts of translation—and interlingually, the play thinks about how we approach language and translate it into our own frames of reference but it portrays this translation as a nontransparent act. In other words, the factors involved are not just linguistic but

extralinguistic: codes, guesses, ambiguities, the unsaid support, or silencing
of power. Translating the memo requires authorization—and not just from
one individual—but from the documents person, the Ptydepist, the translator. When Balaš attempts to get a translation, the system reveals itself (most
of the names were changed in translation, Baláš is Ballas, Mašát is Stroll,
Kunc is Savant, Helena is Helena, diminuitive vocative Helčo/Nellie):

BALÁŠ:	Proč jim to tedy nepřekládá Mašát?
MAŠÁT:	Překládám jen na Kuncovo povolení!
BALÁŠ:	Tak musí Kunc dávat povolení!
KUNC:	Nemůzu, když nikdo nemá materiály od Heleny!
BALÁŠ:	Slyšíš to, Helčo? Musíš přeci jen vydávat ty materiály!
HELENA:	Vždyt nesmím překládat!
BALÁŠ:	Proč jim to tedy nepřekládá Mašát?
MAŠÁT:	Překládám jen na Kuncovo povolení!
BALÁŠ:	Tak musí Kunc dávat povolení!
KUNC:	Nemůzu, když nikdo nemá materiály od Heleny!
BALÁŠ:	Slyšíš to, Helčo? Musíš přeci jen vydávat ty materiály!
HELENA:	Vždyt nesmím překládat!
BALÁŠ:	Proč jim to tedy nepřekládá Mašát?
MAŠÁT:	Překládám jen na Kuncovo povolení!
BALÁŠ:	Tak musí Kunc dávat povolení!
KUNC:	Nemůzu, když nikdo nemá materiály od Heleny!
BALÁŠ:	Slyšíš to, Helčo? Musíš přeci jen vydávat ty materiály!
HELENA:	Vždyt nesmím překládat!
BALÁŠ:	To by mě zajímalo, kdo si tenhle začarovaný kruh vymyslel!
MAŠÁT, KUNC, HELENA (sborově):	Ty, kolego řediteli!
BALÁŠ:	No a? Tehdy byla přece docela jiná situace! Tehdy to mělo hluboký smysl! (Havel 1999: 2: 172–3)

BALLAS:	Then why doesn't Otto translate the memos?
STROLL:	I can translate only after getting an authorization from Alex!
BALLAS:	Then Alex will have to start granting the authorizations!
SAVANT:	I can't, if nobody has the documents from Nellie!
BALLAS:	Do you hear that, Nellie? You'll have to start giving people the documents regardless!

HELENA:	But I'm not permitted to translate!
BALLAS:	Why doesn't Otto do the translating?
STROLL:	I can translate only after getting an authorization from Alex!
BALLAS:	Then Alex will have to start granting the authorizations!
SAVANT:	I can't, when nobody has the documents from Nellie!
BALLAS:	Do you hear that, Nellie? You'll have to start giving people the documents regardless!
HELENA:	But I'm not permitted to translate!
BALLAS:	Why doesn't Otto do the translating?
STROLL:	I can translate only after getting an authorization from Alex!
BALLAS:	Then Alex will have to start granting the authorizations!
SAVANT:	I can't, when nobody has the documents from Nellie!
BALLAS:	Do you hear that, Nellie? You'll have to start giving people the documents regardless!
HELENA:	But I'm not permitted to translate!
BALLAS:	I'd like to know who thought up this vicious circle.
STROLL, SAVANT, HELENA:	You did, Mr Ballas!
BALLAS:	Well, what of it! The situation was entirely different at the time. Then it had a profound significance! (Havel 1993: 111)

The teeth-grinding repetition of the "začarovaný kruh/vicious circle" that Balaš engineered precisely to censor translation as a means to grabbing and retaining power not only acts out the frustration of the process, but also its reality: the different bodies involved, the resistance to transparency, and the power dynamics involved in authorization. Havel might have been inspired by his own dealings with DILIA, but he captures some of the dynamics of the translation process in general (the involvement of different agents in the process), including challenging the notion integral to the business of translation that the purpose of translation is to communicate openly and transparently. Translation is always done in someone's interest, and generally by those who commission it, rather than those who consume it. Balaš wanted them to censor all translations for an "entirely different situation," that is, when he is not involved; translation means something else when the commissioner wants it to.

The passage is emblematic of Havel's style, the rondo of repetition dragging on to the slapstick and then the unbearable. Blackwell translates the repetition of words and phrases; what perhaps cannot be translated is the euphony in alliteration and assonance in the Czech version that serves to emphasize the repetitions and is intricately wrought:

BALÁŠ: Proč jim to tedy nepřekládá Mašát?
MAŠÁT: Překládám jen na Kuncovo povolení!
BALÁŠ: Tak musí Kunc dávat povolení!
KUNC: Nemůžu, když nikdo nemá materiály od Heleny!
BALÁŠ: Slyšíš to, Helčo? Musíš přeci jen vydávat ty materiály!

When he began writing plays in the early 1960s, Havel was immersed in Kafka (whose works had been unbanned by the Communist regime in 1963). We can see the influence here with style and content reminiscent, for instance, of the "memo" passage in Kafka's *The Castle*. K. visits the Chairman who, bedridden, tells him that there had been some written debate between departments about whether to get a land surveyor but:

> this reply seems never to have reached the first department—which I call A—and went by error to another department, B. So Department A was left without an answer; either because the contents of the file itself got lost on the way—though certainly not in the department itself, I'll vouch for that—all that came to Department B in any case was the file folder. (Kafka 1998: 62)

The chairman goes on for a page or so, explaining that the file came with a memorandum written by an Italian, Sordini, that reminds them of the lost meaning in the empty file. Kafka, in a comic nod to his readers, has the chairman interrupt his endless bureaucratic tale and ask K. "Does the story bore you?" "No," said K., "it amuses me" (p. 63). Annoyed, the chairman says the story is not for his amusement: "It amuses me," said K., "only because it gives me some insight into the ridiculous tangle that may under certain circumstances determine a person's life" (p. 63). Kafka uses his style, the seemingly endless storytelling trying to interpret the life of village, even though the messages sent are empty, to think about communication, language, and meaning. He fixes on the comedy of the attempt and the tragedy of the reality, as he communicates to the reader the effort of interpreting the uninterpretable life around us. The style itself amuses, frustrates, and bores us but challenges us to actively interpret the novel.

This cohesion of style and content lifts Havel's language out of the nonsensical or comically absurd; he tests the limits of our endurance to frustrate us in the same way that the characters on stage are frustrated, to push language to its edges. Rather than have a character tell us that translations are not permitted, we have a chorus of censors, persuading themselves as much as us that they cannot allow it to happen; language has taken them over. Ken Tynan, coming out of a performance of Brecht's *Mother Courage*, overheard a fashionable young woman saying she was bored to death by it. "Bored to life was more like it," he writes. And here, Havel pushed us to be bored to life.

Tynan considered *The Memorandum* for the new English National Theatre, where he was the literary manager, but after it had gone "the rounds of this organization," he wrote:

> I'm afraid the general opinion is that—for English consumption—it doesn't quite work. The principal idea is superb, and ideal for a one-act play; but it's our feeling that it goes on too long for what it has to say. (VBA Memo, 10/11/65)

Tynan was not necessarily speaking for himself; according to Blackwell, she had heard from a number of people that "Tynan promoted it honorably and completely" (VBA 3, 11/17/65) in discussions at the National Theatre. But, she added, he was in a weak position there because of his own protest against censorship: "Tynan is in the midst of a terrible storm and it's not impossible that he will be forced to leave the National Theatre. (He said a dirty word on television and an enormous campaign has been organized against him, it has even reached Parliament.)" (VBA 3, 11/17/65). According to Tynan's wife, Kathleen, a month earlier "in a memo" to Laurence Oliver (then running the National Theatre), "he proposed midnight readings [. . .] to pull in students and Royal Court supporters, and suggested that Václav Havel's *The Memorandum* might fit the bill" (Kathleen Tynan 1988: 225).

But the language he uses reveals the prejudices at the theatre. They did not believe it compatible with the reality of "English consumption," that is, that it did not fit national tastes of the time and therefore would not make money (the audience is defined as consumers), despite Tynan's remit of changing tastes and the role translated theatre would play in that. Equally revealing is the next comment that though the idea is "superb" it should be "a one-act" because "it goes on too long for what it has to say"—the aesthetics are flawed because it does not fit the norms of English theatre and is being judged by them. The hegemony of realism on the British stage supposes that other styles are aesthetically deficient or bad and blinds them to the actual aesthetics of the play, that the form—the length and verbosity, the repetitions and circularity—has a point and is tied into the content of the play. The notion that "it goes on too long for what it has to say" presupposes a reading and a message in the play about Communism and Communist bureaucracy that seems self-evident—the obvious "between-the-lines" reading that requires less verbiage to put its point across.

The Memorandum received its British premiere on BBC radio (it would not be staged in England until after Havel's arrest in 1977 and was staged as a result of that arrest). Blackwell had sent a copy to Martin Esslin, then head of the radio theatre department a week after Tynan's rejection (VBA

1, 11/16/65) and it was produced the following year. In January 1967, the BBC Audience Research Department produced a memorandum on audience reaction. "0.1 percent of United Kingdom" listened to the play (around 5,500 people) and it received favorable reactions: 13 percent gave it an A+; 39 percent an A; 36 percent a B and the rest C or C–. The majority "were evidently much intrigued" by the play and said that it "combined serious satire with considerable humour, even fun (as there were a number of comic scenes)." (Though one audience member thought the humor "elephantive" (sic)." The surprise at the humor lay in their expectations of the play as a political one (possibly amplified by Blackwell's radio lecture before the play that contextualized it).

One audience member expressed surprise that such a "biting play" would have been allowed in Czechoslovakia and several suggested that it was "a courageous sort of play coming as it did from a dramatist in a communist country"; the subtext in other words was obvious, the play's petticoats were showing. Given that the assumed message was a "serious satire" of the Communist regime, some considered it too "drawn-out and repetitive in places, or on the long side as a whole for what it had to say." The echoes of the National Theatre's critique—the play "on the long side as a whole for what it had to say"—suggests that the National Theatre were correct about "English consumption," that the style was seen as obfuscating the clear political message of the play. The audience *got* it, they did not need "drawn-out and repetitive" language and scenes to underline the perceived political underpinning of the play.

The "Farm Estate Secretary," "mathematician (who works with computers)," and the "housewife" listeners to BBC Third Programme were likely average middle-class listeners with certain expectations; Tynan's "memo" to his colleagues at the National Theatre suggested that they should aim the play at a younger ("students") and more adventurous ("Royal Court supporters") audience because they might be more open to engaging with various aspects of the play. In other words, Tynan felt strongly that emphasis had to be put on the audience as readers; either audience who were not calcified in a stagnant British tradition had to be found, or, they had to be "re-educated." As Stalinist as that sounds, his sense was that audiences had been fed so long on the "ghastly norm" that they needed exposure to different forms of plays in order to be "bored to life." But not all at the National Theatre agreed; he was not the sole gatekeeper and had recently, with his "dirty word" *fuck*, shown to have some offensive taste.

For Havel and Blackwell, the fear was that *The Memorandum* would have to be "adapted" to gain a British audience which would evidently involve cutting the repetitions and verbosity to cater to English tastes. Havel advised Blackwell to "keep going on the translation" and not to "show it to anyone" except Tynan, who Blackwell had given a synopsis of the play. He supposed that if they had a "final and completely finished translation" it would be "an already prepared and tangible product" to offer producers, one that might not "provoke adaptations" (VBA 1:3, August 1965). Havel's language shows a steep learning curve in the West, calling the translation a "product" or "goods"/"zboží"; if it was perceived as such, it might be more palatable to producers. But the problem was that these "goods" were too avant-garde, too unreadable in their form, and therefore too much of a financial risk.

Radio was one place the plays were performed without adaptation. Martin Esslin, Head of Drama at the BBC (1963–77), premiered most of Havel's plays in English on radio. Richard Imison, his Deputy at the time, wrote that the cheaper format of radio allowed greater experimentation in bringing unknown foreign playwrights to English audiences. Esslin drove the experimentation (Calder 2002), describing his "impatience, even rage, with theatre critics who seemed to me to have missed the importance and beauty of plays that had deeply moved me when I came across them, almost by chance, in little theatres on the Paris Left Bank" (Esslin 2004: 11). Imison noted in 1991 that: "Listeners to British radio who are over the age of fifty . . . had the opportunity to hear most of the plays of Václav Havel before he shot to political prominence" (Imison 1991: 291), that is, that Esslin produced Havel before it became fashionable to do so, on the basis of his playwriting rather than his dissident fame. Esslin not only produced Havel's plays on radio but was instrumental in recommending and disseminating the plays to publishers and theatres. When he traveled to Prague in 1965, Blackwell wrote to Havel that he should meet Esslin at the airport and perhaps arrange a party at the Theatre on the Balustrade for him: "All the contacts—including Lincoln Center—that we've received have been through Esslin, every letter I've received about *The Garden Party* start with "On the recommendation of M.E."—it would be good if you took care of him well" (VBA 3, 10/8/65).

Blackwell felt strongly that Esslin understood the plays because he was *not* English or at least that he had been exposed to, and was an expert on, what she saw as the European tradition. Writing to Havel's agent in Germany, Klaus Juncker, she said:

Martin is a continental and hence 'on our side', and the BBC can be instrumental in breaking the British ice. Clearly, there's no need for me to enlarge on English insularity and on their reluctance to accept the Continental style of writing, particularly when it's laced with Central European issues, and also somewhat out of step with current local output. (VBA 2:3, 8/7/76)

At this point—1976—Blackwell had been trying for over a decade to get the plays produced on the professional British stage and was increasingly convinced that this "English insularity" prevented a genuine and informed appreciation of the plays; they were too embedded in a "foreign" tradition and calling something "foreign" or someone "a foreigner," she wrote to Havel, "is an insult in the English language" (VBA 3, 12/9/71).

Esslin understood the import of Havel's style, including him in the second edition of his seminal book, *The Theatre of the Absurd* and calling him "a master of the ironical, inverted repetition, of almost identical phrases in different contexts" (Esslin 2004: 325–6). But Esslin, as discussed above, also saw the plays as fundamentally political in their purpose, and makes the distinction in *The Theatre of the Absurd* between "Western" and "Eastern" absurdist playwrights, with the former being more universal and the latter more tied into their contexts, and thus, by implication, lesser talents.

Havel was aware of the hermeneutic difficulties the play found in translation, "I was at the premiere in Berlin," he wrote to Blackwell, "it wasn't a bad production, the actors were good, it was successful, nevertheless I sensed that the play was not fundamentally understood: for them it's just a slightly exotic satire on Eastern bureaucracy" (VBA 3, 1/1/66). This was one of only a couple times Havel was let out of Czechoslovakia to see his own premiere, and it made him wonder whether you needed cultural experience of living in Czechoslovakia to fundamentally understand the play:

> In theory, Gross is a universal theme, in practice though maybe this theme isn't well understood and—I fear—cannot be understood without Czechoslovakian historical experiences. It's strange, I thought this play would have a greater chance of being comprehended in the West than *The Garden Party*, but as it turns out, it's not so simple. Indeed in a sense, it confirms the reaction of Tynan, Esslin and others abroad, who saw or read about it here—they say it's cleverly thought-out, sharp, funny, the ptydepe theme is apposite, it's well-constructed, but some real socio-historical-psychological dimension of "Grossism" doesn't seem to me to be understood—for them the play acts like a tedious enough amplification of one idea. (VBA 3, 1/1/66)

The issue was not whether the West could understand the experience of Czechs under postwar Communism, but whether they were prepared to understand the universal applications of that experience. Gross's inability to read the message, his willingness to work the system to uncover the message, his reappointment as the "Staff Watcher" surveilling his fellow employees, and then his reascension to Director and willingness to sacrifice the translator who aided him, is not just a social message relevant to Czechs who might have compromised with the regime, but suggests an innate fallibility in man's relationship to language and power. Jan Grossman, who directed the play in Prague, wrote that:

> The story of an artificial language, as it's shown in *The Memorandum*, has never occurred and probably never will. But the plausibility of the dramatic material and the consistency of its composition persuade us that it *could* happen sometime. (Grossman in Havel 1999: 2: 1009–12)

Grossman asserts that this is a story that "has never occurred," that is, that the play is not simply a satire on Communist cant and collusion, but rather that Havel, inspired by the gap between reality and illusion in ideological language, posited the potential endgame of such rationalization of language and understanding. In attempting to eliminate the ambiguities and misunderstandings of human communication, the question is whether this pragmatism dehumanizes human contact. Is misunderstanding, ambiguity and mysteriousness an integral part of human communication, at its heart? Is a recognition and celebration of this a means of resisting absolutist readings of the kind that foster ideological censorship?

"What translation has in common with censorship," Joseph Brodsky wrote, "is that both operate on the basis of the 'what's possible' principle, and it must be noted that linguistic barriers can be as high as those erected by the state" (Brodsky 1987: 47–8). Often the translator is blamed for the "what's possible" principle, making the decisions to cut or domesticate the text, but in many cases, and certainly this case, there is a whole network of people and establishments assuming the "what's possible" principle from the beginning by defining the plays before they are even physically translated or reading them with certain expectations. As Francesca Billiani writes,

> censorship against the penetration of foreign influences, mostly in the shape of translations, subscribes precisely to the assumption that foreign texts can be formally accepted, or rejected, if kept within the parameters, however fluid, of current patterns of taste. (Billiani 2007: 21)

"I'm under no illusions," Havel wrote, "that everyone should like [my plays]," though he suspected that the English response was actually not about inherent quality but about taste and norms. He added, "I already have experience in how capricious and inscrutable the response is to various texts in different cultural conditions" (VBA 3, 1971 undated). But the capriciousness was tied to questions of taste and expectations: Havel received a great deal of interest for a contemporary foreign playwright in England, partly because of censorship. Interest and curiosity was stoked by Havel's "courageousness" under conditions of censorship, but the problem was that this led to readings of the plays as simply political. As such, the plays had cultural worth in the West, in being voices from the inside that opposed its sworn enemy. The problem with Havel's plays was that they were not straightforwardly political enough; their aesthetics made no sense within this model of reading.

In conjunction with reductive readings and subsequent resistance to his plays, was the innate "insularism" of British culture, identified by Tynan as partially being a result of English censorship. Havel's plays, undergoing censorship in Prague, were being translated, at least until 1968, into another culture under the censor's hand. Because of the emphasis by the Lord Chamberlain's Office on morality and sexuality, Havel's plays posed no real risk of overt English censorship. Yet, they did meet some "diluted forms of control" (Billiani 2007: 3) or "external constraints" (Tymozcko 2008: 38) in England. The RSC first approached Blackwell about *The Garden Party* in 1964 but the first professional production of a Havel play in England was not until 1977, and then, was in a tiny theatre above a pub in suburban London.

Meanwhile, by March 1966, Havel wrote to Blackwell that *The Garden Party* had been performed in: 18 theatres in Germany, Vienna and Graz, Zurich and Basle, Budapest, Belgrade, and Stockholm. Performances were due in Bulgaria, Romania, Finland, and Holland as well as four theatres in Czechoslovakia. Gallimard was publishing the play in France. *The Memorandum* was playing in ten Czechoslovak theatres and in Berlin, and was due for production in Vienna and Switzerland. It had been translated in to French and Yugoslavian. "With such a list," he wrote wryly, "I should be as rich as Sophia Loren but surprisingly I'm not. Oh well, I'm not doing it for the money . . ." (VBA 3, 3/20/66).

Spraying the bedroom: The United States

But Joseph Papp optioned and then produced *The Memorandum* in the first season of the new Public Theater in New York, with a cast including Olympia Dukakis and Raul Julia. The same season (1967–68), he produced a hippie musical called *Hair*. Havel unexpectedly got his travel visa and saw his play on the New York stage: "People laughed or applauded in the very same places," he wrote in 2005, "which particularly surprised me given the fact that the translation was probably not great and there are some things in my plays that are simply untranslatable" (Havel 2007a: 7). Havel's retrospective critique of the translation, however, belied the fact that Havel, Papp, and the reviewers treated the translation as very successful at the time, especially—for Havel—because it had not been adapted. The Prague Spring gave it newsworthy interest and political topicality, and it seemed to speak to the convulsions in American society too in what reviewers read as its "anticonformity" message. An NYU professor described the play in the program as a "product of this decade's cultural thaw [. . .] already an East European classic," but posited it as relevant to the American counter-cultural zeitgeist: "The act of producing, or attending Memo is a struggle with the automation of the mind, in which we are all engaged today, whether in the shabby and shiny bureaus of power, in drop-out psychedelia, or in pleasurable beds" (VBA 9:5).

Blackwell's American agents started contacting Broadway for Havel's next play, *The Increased Difficulty of Concentration*, but, even after the Soviet invasion in 1968, Broadway was not interested. It was, however, produced on the experimental stage of the Lincoln Center in December 1969, to generally good reviews that explicitly read it as a political play because of the recent events in Prague. The play won two Obies and, according to the *Village Voice*, at the award ceremony, Jules Irving accepted the award for Distinguished Playwright for Havel and made a speech about the "Czech government's harassment of Havel."

But, suddenly, he was "heckled loudly" by a "beery voice" that shouted out "we want more American playwrights" (VBA 9:2, 28/5/70). "The jingoistic heckling continued" when the English playwright Joe Orton's *What the Butler Saw* was announced as Best Foreign Play (jingoistic even though the best "foreign" play was an English-language one). The edge of xenophobia and nervousness surrounding the goodwill and success of the two Havel plays in America can clearly be seen in one of the reviews of *The Increased Difficulty of Concentration* (by an unnamed reviewer) in the fashion magazine, *Women's Wear Daily*, that compared Havel's plays to an infestation of cockroaches:

> For a couple of years, the New York Shakespeare Festival's Public Theatre harangued its audiences with post-Kafka satires of bureaucracy in the totalitarian state. Joseph Papp's theatre finally rid itself of these naïve, middle European anti-conformity plays (which, ironically, conformed remarkably to each other) and went on to more original projects. But like cockroaches, which move into the bedroom when you spray the kitchen, these plays just turned around and marched uptown to Lincoln Center. Now there's no reason to suspect that Václav Havel's *"Increased Difficulty of Concentration"* is the first of a series of such plays at the Forum Theatre, but it may be wisest to head the roaches off at the pass.

The shocking language of infestation not only shows the cultural arrogance of the reviewer, with awful echoes of Nazi propagandistic portrayals of Jews as vermin (especially with reference to Eastern Europe; a site of large Jewish emigration to the United States), but also the fear of infestation, that somehow the American theatre might be overcome by the foreign. The insistence that these plays conform "remarkably to each other" carries overtones of racism of the "they all look like each other" variety, without any self-awareness that perhaps it is the viewer/reader who is unable to see/read or, more appropriately, refusing to. That Kafka is mentioned as a precursor suggests that the roach metaphor is not only frightening—the idea of the metamorphosis of Gregor Samsa (maybe us!) into these Eastern European cockroaches—but unconsciously awakens the image of his brutal family whose reaction to him condemns him. The discomfort with the non-domesticated is transformed into a sense of overfacile interpretation: these "naïve" plays are of course about Communist "bureaucracy." The reviewer, here, perhaps betrays what is going on at large, that the only way these plays make the stage are because they are read and presented as such. The reviewer does admit that some elements of the show were good, the "occasional comic moments" and "its reasonable interest, just as a story" but these are only attributable to the Americans in the production: "This isn't to the play's credit as much as it is to the director's [. . .] Unfortunately, they [the actresses] were much more delightful than the play" (VBA 9:3, 12/5/69). "Now to spray the bedroom," the reviewer concludes, and you can hear the rattle of the aerosal can.

Although this review was extreme, it is revealing as the end result of a reductive reading of the plays as just East European satire and thus, radically othered, from American society (even though the dismissal of its "anticonformity" hints at anxieties about the American counterculture). The connection of the two can been seen in Lincoln Center's program for *The Increased Difficulty of Concentration*, where the biography (despite Blackwell forcing them to tone the politics down) presents an utterly political picture of Havel whose "passport was revoked because of his outspoken resistance to the Communist invasion and the popularity of his plays abroad"; it tells playgoers that he is "at work on a play about Stalinism" and the "security police visit him three or four times a week" (VBA 9:3). The Czech government was harassing him and they did revoke his passport, but that information was largely irrelevant to the play at hand, other than to provoke interest and, perhaps, sympathy—to give playgoers reasons to see the play.

On the very next page of the program is a full-page ad by the US Travel Service that informs Americans about how to help foreign tourists and on "how to become an unforgettable American memory" for those foreigners. It gives a striking portrait of attitudes toward the foreign and how interactions with the foreign can be commodified, if not understood. "1. Keep an eye out for foreigners," it says. "2. Go up to one. 3. Speak slowly" (VBA 9:3). It tells Americans to help foreigners find their way (No. 4), help other Americans help foreigners (No. 5), and to show foreigners "bargains" because the United States was "a lot cheaper than abroad" (No. 6). "Get *their* phrase book" (my italics) if you still cannot communicate, and, finally, tells an anecdote about how a waitress, who couldn't communicate with a foreigner, drew a picture of the food on offer. Her kind act resulted in the "foreigner" sending people from his hometown back to the restaurant on their holidays. Kindness and communication means profit. There is no sense that the American might learn something—anything—from the tourist. It is a document from another age, but it gives an indication that, despite the seemingly ascendant world of the hippies and antiwar protests that Havel saw on his trip to New York in 1968, there was a real rigidity toward the foreign, unless it could be quantified and commodified within American terms (thus making it less scary). This may speak to wider anxieties in American society (with the war in the Far East, and difference at home in the civil rights and gender rights movements), but it also gives an indication of the world Havel's plays were entering and of the demands and constraints that would be placed on them in the West.

2
Gender censorship

Perhaps this comparison to a psychotic, socially unacceptable character from a Gothic novel is a bit melodramatic, but it is often true that translators, rather than getting equal billing with the authors, may be invisible [. . .] The translators' attic is a crowded place.

PHYLLIS ZATLIN

"I'd like to inform you that I saw you on Czechoslovak television," Havel wrote to Vera Blackwell:

> twice they aired some programme about [Pavel] Tigrid in which there were attacks on this person and that, mainly on [Jan] Procházka (they aired wire-tapped material of him), and also on [Václav] Černý and also on me. And also on you! For quite a while there was a close-up of your face, then finally some surrealist close-up of your eyes and then your mouth; following that a photo of Lane [Blackwell]. With it was some voice-over suggesting that you worked with Tigrid and were a student of Černý's, that you emigrated, that you're a demanding lady (!!) and that you had visited Czechoslovakia. Nothing more than that. Absurd enough. About Lane they said that he is English (!) and that he has some strange contacts. (VBA 3, 4/28/70)

The sudden startling visibility of Blackwell, vilified by the regime on Czech television, presents an almost copy-book example of Laura Mulvey's seminal Freudian and feminist analysis of the close-up in film as fetish.[1] This

---

[1] Laura Mulvey in "Visual Pleasure and Narrative Cinema," writes about the close-up as a means of excising guilt from the male sexual gaze: "the ultimate fetish [. . .] is broken in favour of the image in direct erotic rapport with the spectator. The beauty of the woman as object and the screen space coalesce; she is no longer the bearer of guilt but a perfect product, whose body, stylised and fragmented by close-ups, is the content of the film and the direct recipient of the spectator's look" (Mulvey 2000: 43).

objectification of Blackwell—an attractive woman—suggests anxiety about her and her potential power while attempting to literally take her apart. Lingering on the "surrealist close-up" of her eyes and mouth might imply her dangerous wantonness and *unheimlichkeit* (in the threat of dismemberment and castration), but it also shows her organs of sight and speech, organs of her power as an interpreter and translator.

Milan Kundera, writing about this public airing of the private conversations between the writer, Jan Procházka, and one of the country's most eminent literature professors, Václav Černý (Blackwell's PhD advisor), described it as "the rape of [Procházka's] life" (Kundera 1996: 261). In contrast to this figural feminization of Procházka's fate at the hands of the regime, the regime paints Blackwell as a masculinized woman, "a demanding lady" in the company of men, however suspect. The fact that the regime sought to attack her publicly on television ironically showed how much importance they placed on her as a conduit for Havel's voice abroad. When Havel's works were completely censored and banned in 1970, the regime realized that such a ban would only work within its own borders and to some extent (though not completely) within the borders of the Eastern Bloc. Translation gave Havel a stage and a voice; that the Czech camera lingered on Blackwell's mouth spoke volumes.

The female translator

Reviewing 20 years of feminist translation studies, Luise von Flotow writes that these studies have dealt with issues including "censorship through translation, the silencing of women's contributions to society as translators and writers and, more generally, the non-recognition of women as influential actors in culture and writing" (von Flotow 2011: 2). She calls for a move from the historical analysis of censorship and silencing to a critical analysis of the possibilities and presence of activism and performativity by women translating. In essence, Vera Blackwell's archive reveals a narrative of both censorship and activism, in congruence with each other, and this narrative of what I call gender censorship is not one simply of silence and victimhood.

"[T]he femininity of translation is a persistent historical trope," Sherry Simon writes, "'Woman' and 'translator' have been relegated to the same position of discursive inferiority" (Simon 1996: 1). "Indeed," she adds, "history has not been very mindful of translators whatever their gender," (p. 40) but feminist translation theorists such as Simon and von Flotow have encouraged readings and the unearthing of translation work by women in the past and the present as an act of recovery "that provides a fresh vantage-point into literary practices and their social grounding" (p. 39) and that shows how "translation has at times emerged as a strong form of expression for women—allowing them to enter the world of letters, promote political causes and to engage in stimulating writing relationships" (p. 39).

This "activist translation" (Tymoczko 2007: 217) can involve translating radical political and/or feminist work, translating with a feminist ethic or talking about the translation experience often via prefaces and footnotes; these translator prefaces from early modern literature onwards "were the means by which women found a public voice" (p. 50). Such "metatexts" (von Flotow 1997: 35) that "draw attention to the work of translators" have become more common since the 1970s, making "a concerted move away from the classic 'invisible' translator, the idea of the translator as some kind of transparent channel whose involvement does not affect the source or the translated texts" (von Flotow 1997: 35). These metatexts show women as active readers of the text, interpreting the text exegetically as well as linguistically. "[L]iterary translation can be a way of getting to know [writers] from within," Madeleine Stratford writes, "by crawling under their words in order to reconstruct the fabric of their texts" (von Flotow 2011: 72).

Respecting translation as a form of exegesis rather than a transparent linguistic transfer means a challenge to the traditional charge against translators of infidelity to the original text, a charge itself based on metaphorical and figurative feminization (Chamberlain 1992). Rather, their experience as a close reader and interpreter of the text and often their self-knowledge about how they alter texts in that interpretation (as all readers do) is a locus of "critical knowledge" (Cronin 2003: 126). In addition, an analysis of the "creative nature of the process" (Cronin 2003: 127) of translation, what von Flotow calls, in its end product, "the translator-effect" (von Flotow 1997: 35), is a window into understanding the text. Looking at the translation and the translator's work enables us to revisit and reread the text as an act of "re-membering" (von Flotow 2011: 142).

But Michael Cronin argues that there is a certain societal resistance in market economies to analyzing the activity of translation, in which the consumer just wants product rather than process (Cronin 2003: 94), leading to "a constant, unenviable *censorship of experience*" (p. 94, his italics) for translators. In addition, translators, if they are regarded at all, are viewed as "objects of suspicion" (p. 126) because "by the very nature of their practice [they work] at a distance from their society, culture and language" (p. 126). In repressive or totalitarian periods, translators have been "bound and handcuffed," had to flee, or were killed for their work (p. 93), but Cronin also argues that in free societies, in the era of globalization "another form of censorship and another form of violence" is at work, that "although less dramatic and less tragic in its outcomes [. . .] is much more widespread and more quietly traumatic" (p. 93), that is one of indifference or else "zero translation" (p. 97), in an increasingly monoglossic world.

The suspect quality of translators, however, belies their power; as Maria Tymoczko argues: "If a translator can become a traitor, as the Italian aphorism *traduttore, traditore* suggests, without a doubt it is the political and ideological agency of translators that is the most threatening to those in power" (Tymoczko 2007: 216). One means by which a translator can become an activist translator is in recognizing that they "are the ones who construct meaning in translated texts [. . .] in this capacity they wield considerable power" (p. 265) not only in determining meaning, but also in "explor[ing] and reflect[ing] upon the nature of meaning" (p. 265). However indifferent globalized cultures may appear to translators, they are not only needed and used as linguists, but also as epistemologists. In negotiating with and subverting norms, translators may still be subject to constraints (whether ideological or commercial) but in being self-aware of, and advocating, the kernel of their power as verbal and textual interpreters, they can attain a certain agency and empowerment. Tymoczko advocates the notion of active "self-censorship," a self-reflective and ethical choosing of possible political stances in situations of constraint.

Blackwell, translator

Blackwell was neither a feminist nor someone who professed to hold the figure of the translator in high regard, despite her clear pride in her 20 years of translating Havel's plays (from 1963 to the mid-1980s). "I'm not proud of being a translator," she wrote to Havel's agent, Klaus Juncker, "although I realize I'm good at it and am fully aware of the actual worth of my work" (VBA 2:3, undated); "I've never aspired to being a translator [. . .] I translate some texts of my choice from time to time, but that's a challenging side-line, not my profession" (VBA 2:3, 4/28/76).

Blackwell claimed that she fell into translating by chance, after reading Havel's *The Garden Party*:

> I knew nothing about contemporary Czech literature or drama—and I was fascinated and also astonished by the play—it was an eye-opener for me—I had no idea—then—that things of that sort could be written, let alone produced in Novotny's CSSR—that is, in 1963!—a long time before Dubcek's "Prague Spring." (VBA 2:8)

Although she talked with the BBC about translating other Czech writers, she primarily only translated Havel and indicated that this was a labor of love and perhaps of necessity because of the paucity of qualified Czech speakers: "I honestly don't believe anyone in the US (any more than in England) could find another translator who could do justice to Václav's plays. This is (perhaps an unfortunate) fact, not a boast," she wrote to Juncker, "I translate Václav's plays only because I like Václav, I like his plays and I'd hate to see them distorted by hacks" (VBA 2:3, undated).

Blackwell's defensiveness about her translations and being a translator was perhaps unsurprising, given the era and the culture into which she was translating. From her correspondence with Havel's main agent, Klaus Juncker, as well as potential producers and male agents, it is clear that she was viewed as "only a translator" who therefore should have no power or influence over Havel's texts: her role was relegated to being that of linguistically transferring Havel's plays into English. From the start, however, Blackwell not only translated the plays, but was tireless in trying to interest others in the plays, writing to producers, theatres, and publishers, and producing paratextual material—radio programs, introductions in theatre programs, informational plays, and articles to give some context to the plays. Most of those she corresponded with were men, indicative of the overwhelming gender inequity of the theatre sphere when she was active in the 1960s and 1970s, and from the late 1960s onwards, many of them felt she was too pushy, a "demanding lady," someone who overstepped her mark as a translator. One of the main issues concerned money; from the beginning Blackwell had an agreement with Havel that they receive a 50:50 split on advances, an unheard of agreement at the time and one that would partially lead Havel's agent, Juncker, to persuade Havel to drop Blackwell as his translator in the mid-1980s. Blackwell, who knew she was a good translator, seemed to internalize the disdain for the profession and fear that being associated with it would marginalize herself and her work.

Blackwell is an unknown figure in literary history, because she was "only a translator" of plays that have themselves been marginalized in post–Cold War English-language theatre. However, in recent years, two nonmainstream theatre companies—the Orange Tree Theatre in London and the Untitled Theatre Company #61 in New York have used or recommissioned other translators' versions of the plays. Such a process is inevitable and healthy as new eras often require new translations, but one of the dangers of this is the sometimes automatic assumption that previous translations are necessarily "bad" translations that need to be improved. If the theatre translator is not a famous playwright or writer then they are often consigned to a legacy of anonymity; yet their experience can be salutary and even revelatory about the play-making process when translations are involved and how that reflects the sociopolitical intersection of cultures at a given historical moment. The "forgetting" of translators' experiences, especially those of women, contributes to the continuing "censorship of indifference" toward translators, because it expurgates the actual historical importance and contribution that translators have made to literary and (inter)cultural development, thereby lessening the importance of their role in the present.

Blackwell's experiences are particularly instructive: through her archive we can get a sense of what effect overt censorship has on a translator and not just on the translated text; we get a sense of the murky give and take of totalitarian censorship and its relationship to gender; and of the translator's agency in obviating such censorship. But we also can learn from her experiences as a woman translating in ostensibly free conditions in which interest in her translations was often based on the fact of their censored-in-the-East status: that she faced constraints and resistance as a translator because of the job's marginalized status; that because of this marginalized status her exegetical worth was highly undervalued, leading to reductive alterations to the plays; that her job as a translator involved being a metatexual advocate for Havel, help that was seen as overstepping her duties; that she was seen as an "object of suspicion" in the West politically, sexually, and as a translator; and that her financial demands for equality (with the author) were dismissed as abhorrent except by Havel himself.

Only a translator: Censoring a feminized profession

"I'm well aware of all that you've done for me over the years," Havel wrote to Blackwell in 1978, "and that without you I would probably not exist at all as an author in the Anglo-Saxon world" (VBA 3, 11/29/78). Havel was not just referring to Blackwell's translations of his plays but also all of the promotional work and networking that she'd done for his plays, her help in garnering public support for him, her management of his money abroad, and her representation of him and his work in the English-speaking world. Partly because Havel was unable to leave Czechoslovakia after the Soviet invasion (he was offered a visa out by the government, but it was one-way), and partly because of Blackwell's own drive and energy (Havel called her an "anti-Oblomov" character), her task as a translator did not end on the page or even on the stage, but became a fairly all-consuming passion and job. From her first experience with the RSC, Blackwell knew that it wouldn't be enough to just translate the play text, because the translation needed to be represented and promoted due to the general apathy toward foreign-language plays in the United Kingdom and the United States.

Blackwell, though she'd never planned to be a translator, came from a cultural tradition that valued translators and saw translation as a generative and creative part of a national and international dialogue. In his famous anticensorship speech at the Czechoslovak Writer's Union in 1967, Milan Kundera spoke about "something quite peculiar to Czech literature, which has given rise to a type of man very rare in other literatures, namely the translator as a significant, even a dominant literary personality" (Hamšík 1971: 170). He added, "translators have the status of literary personalities" in Czech culture (p. 170) and translation had "such an important role" because they allowed the Czech language to "mould itself as a language on a par with other European languages and in possession of a European vocabulary" (p. 171). In addition, translations allowed Czech literature to become part of a wider "European literature" (p. 171), thus being central to the nationalists of the Czech Revival in the nineteenth century and postindependence Czechoslovakia in the interwar years. Kundera, of course, only refers to male translators, but in those interwar years, women were actively recruited as translators, thus enabling them to become highly regarded as artists in the interwar literary circles in Prague: translators such as Milena Jesenská, Staša Jílovská, and Jarmila Fastrová. In being active in contacting theatre and publishing figures in the United Kingdom and in the United States, Blackwell was perhaps working from within a particularly Czech cultural heritage that respected the work of the translator as integral to the literary and cultural workings of a given culture.

Havel, too, showed a similar respect for his translator and awareness of her actual work, liaising with both the RSC and DILIA, from the beginning of their relationship. "I would like to really sincerely thank you for everything that you've done from the translation [of *The Garden Party*] to all the tactical steps that we've undertaken together" he wrote in one of his first letters to her, "I feel like I am really your grand debtor" (VBA 1:1, 7/13/64). A month later he again emphasized his gratitude: "I'm grateful that you're working so devotedly on our things!" (VBA 1:1, 8/14/64) and noted that he still had not read the translation, but that his director, Jan Grossman had; in talking to Grossman briefly, the director told him that he "liked it very much" (VBA 1:1, 8/14/64). After a longer conversation with Grossman, Havel wrote to Blackwell: "I'm very happy that your translation is so good—I can't judge for myself except here or there (more optically than semantically), but the opinion of Mr. Grossman is decisive for me—he knows me better than I know myself" (VBA 1:1, undated).

He conveyed his confidence in Blackwell to the director of the RSC, John Roberts, thanking him for allowing Blackwell to work with the adaptor, N. F. Simpson:

> Her translation, as far as we can judge, is excellent. (By the way, it seems to us better than the German, in the exactness both of words and atmosphere.) In personal talks with Mrs. Blackwell we discover that we share our views about theatre and art, so I feel that in every way she can and does speak for me. (VBA 1:1, 11/1/64)

Havel had to rely on someone, given the geographic distance and unlikelihood that the Communist regime would give him a visa to travel (Havel only traveled abroad intermittently in the 1960s, then not at all after the Soviet invasion). But his assertion to the RSC that "she can and does speak for me" assigned a central role to his translator that went beyond the linguistic transfer of the play's contents. That they share "views on art and literature" was vital to Havel, because he viewed her role as an exegetical one; she would embody him as the play's aesthetic representative. Havel was writing in response to Roberts' insistence on an adaptation of *The Garden Party*; in this, Roberts was following theatre norms. He asked Blackwell for a literal translation, a crib, that could be adapted and chose a fashionable contemporary English male playwright for the adaptation. Blackwell wrote to Roberts that a literal translation was impossible because of the nature of the play, some interpretation would be inevitable, pointing out that the

theatre convention of a literal crib is something of a falsehood, as the literal translator inevitably places their interpretation on the translation, even
before it is adapted.

Both Grossman and Havel knew that the play would inevitably change
in translation and were both open to that. Their one fear was that the play
would be adapted unthinkingly and without a real sense of its aesthetic purpose. Blackwell's task was to shepherd the adaptor, N. F. Simpson, through
the ideas bolstering the shape and content of *The Garden Party*, in a way
that an author might. It was a job for which Blackwell was not paid (though
she received 25 guineas for her translation).

Havel's sense of equity with Blackwell, however, did extend to pay and
this would cause enormous problems with others involved in the process.
When Grove Press decided to publish Havel's first two plays, *The Garden
Party* and *The Memorandum*, Blackwell asked of Grove a 50:50 financial
split with Havel. Writing to Havel, Blackwell wanted to make clear why she
felt she deserved the 50:50 split and to emphasize that "this division didn't
come from the top of my head, but was on the other hand suggested by
Tom Maschler, [Fred] Jordan [at Grove] and [Henry] Popkin, with whom
I'd talked about it." She underscored that she had no experience with such
dealings and relied on the experience of these publishers and journalists:

> It's not about the fact that the translations of your plays are difficult.
> Any true translation by anyone is difficult. Rather, it's about the endless
> correspondence about what none of these so-called "agents" are doing—
> including DILIA. (VBA 3, 4/12/67)

Havel had already signed a contract with Grove, which did not mention
any payment amount to the translator. But Havel wrote to Blackwell that he
would write to Fred Jordan at Grove, saying that:

> he should pay you the same as he pays me because it's no joke translating
> this kind of play. Whether that will work, I don't know [. . .] If, however,
> Grove really wants to pay you only a small amount in order to publish it,
> there might be another possibility: I would privately give you a part of my
> payment, so that the whole—including your payment—would be split in
> half. Please believe me, that I don't have any notion of stealing from you
> and I'm open to whatever agreement—but it's hard for me to ensure that
> Mr. Jordan won't rob you. So: I'll simply write to Jordan, reminding him
> again that you are the authorized translator in the English speaking world,
> that you're working on the definitive translations right now (the earlier
> versions were just working versions and shouldn't be published) and that
> he should pay you the same amount as me. (VBA 3, undated 1965)

Havel clearly felt that Blackwell deserved 50 percent of the advance because
he understood "it's no joke" translating his plays, that this was not just a

question of a straightforward linguistic transfer but a thorny act of interpretation. Havel went against the English-language norms of the time by supporting financial equity for his translator, and financial equity for a woman in a profession, but he clearly felt that it was a point of fairness in terms of the amount of work involved at the stage of translation, even offering to pay Blackwell privately from his own share to render this equity. Both he and Blackwell assumed from then on a 50:50 split for stage and page payments.

The idea of financial equity for the translator upset DILIA, and outraged Havel's main Western agent, Klaus Juncker. In 1967, DILIA wrote to Blackwell:

> We have never completed a 50:50 contract between an author and a translator. This is a practice, according to our information, that is also not normal in the West. We have news from the US, for example, that the most they pay is $15 per 1000 words and in England the maximum payment for the translation of a literary work is 80 shillings for a 1000 words. As far as we have completed joint contracts between the author and translator (and these are the exception) we work on a 2:1 basis in favor of the author. We understand that the case of Havel's plays is anomalous, nevertheless we cannot rid ourselves of the feeling that even in this case the translator shouldn't be placed on the same level as the author. (VBA 2:6, 3/24/67)

Blackwell defended her position by pointing out that her work for Havel extended beyond the bounds of the textual translation (and the complexity of that task) and that it wasn't a completely unusual arrangement:

> I fully understand that the 50:50 split between the author and the translator isn't common. On the other hand, it's not unheard of [. . .] in the case of future translations the percentage split should depnd on how much work is invested not only into the translation, but also into the promotion of the work. (VBA 2:6, 4/10/67)

As proof that it wasn't a completely new type of arrangement, she referred to a letter sent by Jonathan Cape publishers to DILIA 3 months earlier, in which the well-known editor, Tom Maschler, who had bought the rights to publish Havel's two plays in the United Kingdom, defended the 50:50 split and claimed that "I originally suggested to her that, subject to your agreement, the earnings from the plays should be divided equally between Mr. Havel and herself." He confirmed to DILIA that, "We have in the past come to similar arrangements with translators" and made the case for Blackwell in particular deserving equal payment:

> I would say that in this particular case VB has, of course, earned fifty per cent in that she has done so much more than simply translate Havel,

for she has contributed substantially towards making him known in this country. (VBA 2:6, 1/17/67)

Blackwell had herself contacted Cape about publishing Havel's plays, she was in constant contact with the BBC, especially Martin Esslin, offering them translations of his new plays, she gave a script of *The Memorandum* to Joe Papp at a PEN meeting in 1966 that led to the first professional production of his plays in English (at the new Public Theater in 1968) and a long-term US home for Havel's plays, and she was sending out the translations of *The Memorandum* and *The Increased Difficulty of Concentration* to various theatres, journals, and publishers. In addition, she was handling payments for Havel, trying to work out ways in which to keep DILIA from playing politics with such payments, that is, withholding them as punishment or demanding extra percentages.

Despite a fairly tortuous back and forth with DILIA through the sixties, and their questioning of payment equity, both Blackwell and DILIA realized that her promotional activities were worthwhile and helping Havel. After 1970, however, DILIA were told to crackdown on Havel and actively prevent foreign deals on his plays, but one of their employees suggested to Havel that he do his business through a Western agency instead, and Havel chose his friend Klaus Juncker, at the leading German agency, Rowohlt.

Throughout the 1970s, Rowohlt repeatedly tried to stop Blackwell doing anything other than translating the plays, and, even then, were suggesting to Havel that she shouldn't be the translator at all. When Rowohlt were sent a contract from Methuen for the publication of two of Havel's plays, *Audience* and *Private View* (published together under the title "Sorry. . .") in 1978 that divided the royalties, they refused to sign it. One of their agents, Malte Hartemann, wrote to Blackwell's agent that, because Rowohlt was taking a cut from Havel's half: "It really is hard to see why the translator should get more that the author, who has done a job that is much higher to estimate than the translator's" (VBA 2:2, 8/14/78). Blackwell, in a furious letter to Havel, wrote that Juncker had phoned her and repeated "Liebe Vera, Sie sind doch nur eine Übersetzerin," insinuated that she was "stealing" from Havel and that he had approached the BBC "*ordering*" them not to pay her 50 percent, even though he knew this was not BBC practice (VBA 3, 10/31/78). Juncker went further, claiming that Havel told him he had never agreed to pay Blackwell 50 percent and demanding Blackwell show him evidence of Havel ever agreeing to such conditions:

> I have had several long telephone conversations with Václav and discussed all the issues. He stated unequivocally that he *never* gave permission for a 50:50 split of the English royalties which were worse conditions for the author than the translator. Show me, please, a contract or a letter stating this [the 50:50 split]. Someone must be mistaken. (VBA 2:2, 10/18/78)

Blackwell was horrified at the implication that she was a liar and deliberately attempting to cheat Havel. She sent a strongly worded reply to Juncker:

> Re Václav's alleged statement, quoted in your last letter, that he never (your italics) agreed to a 50-50 split between him and me—I'm astonished. You challenge me as follows: "Zeigen Sir mir doch bitte einen Vertrag oder einen Brief, falls es so etwas gibt" (my italics). Well, there's a lot I could show you, but since you ask just for ONE piece of evidence, so be it. (Anyway, I've neither the time, nor any obligation whatsoever to xerox for you my whole file.) Apparently, you've brought us to the point where gentlemen's agreements are no longer honoured and friends' words are no longer trusted. (VBA 2:2, 11/2/78)

Blackwell enclosed a copy of the contract with Grove Press from 1966, "in which the 50–50 division of the total royalties is agreed to and signed by Havel" and reminded him that he received copies of a 1972 contract with the English National Theatre for *The Conspirators*, which also explicitly showed the 50:50 split. "Why didn't you raise the issue then, I wonder?" she wrote. She felt it was an attack on her "integrity" and that she could not defend herself when Juncker had repeated on the phone that "Ich glaube nichts was Sie sagen" (VBA 2:2, 11/2/78).

Blackwell's assertion that "gentlemen's agreements were no longer honoured" points to the world in which she was working: both in the patriarchal terms in which she worked and a sense of inclusion she had in that world that proved to be superficial. Writing to Havel, she expressed her shock at being "screamed at" by Juncker; "under capitalism" she wrote, this is allowed, when it would not happen to a "milkmaid" in Czechoslovakia. Her language was telling: she felt she was the hired help and was meant, as such, to keep quiet and to be paid in accordingly subservient terms.

Juncker, of course, was working within the norms he expected: the translator was there to provide a linguistic transfer and nothing else; she was unimportant in terms of the play and the author. Havel, in trying to assure Blackwell about Juncker in 1973, wrote that Juncker was a "pragmatist" whose only concern was for the "thing" itself, that is, the play, and if unusual demands were presented to theatres or publishers, regarding the translator (i.e. insisting on a particular translator or demanding a 50:50 split), then Juncker worried that this might jeopardize the chances of the play being produced or published (VBA 3, 9/18/73). The care and "caution" that Havel felt was Juncker's trademark revealed the world they worked in with a sense that, with already existent hostility toward translated plays, any extra demands might scupper the chances of these plays and certainly these demands should not originate from the translator.

Bad feeling had arisen over the putative production of *The Conspirators*, a play Ken Tynan had commissioned for the English National Theatre in 1971. The play was optioned but it was never produced. Juncker was upset because the National Theatre contract was sent to Blackwell's agent, Peggy Ramsay, rather than him and blamed confusion over who was representing the play to the fact that the play was not produced. In fact, Tynan had had the play translated by a non-native Czech speaker and had not liked it. But Blackwell supposed that Juncker felt that she had been overstepping her place in dealing directly with Tynan and the theatre, whereas for Juncker "from the start [my job] was simply limited to being that of 'only' a translator" (VBA 3, 7/16/73).

For Blackwell, being a translator had meant having to take part in promoting the work and she argued that Juncker had known all along of her involvement in this, and that she didn't enjoy that part of the job. But Juncker's demand that she stick to just translation seemed to her a difficult proposition: "Klaus is now your DILIA," she wrote to Havel:

> Klaus will do the meetings, I'll translate. But it's not as simple as that. Your name is associated with mine here, and not just with regard to translation, but also with regard to agent work and so on; everyone turns to me when it comes to issues connected to you—they don't turn to Ramsay, never mind Klaus. (VBA 3, 7/16/73)

Blackwell's comment that Klaus "is now your DILIA" was telling; she refers to the fact that Juncker would be the one agent controlling Havel's world rights, just as DILIA had, but Juncker had also become an agent of constraint upon her, demanding that she return to his concept of what a translator was. The problem lay in the active work she had pursued before, in pushing the translations and networking, knowing that "just" translating the plays would not be enough in the English-language sphere and that interest had to be generated in the translated plays. Blackwell had done the spadework for Havel in introducing him to the English language theatre and clearly felt that she was in the best position to keep generating interest in the plays.

Blackwell had been closely involved in interesting producers and theatres in Havel's first four major plays and in keeping their interest, keeping pressure on them, offering to help in adaptations, and in interesting the media in the productions. She worked with the RSC on Havel's first major play, *The Garden Party*; she had interested Joe Papp in the next play, *The Memorandum*, which Papp subsequently produced; she had been central in getting the Lincoln Center to produce the next play, *The Increased Difficulty of Concentration* and she had helped, in keeping contact with Tynan, with the National Theatre's commissioning of *The Conspirators*. But once Juncker took control of the English-language rights of the plays, nothing was produced for several years.

Havel was worried: "I'd like to emphasize here that I've got engaged with this and am engaged not only from a sense of some tie to you," he wrote to Blackwell in 1975:

> but also in the interest of my plays: I see all too clearly that when you were translating them and looking after them, they were produced, and from the time Klaus took hold of the rights and has let the tie with you lapse, they haven't been produced. (VBA 3, 8/28/75)

A few months later, Havel included the copy of a letter he'd sent to Juncker in a letter to Blackwell, again stating that when Blackwell was "looking after" the plays that were being produced:

> As I've written to you several times it's not a debate about whether she's proved herself as a translator or that she's looked after my plays well; it's based on the reality that my previous plays were successfully produced in her translations and thanks to her meetings in the English-language sphere. (VBA 3, 1/5/76)

Havel told Juncker that Blackwell knew people in the United Kingdom who might be interested in his new one-act play, *Audience*, but she had only approached them as "a reader" and he emphasized that she had not tried to make any connections, that is, that she wasn't overstepping her mark as a translator.

Havel clearly felt a little frustrated, knowing there might be interest in England in the play and that he had a translator at hand, but his hands were now tied because he was waiting for Juncker to act—to approve Blackwell as the translator and to promote interest in a production in the United Kingdom or the United States. Juncker's reaction to being very gently and diplomatically queried by Havel about his inaction, was to allow Blackwell to translate the play but to remind her that she was just a translator. It is at this point, that Blackwell wrote to Juncker, defensively, saying that "I'm not proud of being a translator" and "I've never aspired to being a translator." As Juncker insisted on constraining her within a traditional concept of the translator, she began to see it as something secondary and shameful, internalizing the hegemonic relationship between writing and translation (and thus also the economic one).

Juncker's strictures on Blackwell did affect Havel's plays; instead of conceiving of her role as an informed helper on the ground, fluent in the two languages in question—Czech and English—with contacts and relationships in both the English and American theatre worlds, built up over nearly a decade, Juncker's sense of what a translator was and did overcame a more common-sense approach. Juncker himself was well-connected in the English theatre world because Rowohlt represented many English playwrights in Germany, but Germany and the German-speaking world was his focus.

Already by 1974, Havel was wondering whether locating all the agent work with Juncker was a "mistake" (VBA 3, 12/2/74), because Juncker was "stubbornly" trying to sell *The Beggar's Opera* in Germany, where no one wanted it because of "Brecht!" (who had written his own version of Gay's ballad opera), and ignoring the English market. He asked Blackwell to engage in a little "intrigue" and to quietly resume her promotional work; "if you have any good friend in some theatre, agency or radio" who might be interested in the play, he asked, would she mind asking them to contact Juncker directly saying that they had "heard about the play," "perhaps directly from you" (VBA 3, 12/2/74). Secretly, Blackwell did and Esslin contacted Juncker on behalf of BBC radio.

Peggy Ramsay warned Blackwell about Juncker in 1970, but Blackwell defended him: "he is a friend, not a rival," she wrote (VBA 9:1, 8/27/70). But their relationship worsened through the 1970s and early 1980s, because of his perceptions of her presumptuousness asa translator. Havel, increasingly isolated in Czechoslovakia was not sure whom to believe and tried to appease both. Finally, in 1984, he was given an ultimatum by Juncker (invoking Joe Papp and nameless English theatre practitioners) that his plays would simply not be performed in English if he remained faithful to Blackwell.

The spy

The anxiety about Blackwell overstepping her role as a translator in the West revealed an issue of power, somewhat related to economics and certainly to cultural capital. The "anti-Oblomov" Blackwell inadvertently showed that a translator could be a significant figure in the literary process, despite cultural resistance to that power being held by a woman and a translator. In Czechoslovakia, her power as a translator was appreciated and used before the Soviet invasion in 1968, then that power—the ability to disseminate banned work abroad—was feared and censored. But the censorship was odd to begin with; the Czech government denounced her on TV, banned her work, and deported her, but also privately (via DILIA) were complicit in enabling her to continue with her job. However, this could only happen under a pseudonym, so that Blackwell underwent a nominal sex change and became "Mr Just." Once she became a fake male translator, some of those in the regime were prepared to enable Blackwell to circumvent censorship of her translations and consequently censorship of Havel, if only in translation.

In the summer of 1969, Havel was brought into the Ministry of Interior for questioning about Blackwell, who had just been deported from the country; there they said that she was not judged to be a spy, otherwise she would have been arrested rather than deported. Instead, they told Havel that she was guilty of passing on information about the Party to Pavel Tigrid, a Czech émigré in Paris who ran an émigré journal, *Svědectví*. Havel told them it was "a gross injustice," that they had no proof of Blackwell's guilt, and that he had no intention of breaking contact with her (VBA 3, 8/7/69). The conversation about Blackwell had started because Havel had questioned them about their wiretapping of his apartment; their excuse was that they wanted to entrap Tigrid or Blackwell (VBA 3, 8/7/69).

In an act of bravery, Havel then sent a letter of complaint on behalf of Blackwell to the Czech National Committee questioning the official reason (broadcast in the media) that Blackwell had been deported because of her work for Radio Free Europe in 1950s. Havel wrote that Blackwell had been officially "amnestied" for this work in 1964, and that she had not written and presented propaganda under the name "Lunáčková" but was an artistic director and actress. He also challenged the other official complaint that she had passed material on to Tigrid, writing that the Central Committee had better ways of getting the material to Tigrid and that Blackwell's two articles for Svedectvi were ones promoting culture in Czechslovakia. Havel underlined how influential Blackwell was in general:

> The expulsion of Mrs. Blackwell inflicted a wound on the cultural ties between Czechoslovakia and England (where Mrs. Blackwell has—in relation to Czechoslovak culture—a considerable influence) and our state has thus very strangely and unjustly rewarded a person, who has for so many years and with so much initiative worked to spread the good name of its culture abroad. (VBA 3, 14/7/69)

Havel accused the Party of trying to set up Blackwell in order to justify its own theories that the West organized the Prague Spring, helped by "agents" like Blackwell. Deporting people from the country engineered false evidence for these false theories (VBA 3, 14/7/69). But Havel and Blackwell knew the main reason behind the attacks on her: she was Havel's translator, and if the regime was going to censor Havel, it had to find ways of censoring her.

Blackwell, nee Věra Jakešová, walked across the Czech border to Germany in 1952, 4 years after the Communist coup, thus becoming a political émigré. She began her working life in the West in Munich with Radio Free Europe, an American government-backed station, which broadcast back into Czechoslovakia and Eastern Europe. There she met her American husband, Lane Blackwell, who spent most of his career as a television executive; her marriage to Blackwell meant she was eligible for American citizenship and, thus, was able to return to Czechoslovakia in the early 1960s, where she met Havel. As someone who "fled" the country, Vera Blackwell was always going to be seen by the regime as ideologically and politically suspect. In this she is an emphasized example of the translator, who is sometimes viewed with suspicion by their native culture because they have left their home culture and language to return changed and capable of disrupting their native tongue or culture. "Translators have been justly celebrated over the centuries for journeying to other cultures," Michael Cronin writes,

> Conversely, translators have also been ignored, disregarded and viewed with deep suspicion. The suspicion stems less from the outward than the return journey [. . .] The traveller who has been to foreign parts is not only *unsettled* but s/he becomes on return an *unsettling* figure for the settled community. (Cronin 2000: 64–5)

In terms of the Communist regime, Blackwell's allegiance was clear and it was not to them, but they did perceive her having an allegiance to Czech culture. When Blackwell organized the US and UK publications of her translations of Havel's first two plays in 1966, DILIA wrote to her: "We consider the English and American editions of Havel's plays to be a huge success for our literature. We want to take this opportunity to tell you again how much we value your effective assistance" (VBA 2:6, 18/8/66). When they were worried that they had upset Blackwell the same year because of various confusions, one of the DILIA bureaucrats, Mr. Kalaš lamented to Havel that he was worried that they would lose an "effective and beautiful colleague" (VBA 3, 23/2/66), highlighting not only her worth to them professionally, but also their perception of her worth as a woman, that is, through her beauty. Havel, rightly, quotes it with irony, aware of the superficial and supercilious flattery, but implies with that selfsame irony that it signals DILIA's anxiety about her agency and effectiveness in the West.

Havel's work was famously banned following the Soviet invasion of Czechoslovakia (with a complete ban beginning in 1970), but the regime was cognizant that his work could still be performed abroad and that he would still receive foreign royalties. The reaction to this was mixed in the very early seventies: Havel supposed that pressure was coming from the higher echelons of the regime to place a blanket ban on giving rights for foreign productions, but DILIA itself seemed persuadable, albeit now demanding 90 percent of royalties coming in for Havel.

Less known is the pressure placed on Blackwell as a means to scuppering English-language productions; she was thrown out of Czechoslovakia in the summer of 1969 and thus cut off from her family (Blackwell's father still lived in Prague), the regime refused to let Charles University grant her PhD, and it initiated several public attacks on her on TV and in the press. In 1970 she was also placed on the regime's "Index" of banned writers, and DILIA officially "refused" to sign contracts if Blackwell's name was on it (VBA 9:1, 6/6/70).

"I'm being constantly attacked in the Czech press and also on radio and television," Blackwell wrote to her US agent in 1970, saying that DILIA were refusing to sign contracts with Havel, their "stated reason" being her, but "[t]he real reason is, of course, an attempt by the authorities to stop Havel's only means of a livelihood—i.e. his income from western royalties"

(VBA 9:1, 6/6/70). Although the main target was Havel, the regime overtly censored Blackwell because they knew that she was effective in disseminating his work and targeted her. In making her utterly visible—her face dissected on state television—they attempted to shame her. They implied that she was working for foreign governments and consequently that Havel was too; she was deemed a spy.

Such a public unmasking of the translator as a suspicious figure, as a traitor, plays into the traditional concept of the *traduttore, traditore*. The translator not only betrays the original text but also their native culture; but the public nature of it, the unmasking of the usually invisible and silent translator concomitantly underlines the anxiety of those judging the betrayal and the actual cultural significance of the translator. After all, the translator has the power to bring censored or banned work into publication or performance, albeit in another language. Czech TV's "absurd" concentration on Blackwell's face with its surreal and fractured close-ups also suggests an anxiety about her femininity, where her "effectiveness" is connected to her "beauty," which is thus something to be attacked. It suggests not only the patriarchal attitude of the regime, but also its fears.

But the situation was even more complicated; at the very same time that the regime was publicly denouncing Blackwell and implying that, having worked for Radio Free Europe in the 1950s, she was a spy, DILIA was trying unofficially to retain her as Havel's translator. "The situation has got a lot worse," Havel wrote to Blackwell in May 1970, but DILIA had proposed a solution:

> it appears that Kalaš was criticized somewhere [for the contract with Blackwell's name on it]. As I understand it, the problem could be overcome if there was simply another translator's name on the contract. I don't know if it will work, I know of course it's an absurdity (when the play is being performed in your translation and its publicly known that you translated it), nevertheless I can attest to the fact that it's the only way, from DILIA's point of view, to solve the situation. They don't want to poke further, they don't care, the only thing they care about is making sure they don't sign a contract that has the name of a spy on it, a spy whom everyone knows isn't a spy. It's only a small example of the kind of nonsense that's happening here in a big way. DILIA is floundering around, trying to fulfill different requirements, regulations and orders from on high, as well as dealing with threats and pressures, and they are trying at least to help authors in the smallest ways. (VBA 3, 19/5/70)

Blackwell passed on the information to her agent, "Dilia is still trying to cooperate, though they have to give in to the pressures from above," she wrote, "They propose to sign a contract from which my name has been removed" (9:1 6/6/70). She then asked if her agent would prepare a "fake" contract in which his "name should be substituted for mine, so it stays in the family" (VBA 9:1, 6/6/70).

A few days later, Havel wrote to her, indicated that there was in-fighting within DILIA, with some hardliners more than happy to follow the party line, while others, specifically, Mr Kalaš, trying to finesse some mutual solution. Nevertheless, he asked Blackwell to translate his next play, "As long as it doesn't bother you, that it will be done by some Ptydepe translator" (VBA 3, 12/6/70). Havel was referring to the constructed language, Ptydepe, in his play, *The Memorandum*; a language that no one in the play, bar one teacher, really understands or is allowed to understand. In the play, the memorandum is finally, illegally, translated by a young woman, Maria, who ends up being the scapegoat, and is fired for making "an improper translation" (Havel 1993: 128). The memo itself delegitimizes the language in which it is written, calling the language "confused, unrealistic and anti-human" (pp. 114–15). The "Ptydepe translator" required by DILIA is both a fake translator, but also resonant of Maria, the one person who ends the play with her integrity and identity intact, a subversive female translator, fired for being one.

Translation carries with it the whiff of imposture. "Is there," Michael Cronin asks, "something about the activity of translation that is vaguely fraudulent? [. . .] Translation at one level, is self-evidently a lie. It is not what it purports to be. It is not the original [. . .] Translation is, however, a supreme fiction in that it is an untruth—pretending to be the original—that is articulating a truth" (Cronin 2000: 108–9). The negativity associated with the fiction perpetrated by translation, Cronin suggests, emanates from "profound suspicion by monotheism" (p. 108), whereas he argues for the embracing of the creative possibilities of translation as fiction where even the "most exact reproduction" is recognized as a "radical transformation" of the original (p. 109). The "Ptydepe translator" both allows the real translator—in this case Blackwell—to survive (in a way that Maria does not in the play) by embracing imposture, but it also seems to signify an embracing of translation as a creative and potentially emancipatory art in the covert admission of the construct of "fakeness" or newness in the translation process, the performativity of gender, and the constructs of language.

To avoid censorship, Blackwell changed gender. There was a practical reason for this: "Rather than inventing a non-existent author of the translation," she wrote, "Václav and I agreed to use the actual name of a real person of Czech origin who has never been involved in any political activity, nor been a member of any émigré organization" (VBA 7:5, 21/8/72). This was "Karel Just," who was a friend of both Blackwell and Havel, and who suggested they use his name. The change of gender was a straightforward ploy to use a "beard" with a wink to DILIA who were averting their gaze. The aversion of this gaze, though, seems symbolic of a cohesion to societal norms; that Blackwell would be less dangerous as a fake male translator; that she would no longer be "a demanding lady."

Havel suggested Just the year before, when he was under increasing pressure not to use Blackwell: "I was told directly (by a good source) that I would be in deep shit, if you translated the play," he wrote to Blackwell, "to

use your translations would be from their point of view a political provocation, because I would be working with a person that this country regards
as its enemy" (VBA 3, 6/30/71). Havel felt that he had to be ethical in his
response to this pressure, adamant that he had to stick to "the principle that
art is not the possession of this or any regime" and he suggested Just: "what
if it was translated by someone, perhaps Mr. Just?" (VBA 3, 6/30/71). He
suggested this "compromise" of a fake translator, so that the agencies in the
West would not baulk at employing Blackwell: "It's not so much the penal-
ties that I'll have to endure, but—as I sensed it—the aversion of our Western
partners to risking any fights with this regime" (VBA 3, 6/30/71).

Blackwell made sure that the contract and any publicity for Havel's
play, *The Conspirators* carried the name "Karel Just," explaining to her
agent that: "As you know, VH wants me to do the translation. However,
to connect publicly my name with that of VH while he is being repressed
by the regime and I remain a *persona non grata* would be most unwise"
(VBA 7:5, 8/21/72). Blackwell was *persona non grata* because of the
regime realized she was dangerous on a political level—as the translator of Havel's plays—but also on a more metaphysical level—in that the
power that she wielded seemed unsettling in its very concept, as a translator and as a woman (the "demanding lady"). That the regime strangely
colluded with the bare disguise suggests that the division between public and private censorship, between fully stated and almost unconscious,
internalized and culturally bound censorships were mutable and sometimes interlocking.

The need for the disguise and textual gender change soon became moot;
in 1972, again at the suggestion of some of those at DILIA, Havel decided
to drop DILIA altogether and work through his Western partners, mainly
Juncker. But it turned out that the Czechoslovak government's political accu-
sations against Blackwell and its attempts to censor her would have a strong
fallout on Western perceptions of her, leading to attempted constraints upon
her work in England and the United States.

La belle infidèle

Havel's play *Spiklenci/The Conspirators* was the "first Czech drama of the
1970s to be classified as a forbidden play" (Rocamora 2004: 113). From this
time on, until the fall of Communism in 1989, Havel was entirely reliant on
his translations, not only to disseminate his work but also for a source of
income. In 1971, Kenneth Tynan made what Havel called "a gentlemanly
offer" (VBA 3, 3/11/71), writing to Havel and commissioning a play sight
unseen for the English National Theatre. "I don't have to emphasize how
gratifying the offer is to me for many reasons," Havel wrote to Blackwell,
including the fact that it would mean that "people aren't forgetting about
me and thinking about me as a dramatist (and not only as a victim of the

regime)" (VBA 3, 3/11/71). He promised Tynan a play by July 1, 1971 and wanted to send *The Conspirators*.

There were still problems; because of his ambiguous position in the "Kafkaesque world" (VBA 3, 3/11/71) of postinvasion Prague: he was unsure how Tynan might send the advance; he was not sure how DILIA would deal with it and Blackwell had been denounced publicly. Klaus Juncker met with Tynan in London and, given Havel's delicate situation in Czechoslovakia (he had already been indicted for an anti-invasion manifesto), they came to the conclusion that ". . . basically they definitely wanted to finalize the contract with me, but that I shouldn't take it as a certainty, but they were deliberating at length about it, taking into account different eventualities from the sanctions here, which I expected" (VBA 3, 6/30/71). Havel, worried that the Czech regime was being effective in scaring off potential collaborators, added:

> Finally even Tynan is showing some hesitation—he is afraid that our government will send a protest to the English government and of possible unpleasantness from the English government (which is sweet coming from an anti-establishment leftie), nevertheless he is still interested and fundamentally wants to do it. It bewilders me a little that my foreign partners in Hamburg and London are more afraid of the regime here than I am, and I'm the one who lives here and is even indicted, nevertheless I don't want to belittle or disparage their fears, because I understand many of them, and I know that several of them are dictated by real worries about me and I also understand reality, that I'm not the only author in the world and that my play is not the centre of the universe and there's no point putting serious things on the line for me or my play. (VBA 3, 6/30/71)

Juncker and Tynan agreed that they would wait until they had read the play and decided then whether it was "worth the risk" (VBA 3, 6/30/71). One of the factors involved was the political risk that Blackwell had become.

In the same June letter, Havel informed Blackwell that his relationship with her was now viewed as a "political provocation" and the Czech regime's attacks soon began to have reverberations in the West. Suddenly, Tynan stopped answering Blackwell's calls and letters and Juncker had to be persuaded that the use of a pseudonym would be enough to neutralize the political risk that he saw Blackwell as presenting. Blackwell, accepting Havel's solution that she become "Mr. Just," wondered aloud how Tynan would take it, whether he would be willing to go along with the pseudonym:

> Mr. Just would be delighted to translate your play and thanks you for your belief in his translatorial skills. But now how to present it to Tynan. Initially he kept calling, he even called me "darling" in every third sentence—and now, in the last month—I've been cut off [. . .] At the beginning

of the week I left a message that I'd received a letter from you and that I wanted to talk with him about it, his secretary told me that they hadn't heard anything from you recently and that he'd be pleased to talk to me, but he still hasn't called. (VBA 3, 7/22/71)

Blackwell was immediately worried that news of her political status in Czechoslovakia had reached Tynan and that this was affecting his relationship with her. She had told Tynan never to mention her name in letters to Havel, and perhaps he had worked out why, "or maybe Klaus scared him, in short, his 'stance' suddenly dramatically changed" (VBA 3, 7/22/71). She wrote that she had "the strong impression that he simply decided not to meet with me in your, or his (who knows?) interest" and worried that her attempts to liaise and meet with him would now be "pointless and even harmful" for Havel's play.

Although she said Tynan had told her that she would be the translator, she now thought that "perhaps he's looking for another translator" and that, if Havel didn't want to go through with the "Just" solution, then Havel should tell Tynan to "choose who he wants as a translator." Blackwell was clearly worried that if Tynan believed she was politically dangerous to Havel or Tynan himself, that it might "disrupt or even prevent such a great chance" for Havel's play to be produced at the English National Theatre. She asked Havel to focus only on what would get the play produced: "Everything else is irrelevant. Even me!"

Blackwell also wondered whether if Tynan even agreed to the Just solution, he would allow Just's "representative" to attend at least some of the rehearsals (as "Just is busy during the day at the office and can't promise such a thing"), something she felt was necessary as part of the translator's job, as well as "consultations" over the text before that (VBA 3, 7/22/71). In her barely coded way (to momentarily confuse those surveilling her correspondence with Havel), she wondered if she was too politically toxic to act as a consultant once the translation was done and in production. This she saw as essential, especially given that Havel was banned from traveling and could not himself consult on issues that might arise in production.

Havel was firm on his decision that she translate the play, but agreed that "Tynan's sudden change in attitude towards you is most probably based on what Klaus or someone else told him about our government's attitude to you, and that frightened him" (VBA 3, 8/3/71). He wished that they had asked him about it, otherwise it wasn't "a fair position," though he wondered if they were afraid to write openly to him about it, as the letters were being read. He knew from Juncker's last letter that there was some "uneasiness" about the situation (VBA 3, 8/3/71).

Blackwell was right to worry. Tynan *had* asked someone else to translate the play, without informing either her or Havel. Blackwell guessed that another Czech émigré, Sylvia Lanova, had translated it, or at least provided a report, "which is a detailed synopsis, a translation of small excerpts of dialogue, plus a judgement about the feasibility, performability of a given work, or a "rough" translation" (VBA 3, 10/15/71). But, she pointed out that the credibility of that report depended on the ability of the person writing it. Lanova was an actress and "a great friend of Olivier's," but Blackwell was concerned, having seen Lanova interpret for a visitor the National Theatre, that she did not have the ability to translate, nor good enough English (VBA 3, 10/15/71).

On hearing this, Havel admitted his was "a little bit nervous" (VBA 3, 11/1/71) and upset that he had not been consulted about the translation, not only because it affected Blackwell and his agreement with her, but that this other translation might affect how the play was read, "if he gave it to someone unqualified, like Mrs. Lang (sic) [. . .] the translation—and consequently the interpretation of the play—could very well turn the play upside down" (VBA 3, 11/1/71). "For that reason," he added, "I wrote to Tynan specifically that a misreading by the translator or director could result in the play being completely misunderstood" (VBA 3, 11/1/71). Havel's frustration was clear; stuck in Czechoslovakia, he could only communicate via letters, and, even then, this form of communication was subject to censorship and some of the letters were not getting through. For him, Blackwell was a guarantee not only of translations he trusted but also of someone who would be his exegetical representative in situ.

But Havel's hands were tied as he was entirely dependent on Juncker and Tynan to get his play produced at all:

> My situation is difficult in that I'm completely in their hands—the contract and everything related to it will be determined by their willingness, benevolence etc., so that I'm not really in the position to dictate terms or put my foot down; all of it depends only on Tynan and Klaus—whether I'll exist somewhere as an author or not and whether or not my plays will be produced somewhere. (VBA 3, 11/1/71)

Because he was considered "subhuman" in Czechoslovakia, his foreign partners could not risk upsetting the Czech authorities and he could not act with any hint of "mastery" or control (VBA 3, 11/1/71). But he was a little disappointed that these foreign partners would not stand up to the regime (though cognizant that this was related to their fears for him); Havel was already hearing about means to get by DILIA, everything was in flux and functioning in gray areas in Czechoslovakia and he felt that those in the West didn't understand this—that you had to play the game rather than take as gospel what the regime said. "The saddest thing about it is the fear of my Western partners from this stuff," Havel wrote ("between you and I"):

> Each one of them is full of compassion for our suffering, each one of them asks with a melancholy face how they can help us, and the one way in which they can help us—by getting on with their work as normal, in

this case as agents—in the spirit of valid international agreements, but until they can get rid of their fear of our regime, then they can't do anything. (VBA 3, 11/1/71)

He asked Blackwell to intervene, perhaps through Ramsay because it might be "embarrassing" to her to do it herself, and to try to persuade Tynan that he should use a competent translator, that Havel and Blackwell had come to a "compromise," that is, the Just solution because of the "political situation"; he hoped that Ramsay might assuage Tynan's fears. Havel, cut off from his native audience, was extremely anxious that this chance to find an audience might be affected by a translator or translation that fundamentally misunderstood his aesthetic and aims. The notion that Tynan made his decision on the basis of politics worried at him: "Do you think," he wrote:

> that Tynan's distancing from you arises from fear of a political risk, or that behind it, there's some kind of personal animosity, or even some kind of intrigue? Why hasn't he explained openly what's happening either to you or me? Perhaps, he's even become afraid of us? (VBA 3, 11/1/71)

The back and forth between Havel and Blackwell, wondering what machinations and political pressures were halting Tynan's decision on the play in fact echoes the themes of *The Conspirators* itself. In the play, a group of intellectuals, politicians, and military personnel conspire to protect their government, but in continuous scenes the group splits into overcrossing and double-crossing factions and, without realizing it, generate rumors of conspiracies they intend to fight which are actually the conspiracies they themselves are enacting. They conspire against their own conspiracies. Through the echoing chamber of the play, in its dozens of contiguous scenes of overlapping conspirators, Havel reconstructs the metaphysical dynamics of conspiracy; its paranoia and the sense that the act of conspiracy becomes a beast of its own.

But, given the difficulties of communication and Tynan's own silence, Havel and Blackwell had their reasons to suspect that Tynan was avoiding Blackwell because of political fears, stemming from a miscomprehension about the actual situation on the ground in Czechoslovakia, which, murky though it was, offered ways and means of bypassing official strictures. Eventually, Blackwell caught up with Tynan, having decided to approach him directly; he "apologized" but said that he wanted to get a "preliminary impression from a different version and that he never intended to use it except for his own information" (VBA 3, 12/9/71). Blackwell was horrified to find out that Tynan had not asked Sylva Lanova to translate, but Lanova's *son*, who, according to Blackwell could not carry on a conversation in Czech, though "Tynan of course claimed that this boy could speak Czech as well as he could speak English" despite the fact Tynan had no means to judge (VBA 3, 12/9/71). Tynan didn't show her the translation, simply saying it "wasn't good" (VBA 3, 12/9/71).

And yet Tynan made his initial judgement of the play based on this translation and it was not positive: "It seems to me that he's slightly disappointed with the play, that he'd been imagining something as exciting, surprising and 'funny' as *The Memorandum* and that he has some qualms presenting the play in its current form to the committee of the National Theatre" (VBA 3, 12/9/71). She added, "His qualms may in part have something to do with the translation. (I haven't seen it, I don't know what it's like, but Tynan said that it wasn't good and he can't use it" (VBA 3, 12/9/71).

One of Tynan's main problems with the play was its use of language; while it had the verbosity of Havel's earlier plays, those plays had been obviously witty, the verbosity had been central to that humor. Blackwell tried to explain to Tynan that the deliberate "unwittiness" of the language in *The Conspirators* was as integral to the ideas and form of the play— that this conspiracy, and conspiracies in general, were not made through action, guns, or politics but through language. The question that had worried Havel—that a noncompetent translation would miss the mechanism and meanings in the play (rather than simply being a question of linguistic ability)—seemed to resonate here. If the translator fundamentally did not understand the play as a reader then it was likely to be misunderstood once translated.

Quite even-handedly and from her own experience, Blackwell realized that it was probably not just the translation that affected Tynan's dislike of the play, but something of a cultural distance to Havel's use of language, which Blackwell saw as alien to the domestic tradition and knew would be judged as too European (and thus bad):

> Remember that the public here are not used to a "subtext" of this sort. A Prague or any Central European public would get it. Here however we live in a foggy island, the inhabitants of which are absolutely against the idea that they belong to the European continent . . . and whatever comes from "Europe" is "foreign". ("A foreigner", as you know, is an insult in the English language.) (VBA 3, 12/9/71)

That Blackwell put the last sentence in parentheses is a little melancholy, since she was a foreigner herself and thus "an insult in the English language"; if there was political uneasiness about Blackwell, there also seemed to be some antipathy toward her as a foreigner. *The Conspirators*, though optioned by the National Theatre, was not and has never been performed in England. But, from 1971 on, Juncker claimed there were rumors in the English theatre scene that Blackwell was not wanted as a translator. Havel, who liked Blackwell's work, presumed that these were unfounded attitudes of "this or that English snob" who might not want to work with "a person who wasn't born in England (that's at least what I think is behind the insinuated dislike for you)" (3, 18/9/73). The next year he wrote to her after a number of letters from Juncker, again claiming that the unamed English theatre figures did not want to work with Blackwell:

the reason for this dislike is not based on doubts about the worth of your translations, nor on any personal grudge against you, but something completely different. At first, Klaus based it on the fact that in English theatre circles he met with a definite distrust of you (perhaps as a foreigner?), and he had to take that distrust into account, later he based in on the fact that my ties with you, as he was it seems privately informed, were hurting me. (VBA 3, 10/23/74)

Juncker's doubts about Blackwell, based on unsubstantiated rumors about her, suggest that the distrust of her as a foreigner was linked also to a political distrust of her, that she was inherently suspect as someone who was not English and doubly so, as she came from Eastern Europe. Tynan himself had long criticized the insularism of British culture, and the country at the time was exhibiting a certain strain of xenophobia, just a few years after Enoch Powell's famous anti-immigration "Rivers of Blood" speech. In 1966, Havel had celebrated the fact that he had a translator who was intimate both with the Czech and English languages and cultures (and, it must be noted, the American—married to an American, Blackwell had a Masters degree from Harvard and lived in the United States from 1976 until her death). A knowledge of both languages and cultures would seem a central qualification for a translator, but it also made her "not quite" Czech and certainly never English. Havel suspected that the very qualifications that made her a skilled translator would also generate the kind of "dislike" and distrust that might end her career. Havel protested to Juncker that these were the attitudes of "whisperers" and said that he regarded them as "stupid"; he wrote to Juncker that the idea she was politically dangerous to him, "couldn't come from anyone else, but the ruling circles here, who want to use the German ignorance of the situation here to hurt me, pretending that it's a matter of my welfare" (VBA 3, 10/23/74).

He argued that Blackwell's skills and past success were proof of her reliability and worth, reminding him that "he knows that your service to my previous plays is indisputable, that he doesn't know of anyone more suitable who could take over your role"; above all, Havel added that his own positive opinion about Blackwell should be worth more than the "voice of his unnamed whisperers" (VBA 3, 10/23/74). Juncker seemed to take this into account but Havel was now unsure because of his "silence" and, certainly, from this point on actively argued against Havel's use of Blackwell as a translator. Juncker was acting out of genuine concern for Havel, but he did not seem to question the origin or attitudes behind such rumors.

The condescension toward Blackwell as a foreigner led to a questioning of her skills and knowledge from the beginning. Her first agent, a woman, Dina Lom (wife of the Czech-born actor, Herbert Lom), questioned Blackwell's ability to use and understand English, in front of clients. Writing in protest to Lom, Blackwell reminded her that:

Recently I rang you up to point out that I didn't consider my version of *The Memorandum* a "draft" as you had called it in talking to Mr Midgley. You said that perhaps I didn't understand the word. Another time we had a similar exchange as to whether I understood the word *cliché*. When we met together with Robin Midgley, towards the end of our talk, you said—no doubt with the best intentions—regarding my English, "I'm sure Mrs. Blackwell understood what you said." (VBA Memo: 1, 4/21/66)

Blackwell's clearly fluent English in this, and all her English-language letters, enabled her to articulate her frustration at assumptions that because she was a foreigner she was somehow less skilled than an English-born translator. Part of this, of course, is based on a comprehensible anxiety that she was not a native English speaker, but she was fluent and a native speaker of the language from which she was translating.

The reported remarks of Lom's also reveal a couple of telling elements that do perhaps, on the other hand, show some ignorance of the domestic scene on Blackwell's part. First, that Lom would assume that the translator's text of a play was a "draft." Blackwell reminded her in a phone call that she had a "rather strong opposition to your view that my rendering of *The Memorandum* is 'a draft'," or a literal translation, but the norms of the time—and the norms today—tend to assume that the translation from the source language is a crib or a draft that will be artfully rendered either by a (famous) playwright or the director and actors. It assumes that the "literal" translator can perform the unfeasible, that is, a translation that does not involve any interpretation of the original language text. Blackwell's protest against this points to a fight for recognition of her talents and status; she was insulted because she thought Lom was questioning her abilities as a translator in only being able to produce an inferior first "draft," but, in fact, it was perhaps nothing personal, just an assumption about the entire profession.

The second issue is gender: Midgely was a well-known director for the BBC and the RSC in its early days; as *The Times*' obituary stated, he worked for BBC Radio, "at that time buzzing with bright young men hoping to work eventually in the theatre" (*The Times* 2007). The bright young women at the time might be actresses, translators, agents, and occasionally—Joan Littlewood, for instance—directors, but it was largely a male world. Lom's remarks to Midgely suggest that she identified herself with him as an Englishwoman (by pointing out Blackwell's foreignness, particularly "her heavy Czech accent") and identified with patriarchal structures when it came to the translation (assuring Midgely it was only a "draft"). Lom, unconsciously, uses Blackwell to prove that she is capable of being one of "us."

This issue of internalized patriarchal assumptions and norms, a censorship of the self, is one that Blackwell also exhibits. Blackwell's archive reveals how few women were working in any decision-making capacity in the theatre world at that time in England; when she comes across them, she can often be derogatory in a clichéd patriarchal manner. So, her next agent Peggy Ramsay is "hysterical," and Sylvia Lanova is a typical actress of "primitive construction," that is, not that bright. Sensing Lom's competition with her in this male world, Blackwell comes out fighting, arguing that she was doing a better job as an agent than Lom was: she claimed Lom had only sent out *The Memorandum* to one client whereas she had sent the translation out to the Lincoln Center, Tynan, Esslin, and Henry Popkin. This letter to Lom, from the later 1960s, suggests that women had to compete with each other under the constraints of male terms in order to be taken seriously or listened to. With "her heavy Czech accent," Blackwell had to prove herself because she was a foreigner, a woman, and "only a translator". And all three identities were suspicious.

Speakability, voice

Lom's contention that "[i]n spite of her heavy Czech accent (and of being married to an American), Mrs Blackwell has lived in this country long enough to be able to write British office jargon" in her translation of *The Memorandum*, points to the thorny question of playability or speakability in translations. David Johnston argues that playability is central to a successful translation "translation for the stage is about giving form to a potential for performance. It is about writing for actors" (Johnston 1996: 58). Without this sense of an ear for the target language and target audience, a translation can end up being wooden and unnatural; often until a translation is being staged (like a native language playscript), the question of rhythm and naturalness may not be entirely clear. Ideally, a translator can be involved in the rehearsal process to work with changes and adaptations to ensure that there is some fidelity to the spirit of the original text and some expertise in the room about linguistic and cultural issues. However, in the hierarchy of the theatre world, the low status of the translator as an exegetical partner means that decisions are often taken by directors, actors, producers, or more famous adaptors, and are often taken not only for aesthetic reasons but also for commercial ones.

Lom expressed "enthusiasm for a big commercial production" of *The Memorandum* and was concerned that Blackwell could not write " 'saleable' English" (VBA Memo: 1, 4/21/66). Her wording indicates that this was not an issue of idiomatic English since Blackwell had "lived in this country long enough" but of a kind of English that could make the play commercial. In Lom's terms, the search for linguistic "playability" was not related to necessary acculturation (because of cultural differences in the languages) nor was it a question of naturalness or artistic collaboration normal to the stage; rather, it was a question of aesthetic adaptation, implemented to make a play more commercially viable. In some ways, this is inevitable, of course, and theatres and producers want to stay afloat financially, but the intent and agenda behind a call for alterations in the translation for commercial reasons needs to be recognized and assessed, because it results (and resulted) in alterations that had nothing to do with aesthetics or cultural and linguistic compatibility. Blackwell protested that what she, Havel, and DILIA wanted was "not primarily a commercially successful production, but a right production" and by "right" she meant a production that was "as faithful to the original as is consistent with having a critical success" (VBA Memo: 1, 4/21/66). She understood that changes and alterations might have to be made for the play to be understood. This would make it a "critical success" but the hope would be that the bottom-line of such alterations would be aesthetically rather than commercially based. After her experience with *The Garden Party*, where the RSC had found her translation "remarkable" but still wanted a wholesale adaptation by a male playwright into an English cultural idiom (the holiday camp and an English tradition of the absurd, i.e. farce) that, finally, didn't work, Blackwell was wary of the agendas behind such alterations for comprehensibility and playability.

Exhibiting what seemed to be inordinate sensitivity when it came to theatres changing her translations, Blackwell always protested and claimed her authority via copyright. Her intransigence in this led to problems with both agents and theatres, and eventually was cited as a reason for dismissing her as a translator. She reluctantly acknowledged that changes might have to be made for various performances, especially in the United States (altering "Britishisms"), but felt that she should have approval of those changes. The attitude of the agents and theatres was that, following theatre norms, they should be able to alter the script as needed for reasons of speakability, and that she should be cognizant, if not expectant and acceptant, of that. Her demands seemed abnormal for a "literal" translator. Blackwell was defensive and touchy about the requested changes, many times feeling these requests were judgements on the quality of her translations, but she was also defensive—and rightly so—about changes made to the translation that were actually changes made to Havel's text that compromised both form and content of the plays either for commercial or for ideological reasons. In 1968, following the Soviet invasion, Havel had given her Power of Attorney:

> to act for me and in my name in contractual and administrative and editorial matters related to my plays and other writings, and to receive, hold, and disburse any and all royalties, license-fees, et cetera on my behalf and for my account. Her signature shall be equivalent to mine on contracts and agreements. (2:2, 15/11/68)

It was a position she took very seriously; in Havel's absence, she felt that she should be the one to defend the integrity of his plays in all "administrative and editorial matters." This included the times when he was in prison and incommunicado. During his second extended period of incarceration, following his coauthoring of Charter 77, a document asking for freedom of expression, goodwill, and interest in his plays exploded in the West and, for the first time, in England. The translations, previously noncommercially viable, were suddenly hot news, and Havel wrote three one-acts, *Audience*, *Private View*, and *Protest*, which seemed more accessible to English audiences because of their brevity and apparent realism, plays with a protagonist that could "be interpreted as an autobiographical portrait of Havel" (7:1, May 1980).

Of these three "Vaněk plays" (the main character in all three carries the diminuitive name, Vaněk), *Protest* was the last. Written in 1978, and translated by Blackwell, the play portrays a meeting between Ferdinand (Vaněk) and an old friend, Staněk. Vaněk is a "dissident" whom Staněk has avoided for a while, being a writer, now working in television, who decided to collaborate with the regime in order to retain his life and income. Staněk has lived in the country and is passionate about "cultivating his garden" (echoing Volatires's advice in *Candide* about the good life), but his daughter has become pregnant by a singer, Javůrek, who has been arrested for making a joke during a concert. Staněk, having studiously avoided putting his head over the parapet, phones Vaněk, who is just out of prison, to ask him how to go about a petition for Javůrek, but only after a lot of shilly-shallying about his real reason for the reunion with Vaněk. Vaněk, on hearing the request, pulls a petition out of his briefcase that he has already begun and Staněk, relieved, begins wondering aloud what effect signing such a petition would have on his life and career in a four-page monologue. He finishes: "Should I be guided by ruthless objective considerations, or by subjective inner feelings?":

VANĚK:	Seems perfectly clear to me—
STANĚK:	And to me—
VANĚK:	So that you're going to—
STANĚK:	Unfortunately—
VANĚK:	Unfortunately?
STANĚK:	You thought I was—
VANĚK:	Forgive me, perhaps I didn't quite understand—
STANĚK:	I'm sorry if I've—
VANĚK:	Never mind—
STANĚK:	But really I believe—
VANĚK:	I know—
	(*Both drink . . .*).
	(Havel 1993: 264)

Both interpret the speech differently: Vaněk believes Staněk has convinced himself to sign but Staněk has convinced himself *not* to sign. Staněk goes on the attack, thinking that Vaněk will judge him, but then receives a phone call telling him that Javůrek has been released. Vaněk is overjoyed the petition wasn't needed and Staněk ends the play reminding him that these petitions can do more harm than good, and leads him to the garden.

Written a year after the Charter 77 petition and the same year of Havel's seminal essay on personal responsibility and nonviolent resistance, "The Power of the Powerless," Vaněk can be, and has been, read as a "moral" figure (Pontuso 2006: 90) who "pursues the highest form of responsible behavior" but who "does not arrogantly condemn those caught in the web of an evil situation" (p. 92). Imprisoned for writing petitions and being a dissident, Vaněk can be read as doppelgänger for Havel (when the play was first performed in London (1980) and New York (1983), Havel was serving 4½ years in prison for his Charter 77 participation and political resistance to the regime), and a moral compass in the "post-totalitarian society" in which he lives. But, as Marketa Goetz-Stankiewicz points out Havel denied it was a "self-portrait. Rather he is a dramatic principle which causes his environment to react and reveal itself" (Goetz-Stankiewicz 1987, p. xxvii).

The notion that Vaněk is a "dramatic principle" is important because rather than using him as a grandstanding avatar, Havel makes him an almost silent antihero, one "who does not wield the word," who "hardly acts, a suspect model because he knows better what *not* to do than what to do" (pp. xxvii–xxviii). His silence is his "chief defence against the falseness of language," a silence that becomes "a more eloquent tool of communication than the thousands of words used by the others" (p. xxi). So, *Protest* is not a simple black and white story of the brave and "good" dissident versus the craven, "bad" collaborator and the corrupted morals of the post-totalitarian society, but is an analysis of how language shapes our reality, how it betrays us into false realities.

Central to this rumination of language is the way it is used in the play: Vaněk's ineloquence makes him a "dubious hero"—regarded to be intelligent and a writer by the others—we don't see it as an audience, his lines are full of hesitation, echoes, and dashes where his short bursts of speech break off. The rhythm of the play moves between Staněk's longer passages that reveal him justifying his changing positions to short bursts of dialogue where the linguistic castle in the sky breaks apart and Staněk can no longer sustain the unreality of his position against Vaněk's silence. So, Staněk's lengthy monologue where he considers the consequences of signing the position breaks down into the brief dialogue above where what is being understood is being understood in silence.

Protest opened at the English National Theatre in January 1980, directed by Michael Kustow. In early January, Kustow wrote to Blackwell, "to tell you that we have made a few changes in your text (which anyway is the radio adaptation) in the interest of greater colloquialism and suitability for the actors concerned" (VBA 7:1, 1/7/80). These changes arose during the rehearsal period and Kustow pointedly added that alterations to translations was normal practice: "I'm sure you'll appreciate that this happens [. . .] I just wanted you to be forewarned in case—as I hope you do—you are in London when it's playing" (VBA 7:1, 1/7/80). Kustow's version was used for the radio broadcast and for a "Havel Afternoon" alongside a reading of Havel's open letter to Gustav Husák (read by Harold Pinter) and a dramatized version of Havel's Charter 77 trial (VBA 7:1) sponsored by the Writer's Guild of Great Britain, an act of solidarity and publicity for the imprisoned Havel.

Blackwell wrote a detailed attack on Kustow's "few changes" to the script, arguing that however small the individual changes were, that they misread the play and focused on a political message rather than on the rhythms and language of *Protest*. "I consider Kustow's version a parody of Havel's PROTEST," Blackwell wrote, "Hence my protest" (VBA 7:1, May 1980). She contested the claim that there hadn't been many changes, that it wasn't just "routine alterations of a few lines here and there so they would 'speak better'," but in fact the changes "actually affect some 80% of the original" and their "total impact constitutes total misrepresentation of Havel's PROTEST" (VBA 7:1, May 1980).

Upset that neither the National Theatre nor the BBC (who used the National Theatre version for a radio version) had "requested" or were "ever granted" the right to alter the translation, she claimed that they had "therefore committed breaches of their contracts" with her. But it was a *fait accompli*, and Blackwell wrote her "protest" after the fact to other practitioners interested in producing the play (including the Orange Tree Theatre who did, in Blackwell's original translation). Coming out fighting was not a strategy that would endear her to directors like Kustow or institutions like the BBC or the National Theatre, and she was not shy in her criticism. Kustow was following normal behavior for directors in assuming that the translation could be changed and probably felt he had done enough by indicating that the script had changed in rehearsals. But, as Havel was in prison and Blackwell was now living in New York, Blackwell's defensiveness probably lay in the fact that there was no one present to collaborate with the director and actors in discussing the fidelity (in terms of the author's style and aims) of such changes.

Arguing that it was not the alteration of the translation that was the problem, but the changes to "Havel's original," which was "radically altered" by deformations of the "structure plus the content of Havel's play, and the personality of Havel's characters," Blackwell focused, among other elements, on cuts to Staněk's long monologue and changes to particular "awkward" words. As with Havel's earlier plays, English-language theatres balked at the verbosity of certain sections, and the very lengthy monologue read literally reads as if it is full of superfluous content, but the point of the verbosity is to reflect the state of the character's mind and soul, as Blackwell argued:

It reveals, strips bare his hang-ups, his pathetic wangles, his regrets, indeed his real sufferings, his painful swayings between the man he would like to be (a man living in truth) and the man he actually is (a man accepting the ever-present lie), the man as seen by his own children and the man as he'd dearly love to be seen by them, the man as he's seen by the dissidents and the man he almost begs the dissidents to see, the shrewd man who manages to swim with the tide and the man Staněk can't help seeing in the bathroom mirror every morning as he shaves.

All this—and much more—is presented by Havel in Staněk's speech with infinite skill, great subtlety and with irony—sometimes gentle and sometimes so sharp it cuts this Staněk to shreds. (VBA 7:1, May 1980)

Blackwell, in her defense of Havel's writing, echoes it to make her point: the repetition of "the man" indicating the battle between Staněk's different identities coexisting in a mutable atmosphere. In having "slashed" the monologue, Blackwell felt that Kustow had missed the point of the language and the length, that the "subtleties" of the speech were lost:

his skillfully and strategically deployed clauses and subclauses, concepts and words which not only mirror each other, but in fact shift (sometimes slightly, sometimes radically) the previously reflected picture in such a way that what might at first have appeared as a true reflection of a man now becomes a caricature image, a parody of a man. The way Havel handles this speech by Staněk (and indeed all of Staněk's speeches) can be likened to the tragic wandering of a man through a "laughing gallery", lined with misshapen mirrors; he hits a real mirror from time to time, only to flee from it deeper into the corridor where the grotesque reflections are supposed to make him laugh and where his greatest tragedy consists in his actually managing a laugh—when he closes his eyes,

All this has been rubbed out, flattened both by the massive cuts and by the pedestrian alterations in the remaining lines given to Staněk by Kustow. The complex picture of the dissidents' situation becomes a dull, straightforward statement. Staněk becomes just a mildly amusing bastard. (VBA 7:1, May 1980)

Blackwell's emotive language of "deformations," "parodies," "caricatures," "slashed" may be overstated, but was genuine: "When one sees what has been cut—here and elsewhere—one could really weep" she wrote. Behind the emotion was not only a protectiveness about her translation but also about Havel's play, that it was being misread at a fundamental level when the play talked about language.

Substitutions of words and lines so that they would "speak better" meant that "in some cases their changes indeed appear smoother" but that this "smoothness is not always the greatest virtue." She argued, "Some of the words and lines in Havel's PROTEST sound awkward in the original Czech and were introduced by Havel for a particular purpose." She felt the assumption was that the awkwardness was a product of bad translation rather than the intent of the author to say something about how language defined a person and a character, and pointed out that "the English equivalents [. . .] were chosen by me with great care," emphasizing her role as someone who was interpreting the text as she translated.

She gave two particular examples: first, the multiple use of one word by Staněk in his monologue, "subjective," when he is analyzing himself. He repeats the phrase "the subjective side of the matter"/"subjektivní stránku věci" (Havel 1999:2: 666); Kustow changed this to "personal" which Blackwell agreed "spoke better": "But this is not the word Havel wished Staněk to use. Havel wished to inject into Staněk's lines some awkward words to signal to his audiences that Staněk was weaned on a particular ideological jargon" (VBA 7:1, May 1980). The use of such jargon, or "dead language" (Goetz-Stankiewicz 1987: xxviii) suggests Staněk 's internalization of the world in which he lives, the reality of which he supports in using the language.

Secondly, she points to the changes in punctuation with reference to Vaněk. Havel uses dashes throughout the three Vaněk plays to underline his hesitation and silences, important because Vaněk can no longer trust language as a means to communicate his sense of truth; silence and the words of others reveal the truth of their fragmented, muddled, and untruthful realities. The question of talking and not talking comes up when Staněk probes Vaněk about his prison experience:

STANĚK:	Ale nějak zlomit se vás jistě snažili—
VANĚK:	No tak—
STANĚK:	Jestli o tom nechcete mluvit, tak nemusíte—
VANĚK:	Vjistém ohledu to je vlastně účel vyšetřovací vazby—srazit člověku hřebínek—
STANĚK:	A přimět ho, aby vypovídal—
VANĚK:	Hm—
STANĚK:	Kdyby mě někdy pozvali na výslech, což mě dříve nebo později nemine, víte co chci udělat?
VANĚK:	Co?
STANĚK:	Prostě nevypovídat! Vůbec se s nimi nebudu bavit! Je to totiž nejlepší: člověk má aspon jistotu, že jim neřekne něco, co nemá—
VANĚK:	Hm— (Havel 1999:2:650–1).
STANĚK:	But surely they tried to break you down somehow!—
VANĚK:	Well—

STANĚK:	If you'd rather not talk about it, it's all right with me—
VANĚK:	Well, in a way that's the whole point of pre-trial interrogations, isn't it? To take one down a peg or two—
STANĚK:	And to make one talk!
VANĚK:	Mmn—
STANĚK:	If they should haul me in for questioning—which sooner or later is bound to happen—you know what I'm going to do?
VANĚK:	What?
STANĚK:	Simply not answer any of their questions! Refuse to talk to them at all! That's by far the best way. Least one can be quite sure one didn't say anything one ought not to have said!
VANĚK:	Mmn—
	(Havel 1993: 246).

The short extract is tragic and funny; Staněk who is thinking about a petition for Javůrek is trying to find out from Vaněk what prison and interrogations are like—his selfishness barely tinged by empathy and containing a certain titillating curiosity. Staněk, here, is also us, thinking about what we might do in such a position, thus not necessarily making him a villain. In the Czech version, the use of dashes shows him moving from curiosity and fear ("But surely they tried to break you down somehow—") to a slightly faked compassion ("If you'd rather not talk about it, it's all right with me—"), to real fear when he hears something concrete from Vaněk ("And to make one talk—"), all of which he is unsure about; the dashes underline his tentativeness and the mix of emotions. Vaněk's lack of language (apart from one longer line) allows those emotions to keep changing so that he moves then into bravura and more forceful punctuation—the commas, question marks, and finally exclamation marks ("Simply not answer any of their questions! Refuse to talk to them at all!"). But Staněk double-checks his bravura right at the end of the extract ("At least one can be quite sure one didn't say anything one ought not to have said—"), waiting to get Vaněk's approval.

Here we have Staněk wondering how he will react to interrogation and asserting that he will refuse to speak, not through any courage or resistance, but so that he cannot incriminate himself. But of course the joke, apart from his cravenness, is clear: he can't *stop* talking in the face of Vaněk's silence. What makes him not just a caricature or a joke of a character is the portrayal of the wavering human emotions threaded through the extract, ones with which we can identify: he feels for Vaněk, he's curious, he knows he's not brave, he fantasizes about a courageous self.

Blackwell clearly changes the punctuation herself, inserting exclamation marks in Staněk's first two lines in this extract and, in doing so, dilutes the subtlety of Havel's representation of him; it makes the character in this extract more jovial, less melancholic, and less hesitant. But she was aware of how such changes could affect the play, however small, and criticizes Kustow for his rendering of part of the extract, which she quotes in her "protest":

VANĚK:	Look, in a way, that's the whole point of pretrial interrogations, isn't it? To take you down a peg or two—
STANĚK:	And to make you talk!
VANĚK:	Yes!
STANĚK:	When they haul me in for questioning . . . you know what I'm going to do?
STANĚK:	I just won't answer any of their questions! . . . That's the best thing to do, at least you're sure you haven't said anything you shouldn't!
	(Kustow, quoted in VBA 7:1, May 1980).

For her, the fact that Kustow changed Vaněk's answer "Mmn—" to "Yes!" underlined a basic miscomprehension of the character. "It is simply unthinkable that this Vaněk would actually respond to Staněk's innuendo by endorsing it!" she wrote;

In all the Vaněk plays, including PROTEST, one can hardly find a full-stop, let alone an exclamation mark, after any of the vague, evasive, meek responses with which Vaněk punctuates the "monologues" of the other characters. Vaněk's very function is to look at the other characters, say as little as possible, grunt from time to time when absolutely necessary (thus signalling to all and sundry he is actually following what's being said) and watch as—little by little—the others reveal themselves. The crust of their outward hypocrisy is shattered precisely because it keeps colliding with the immovable wall of Vaněk's silence.

Any definite statement from Vaněk (even a slight indication of his sympathy with his interlocutors' predicament) would make them assume again the mask of the false persona they keep tearing to shreds under Vaněk's silent gaze [. . .] The condition of Havel's compassion is Vaněk's vague, non-descript response, and above all his silence. (VBA 7:1, May 1980)

She also questioned the substitution here of the pronoun "one" by the generic "you"; while Kustow might have been seeking less formality in the language, the use of "you" clouds some of the dialogue because it can be mistaken for second person singular. Thus, Staněk seems to be implying that

Vaněk was made to talk "And to make you talk!" consolidated by Vaněk's now affirmative answer. Also, although she doesn't point it out, a cut is made in Staněk's last line in this extract, when the second sentence is excised. In the Czech, he says:

STANĚK:	Prostě nevypovídat! Vůbec se s nimi nebudu bavit! Je to totiž nejlepší: člověk má aspon jistotu, že jim neřekne něco, co nemá—
STANĚK:	Simply not answer! I won't put up with them at all! It's for the best: a person is at least clear that they're not telling them anything they shouldn't—(my translation)

Kustow's and Blackwell's versions are as follows:

STANĚK:	I just won't answer any of their questions! . . . That's the best thing to do, at least you're sure you haven't said anything you shouldn't!
STANĚK:	Simply not answer any of their questions! Refuse to talk to them at all! That's by far the best way. Least one can be quite sure one didn't say anything one ought not to have said!

In terms of content, it might seem understandable to remove the second sentence; in terms of information, it does not add anything more to Staněk's exclamation. What is important, however, is that the second sentence functions as a motor of his bravura, it emphasizes his sudden confidence, and it plays into the joke of his verbosity even while he is denying that he will talk. While these small changes "might appear insignificant at first sight" Blackwell writes, they can "in fact, twist the characters, the structure and the meaning of Havel's play."

The complexity of translation and adaptation for the stage reveal themselves here; Blackwell does not always practice what she preaches, but it is evident from her long "protest" that she understands the implications of the smallest alteration and had an intimate sense of what Havel was trying to achieve (as she could read the Czech and had translated several of his plays). While it was, and it is, acceptable practice to make translations more speakable, without recourse to the translator, the practice has its issues, one of which is an assumption that the translation and translator has no exegetical authority and is providing only a literal crib that can be changed according to the whim of the adaptors. Of course, this can result in wonderful new works of art, but still at issue is the question of whether the newness of the source language text is being attenuated or lost.

Havel's unusual punctuation for all three Vaněk plays is not normal for Czech plays, or even for Havel's other plays, though it is influenced to some extent by Beckett. Beckett's (and his estate's) insistence on the exact reproduction of his scripts makes sense here and, as his plays are now regarded as modern classics, the idea of changing Vladimir's and Estragon's repartee would seem scandalous and unnecessary even though *Waiting for Godot* is a translation (albeit done by the author). It is an aspect of the play, *Protest*, which is translatable and, though textual, is incredibly important in terms of understanding the characterization of Staněk and Vaněk, and in terms of indicating enunciation for potential actors.

It should be said, also, that *Protest*, published first in *samizdat* (in 1979 in the underground journal *Edice Expedice* (Havel 1999:2: 1036)) was going to be read (illicitly) in Czechoslovakia rather than performed, and thus, the textual markers and the conciseness of the language are also related to an awareness of the play as a text as well as a play text. Havel is self-referential in *Protest* about how his plays were disseminated: Vaněk tells Staněk that he's writing a play:

STANĚK:	A play?
VANĚK:	A one-act play—
STANĚK:	Another autobiographical one?
VANĚK:	More or less—
STANĚK:	My wife and I read the one about the brewery the other day. We thought it was very amusing—
VANĚK:	I'm glad—
STANĚK:	Unfortunately we were given a very bad copy. Very hard to read.
	(Havel 1993: 248)

Making fun of himself for his "more or less—" autobiographical one-act plays, one of which was set in a brewery (*Audience*), Havel underscores the means by which the plays were consumed, referring to the "poor quality" of the *samizdat* texts, the "very bad copy" being perhaps "the sixth carbon copy on onion skin" (Blackwell in Havel 1993: 248). So says Blackwell, in a footnote, in the published Grove Press version of the play, and in some ways it is a fitting emblem for the hazards of adaptation; that we have to squint at the text to get a sense of what the first copy was.

The anger with which Blackwell approached her "protest" is not entirely fair; Kustow evidently approached the production with goodwill and care, and working within the norms and expectations of the time. In addition, of course, Blackwell did not always follow her own doxa when it came to the translation, but she was right to point out that the practice of altering a translation for playability can radically alter the aesthetics and authorial style of a play, thereby neutralizing its impact for newness and actual creative engagement. That Kustow's version of *Protest* was used for the politically charged "Havel Afternoon" suggests that the play was conceived in the National Theatre production as a dissident play and therefore the cuts and alterations reflected what the production wanted to get out of and convey with the play. But the "dissident," "more or less" autobiographical aspect of the play is only a departure point for Havel's engagement with the boundaries, possibilities, and traps of language.

Can the demand for speakability or playability be a coercive constraint? Ideally, no. If those involved with the production work with the translator and/or author, or are schooled and have experience in the work of the author, then the possibilities of a striking new work of art are manifold. Because of the accepted norms in attitude toward the so-called literal translation, however, there is a sense that this translation can be used in any way the adaptor wishes; this can produce a real engagement with the aims of the source language play, but it can also veil those aims and aesthetics, thereby perhaps offering a wonderful work in the target language theatre that, at the same time, obscures more radical possibilities that the source language offers. In Havel's case, his plays were deemed relevant because of their newsworthiness and through genuine sympathy for Havel's plight, but this has also meant that his plays now seemed outdated and, as Remnick said, "emblems" of a past era. The element of newness in them, Havel's consideration of language as something that is manipulated by and manipulates humans was in fact entirely relevant to English-language culture and, of course, to the translations. In *Protest*, Staněk rails against the "selfishness, corruption and fear" of the people and when Vaněk says he doesn't see the situation as bleak as that, Staněk describes how the environment he lives in affects his work in television:

VANĚK:	There was a piece by you on the TV the other day—
STANĚK:	You can't imagine what an ordeal that was! First they kept blocking it for over a year, then they started changing it around—changed my whole opening and the entire closing sequence! You wouldn't believe the trifles they find objectionable these days! Nothing but sterility and intrigues, intrigues and sterility! How often I tell myself—wrap it up, chum, forget it, go hide somewhere—grow apricots—(Havel 1993: 245)

Staněk tells Vaněk that he is lucky living in his "environment," where his work isn't censored, and the irony is that although Havel's *Protest* was subject to the Czechoslovak regime's blanket ban on Havel's work, it was published underground in *samizdat* (in three different *samizdat* editions), and underwent none of the cuts and changes it would see in its first English-language production. These cuts and changes not only altered the form of the play, but also its meditation on censorship. Staněk here not only bemoans the external censorship his art faces, but he also enacts censorship, both in his internalization of the jargon of the day, substituted for real thought or ethics and—as shown in his final, long monologue—censors his own life, the skein of sophist thought showing that censorship in action. Vaněk, too, censors himself, in his pauses and hesitations. The art of Havel's plays lies in the contrapuntal effect of these two censors, unable to talk transparently in any language of truth, letting the audience or reader divine it for themselves.

But the question of constraints weighs as heavily in the case of the perceived "literal" translator. Cronin's notion of the "censorship of indifference" applies here, where the position of the translator who makes the initial translation is seriously undervalued and not respected, or, thought of as an exegetical act. Blackwell's problem was not related to the quality of her translations, but to her vociferousness. The Czechoslovak regime condemned her as a "demanding lady" and this quality also met with resistance and disapprobation in the United Kingdom and, as we shall see, in the United States. The fact that she demanded her rights, visibility, respect for her knowledge of the language, culture and Havel's aesthetics, and an equitable payment got her into trouble because such demands were not acceptable. The issue of speakability relates to the needs of the target culture but it brings up the question of what or who is silenced in order to achieve naturalness and voice in the target language. For speaking up, Blackwell would be silenced.

The art hiding art

In November 1983, the Public Theater in New York presented a production of Havel's three one-act plays, in Blackwell's translation, under the combined title of *Private View*. The production received outstanding reviews, with *New York Theater Voice* declaring it: "a miniature of mankind that makes you proud to be a member of the species" (VBA 6:2, December 1983: 20). Blackwell's translations were not only mentioned, but also garnered good reviews: Clive Barnes in the *New York Post* wrote that the plays were "delicately and seemingly idiomatically translated by Vera Blackwell" (VBA 6:2, 11/21/83); Muriel Broadman in *Backstage* called them "admirable"; John Beaufort in the *Christian Science Monitor* wrote that they had "a colloquially contemporary ring" (VBA 6:2, 11/30/83: 34). The *New York Tribune* praised her for "felicitously re-creat[ing] in English" the "typical cadences of Havel's dialogue" (VBA 6:2, 12/2/83: 1B). Edith Oliver, in *The New Yorker*, wrote: "The performance of these plays, in the impeccable translation of Vera Blackwell, is itself impeccable" (VBA 6:2, 12/5/83: 183).

Havel's brother, Ivan Havel (in England at the time), wrote to Blackwell at the end of the year, quoting Edith Oliver's review, with New Year's greetings "a mnoho dalších 'impeccable translations' "/"and many more 'impeccable translations' " (VBA 2:8, 12/30/83). His excitement that perhaps this production finally meant a breakthrough for his brother in the English-language world, thanks in no small part to Blackwell's translations, comes through in a letter he wrote to her a week later:

> I'm really happy about your success with Havel's one-acts. Of course it was a lot of work but thank God it was worth it, as is evident from the rave reviews in the best American papers and from the fact that people are flocking to it. Perhaps Havel will get wind of it . . . Congratulations, you can be proud of it. (VBA 2:8, 1/7/84)

The translator of Czech literature, Peter Kussi, also praised her translation:

> I want to congratulate you on the translation in which you really succeeded beautifully. The first one-act impressed me particularly, because there are four types of speech—the brewer and the author speak in "two languages". You solved it without making the dialogue seem foreign, inordinately male or too American. In short—art which hides art. (VBA 6:1, 11/22/83)

Kussi's trifecta of praise—not too foreign, not too male, not too American—reveals the hurdles facing Blackwell as a translator and perhaps speaks to her identity as a female foreigner now living in the United States: that she is personally aware of the negotiations going on in a translation, and in a translation of a male author (among the three one-acts, there is only one female character). But Kussi's remark about it not being "inordinately male" points to something else too, rather than producing a boorishness possible certainly in terms of the brewer and his attempt at male camaraderie, Blackwell's also fought for the "feminine" Vaněk, by emphasizing the pauses and hesitations, the nonmacho antihero came through. Kussi, as a fellow translator (and émigré) understood that because the translations were good, the skill would not be seen; it was an "art which hides art"—the censored process that Cronin argues leads to the devaluation of translatorial skills in the globalized world.

Indeed, despite the very public success of the translations, the following year, Havel would write his penultimate letter to Blackwell informing her that Joseph Papp, at the Public Theater "would produce my [new] play, but only on the condition that it would *not* be translated by you" (VBA 3, 10/10/84, my italics). Instead, his new play, *Largo Desolato*, would be translated by another Czech émigré, Marie Winn (thanks to a mutual friend of the Papps, Helen Epstein, who recommended her) and, in England, Tom Stoppard, one of the leading (Czech-born) English playwrights. It was performed at the Old Vic in London in 1986 and the same year, at the Public Theater in New York. The "English version" of *Largo Desolato*, in the Faber edition is Stoppard's and does not cite the name of the "literal" translator. Stoppard was a good choice for a "star translator," not only because he was Czech-born and a friend of Havel's, but because his own playwriting was influenced by Havel's work. He had been interested in adapting a play of Havel's for some time. It is striking, however, that the reaction to Havel's breakthrough success was to change translators and, in the case of England, find an adaptor who was male and a famous playwright, after the 20 years of legwork provided by Blackwell. Blackwell would never again be asked to translate one of Havel's plays.

Havel, just out of prison, felt he was in an untenable situation, in which he was given the choice between sticking with Blackwell or having his plays produced at all. "Please believe me," he wrote:

> that behind my decision is not some atrocious longing for fame and money at any cost (I don't personally care about fame and I don't need money) that would make me jump over corpses just to get my plays put on. Even if it seems silly, the main reason for my decision was based on something of a "higher cause": apart from the world-renowned Kundera, living abroad, and the successful Škvorecký, also living abroad, our literature doesn't have much that would break through abroad, especially from the authors living here. (VBA 3, 10/28/84)

He was extremely embarrassed and asked her not to let it spoil their friendship or the possibility of a "future collaboration," "I've lost too many friends over the course of the last fifteen years" he wrote, and was frustrated that he still did not know why there was such animosity toward her, having heard not only from Papp but also from the English National Theatre that they would not work with her again: "I don't know the reason for this and I don't know whether it's based on professional doubts or some personal animosity or whether there's some political, commercial or other basis." He had to "capitulate" this time. "As you know," he wrote:

> over the years I've successfully fought off those voices against you translating my plays: I pointed to the success of your translations, to your service in getting my plays produced in the English-speaking world, to the nebulous and confused objections against you and to the lack of clear arguments, and so I emphasized my wish to remain as your faithful "translatee", because I cannot forget that you were among the first from abroad who—when I was almost unknown—took an interest. (VBA 3, 10/28/84)

Havel's clear recognition of Blackwell's service faced the ultimatum from others that she could not continue as his translator, despite the fact that no one had given him concrete answers as to why. Blackwell did not blame him, but did blame Juncker: "His dislike for me is insurmountable," she wrote in response, but in an unsent letter: "—was, is and will be—and nothing and nobody will change it" (VBA 3, 12/20/84). Havel had asked her not to blame Juncker, underlining that it was not his fault but that he was responding to what theatres were telling him. Havel also mentions that Papp, who had apparently written to Juncker expressing his refusal to accept Blackwell as a translator, had just visited Havel in Czechoslovakia and had not said anything negative about her or her translations. However, Papp could be mercurial, and Blackwell had worked quite closely with the *Private View* production: her help in that production may have been judged to be interference. Again, she might have been overstepping her mark.

Certainly the lead-up to the US productions was fraught. Between 1969 and 1983 there had been no American professional productions of Havel's work. In 1982, Rowohlt's American agent, Sanford J. Greenburger, contacted Blackwell telling her that "regrettably" they had been trying to sell Havel's one-acts to "innumerable regional theaters as well as several of the better New York production organizations" but that "[e]ven more regrettably, several of these rejections were attributed to a feeling that the existing translations would simply not play well for American audiences" (VBA 2:2, 1/27/82). Peter Skolnik, from the agency, added that Juncker had also "received similar comments from various other individuals." Skolnik added that neither he nor Juncker had had to make "an independent judgment of the suitability of the scripts" because "the marketplace (i.e. the producers) made it increasingly evident that the present versions had become an obstacle to performances here of Havel's plays" (VBA 2:2, 1/27/82).

According to Skolnik, the translations, then, were not being judged for their linguistic cohesion or fidelity to the author's style, but for their commercial viability by the "marketplace" which had no authority—other than financial—by which to judge them. It had nothing to do with skill: the marketplace was essentially seeking a translator who would make the plays more commercially viable and, on a superficial level, this was identified as Americanizing them. As early as 1966, this issue of Blackwell's translations being too British in their diction had been used as a criticism against them and as a putative point of failure in the American sphere. Jiří Voskovec, the émigré Czech actor, who had been interested in translating and producing *The Memorandum* in the United States in 1966, wrote to Havel criticizing Blackwell's translation feeling that she did not have an "instinct for the spoken word" (VBA 3, 12/30/66) and that the translation was "linguistically and idiomatically too locally marked as British." This would not be a problem, he added, if there was a reason for the play to be set in Britain but as it was an abstract location, he said, the "English flavor would be a source of confusion and misunderstanding." He felt that it wouldn't take much to Americanize the Britishisms but that "it had to be done with sensitivity, not too much and not too little" (VBA 3, 12/30/66).

Blackwell's translations were idiomatically British (as opposed to American) at the time when there was much more division between the two idiomatic English-language traditions—see her use of "chum" above which now seems rooted in a particular bygone British era. Her very proper English diction is one reason the translations need updating. But her translations of *The Memorandum* and *The Increased Difficulty of Concentration* were successfully produced in the United States in 1968 and 1969, as were, finally, the one-act plays. Like *Private View*, Blackwell's translations were given good reviews in the United States: her translation of *The Increased Difficulty of Concentration* was seen as a "properly idiomatic translation" of the play (VBA 9:3, *The Morning Telegraph* 12/5/69); she was seen as "successfully employing an easy and familiar American idiom but at the same time avoiding a cheap, slangy approach" (VBA 9:3, *The Record* 12/5/69: D13). *Variety* noted the "sharp dialog, translated with clarity by Vera Blackwell" (VBA 9:3, 12/17/69). Not one review of any of the Blackwell translations suggested they were too alien and British.

Skolnik gave Blackwell an ultimatum: she could either agree to "revisions" of her translations of the one-acts "by someone of our choice" that would "not be made subject to your approval," or, they "would commission completely new translations of the plays" (VBA 2:2, 1/27/82). Having not heard from the Greenberg agency for some time, Blackwell was shocked to receive such a letter out of the blue, effectively blaming her translations for the lack of professional productions of Havel's plays in the United States. She wrote back reminding Skolnik of her legal rights as "the only authorized translator of Václav Havel's plays into English" who "hold[s] the copyright to my English translations. Hence any alterations or revisions of my translations, undertaken without my approval, would constitute a violation of copyright" (VBA 2:2, 2/4/82). Blackwell had written an angrier draft of the letter, following a phone call to Skolnik, where she had asked him for "concrete info" on the "unsubstantiated allegations" against her and had written that she was open to the translations being " 'Americanized' for US audiences" but felt that "I can't agree to any alterations without discussing the problem with the prospective producer in person" (VBA 2:2, 2/4/82).

Knowing that the unnamed producers wanted a more commercial translation, Blackwell wanted to have some say in what would be changed, being especially wary after the English National Theatre production of *Protest*. She was not unwilling to make alterations to the translation, but felt that they should be considered alterations rather than ones for commercial playability. The lack of clarity about who had made the allegations and what exactly their problem about the translations was, made it difficult for her to answer or give any remedy to the situation.

Skolnik would not name the producers who demanded new translations but said that the one-acts had been "seen and declined" by numerous regional and off-Broadway theatres, including the Guthrie, American Repertory Theater, BAM and the Public Theater (VBA 2:2, 2/3/82). He had no textual proof that the translations were the basis for these refusals because "[c]omments concerning the translations were almost invariably made not in letters, but in phone conversations" (VBA 2:2, 2/3/82). He reiterated that Juncker, too, had received "similar comments from several British theatres and qualified critics" (VBA 2:2, 2/3/82). Blackwell's US agent, Lantz, advised her to ask Skolnik "to cease dishing out generalities and present you with specifics, including critical specifics that you can act upon if you agree with them" (VBA 2:2, 4/12/82). Blackwell had already asked; she wanted Skolnik "to reveal to me the identity of the Off-Broadway theater which offers to option the plays in question 'conditional upon revisions in (my) translations'," (VBA 2:2, 2/10/82) and had reiterated that "I'm prepared to co-operate with any producer and/or director in the matter of possible adjustments [. . .] however, I must first know who these persons are and hear from them directly what precisely it is they feel ought to be altered and why" (VBA 2:2, 2/10/82).

The off-Broadway theatre was probably the Public, since it eventually did produce the one-acts and Papp would later, apparently, express his dislike of Blackwell's translations. But, in fact, it had been Blackwell who "urged [Skolnik] to follow Papp's interest in the plays after the unscheduled reading of *The Audience* by the Public Th. actors" in the late 1970s but "Skol said he'd place it on Broadway!" (VBA 2:2, undated notes). In notes to herself, Blackwell also pointed out that despite what Juncker had heard in England, her work there had led to plenty of mostly amateur productions—though also professional productions by the National Theatre, the BBC, and the Orange Tree Theatre, as well as publications of the one-acts: "contrast it with the deafening silence in the USA after 2 productions I sold (obies)— ever since the matter was in your hands" (2:2 undated notes). Blackwell had backed off from promoting Havel's work in the United States, even though she now lived in New York, because of Rowohlt's request and since that time no production had taken place. Skolnik said that it was a deliberate decision "during the past years when I was instructed not to circulate Havel's plays (as this was considered antithetical to his interests)" (VBA 2:2, 2/3/82), implying a political decision by Juncker not to offer the plays in case it might do harm to Havel, who was in prison. But, in the very same period, Havel's plays were being offered and produced in England and Europe. "Klaus didn't want me to act of Havel's behalf in the US," Blackwell wrote, "although he knew full well I have many friends who could have helped what ought to be our *common* endeavour: the placement of Havel's plays in the USA and hands of good producers" (VBA 2:2, undated notes). She had phoned some of those friends, some "leading NY producers and directors" and, according to her, Skolnik had not approached any of them (VBA 2:2, undated notes).

The quality of Blackwell's translations were being impugned via the comments of unnamed producers, but it seems that some other elements were at issue: control over the texts (whether by translator, agents, theatres, or producers) and Blackwell's outspokenness about her position as translator. The two were linked: when Blackwell asserted her copyright on the translations, Skolnik rebutted her claim by reminding her "of how unusual, even extraordinary it is to have the sole right with respect to a given language" and that she, as a "professional dramatic translator," should know this, that is, she should be conversant with and abide by the norms (VBA 2:2, 2/3/82). He added that they had honored "an informal grant of exclusivity" but would not longer do so (VBA 2:2, 2/3/82). In fact, as Blackwell pointed out in her draft (and not in her final letter to Skolnik), she had a *formal* grant of exclusivity in the power of attorney. Lantz made this point, saying that while Blackwell was willing to collaborate with a reviser, the one thing they were "not prepared to allow is an invasion and diminishing of her established legal and moral rights" (VBA 2:2, 3/4/82). One of these rights was a financial one; he reminded Skolnik that, due to the "underlying agreements" with Havel, they could not "unilaterally appoint a new adaptor or translator, and arbitrarily reduce Dr. Blackwell's financial participation" (VBA 2:2, 3/4/82). When Skolnik had told Blackwell that she would have to allow a reviser to work on her translations, he added, "the old division of proceeds (60% to Havel, 40% to you) would, of course, be revised. The new division would be 60% to Havel, 20% to you, 20% to the reviser" (VBA 2:2, 1/27/82). Once again, the 50:50 split was being whittled away, and at a time when Blackwell's financial position was "precarious" (VBA 3, 5/30/84). Her husband had not worked for 3 years and she was freelancing "here and there" so they were "surviving as we can," adding "Please understand that in this situation, Klaus's attacks were especially stinging" (VBA 3, 6/6/84).

Her personal welfare was always superseded by Havel's. On the face of it, this makes sense. He was imprisoned between 1979 and 1982 and in poor health. Skolnik inferred that she should not make a commotion and should accept their terms because Havel's welfare was tantamount: "Václav's income and the urgency of bringing his work before the American public must take priority over all else" (VBA 2:2, 1/27/82). On the face of it, this was a reasonable and humane request, except that it implied that Blackwell did not have Havel's interests at heart despite her 20 years of work for him. "Re your professional concern for Havel's welfare—versus mine," she replied, knowing that connecting her demands and Havel's situation was a false equivalency, "I'm sorry, but I honestly don't want to argue the point with you" (VBA 2:2, 2/4/82). Havel's situation was, in essence, used to enforce the restrictive norms of the translator–author relationship that Blackwell challenged.

In the end, after negotiations between Greenberger and Lantz, Blackwell won out and actively took part in the rehearsals for the Public Theater production of the three one-acts and felt that her presence at those rehearsals was useful because "neither the director nor the actors (before my supplementary 'schooling') fully and fundamentally understand what it was about." "The director of course didn't know anything either about you or the background of the plays," she wrote to Havel, and described to him how she went about giving them some context, including making them listen to the original language in a recording made of the play, *Audience*, in which Havel himself had performed:

> so when I was finally called to appear at the rehearsals, the actors flitted round me, and I had to talk to them. They wanted to know who was who, what Landovský and Kohout looked like, they wanted to see your photos and find out everything about you. Along with all sorts of documents, I'd also brought them a recording of *Audience* with you and Landovsky: they listened to it intently, then Vaněk and Staněk [the two characters in the play] went to the stage and performed in it *Czech*. It's a pity I didn't record it, because it was hilarious: they performed it exactly according to the text that they knew, only they used words that—as they had heard it—seemed to be Czech. (VBA 3, 6/6/84)

The scene is suggestive with the actors mimicking the sound and rhythms of the Czech language that, on stage, means nothing semantically, getting to heart of the very strangeness of it. But the exercise, however humorous, was useful; Blackwell got them to listen to the source language, to understand it as a translation, and to listen to those rhythms, hesitations, and pauses. Her "supplementary schooling" not only gave them cultural and social context but also a sense of how language functioned on an aural level in the play. Blackwell's use of various documents, photos, the recording and personal anecdotes seemed to be a fruitful schooling, given the rave reviews the production and the translations heralded.

Blackwell told Havel that she agreed to changes in the scripts with the director, as she had indicated she would do in her correspondence with the Greenberger agency. The angst surrounding the demands for flexibility and her intransigence were finally solved by what she had suggested, that is, her working with the director in order to talk through alterations instead of alterations implemented, without knowledge of the context and aesthetics, just for the sake of speakability. Even more, Blackwell used the opportunity of attending rehearsals to share her experience and knowledge as an expert on the plays. The positive effect of this, as it seems, on the outcome of the production, however, possibly made her too visible and too involved.

In one of his last letters to her, Havel wrote again that he could not judge her translations himself: "not because my knowledge of English is so poor but even if I did learn English better, I'm not a native Englishman or American and I could never judge the sound, melody, oral gesture, type of humor and irony etc. of your translations" (VBA 3, 8/10/84). But he could judge the translations on the basis of their success by "what you've translated of mine has met with success, received prizes, wonderful critical praise underlining above all and explicitly the quality of the translations, it speaks of the benefits of your translations" (VBA 3, 8/10/84). He asked her not "to get angry automatically" at those who criticized her translations, and compared it to his own experience with criticism of his plays—that he always heard the negative more than the positive criticism. "When I wrote to you that I would stay faithful," he added, "I didn't mean as a friend—that's a given—but as your translatee" (VBA 3, 8/10/84).

But, in 1984, Havel was in a difficult position and was "still adapting and getting used to—a prison disease—the weight of freedom" after 4 years incarceration (VBA 3, 1/20/84). "Prison does enough to shake up a person, it's like the smallest storm that blows over life and doesn't leave anything its place. Finding a new balance, rhythm, way of life, way of work, etc. isn't—at least for me—easy" (VBA 3, 1/20/84). There was some sense of strange political calm and real humor; Havel, living in his country cottage, Hrádeček, was working on repairs:

> You wouldn't recognize Hrádeček, it has really, really changed over the years, so that now it's almost a stately residence, almost like a luxurious pension [. . .] the police are still watching me, they built their own little cottage for that purpose, but they're leaving me in peace, since February I haven't been interrogated, followed, the house hasn't been searched, no controls, no persecution, nothing. I've begun to get suspicious of myself. (VBA 3, 8/10/84)

In the strangely mixed repressive and idyllic atmosphere, Havel was largely cut-off from the outside world, receiving word via letters and sometimes phone communication or personal messages via intermediaries from Blackwell and Juncker. Hearing different versions from both sides, Havel said that he did not want to become "mixed up" in their differences and that "more pragmatism and less emotion" was needed on both sides. He did not want to become an "investigator, who investigates who said what when" and could only "call on all sides for calmness, pragmatism, detachment, openness to the other's will"; "You know what Lenin said," he added wryly, "we have to work with people as they are" (VBA 3, 1/20/84).

But, coming back to the stand-off between Blackwell and Juncker in another letter, Havel wrote that what threatened his fidelity to her as his translator was not the translations themselves but the "eternal tension with Klaus" (VBA 3, 8/10/84). He did not think that Juncker was the "bad guy" she painted him as, just someone committed to their job. "He never expressed any personal repugnance about you," Havel wrote, "if there was any criticism, it was always in relation to some agenting worries" (VBA 3, 8/10/84).

Papp had asked him for another play and "I've of course be happy if you would translate it," Havel wrote, "But what to do when your relations with Klaus are on the level of today's relations between the two superpowers?" Havel came up with a solution, to include a "third—disinterested—party," Tom Stoppard. He envisaged Blackwell and Stoppard working on the translation together, which would perhaps mean that her translations would no longer be "undervalued" and would "knock the gun out the hands of the potential doubters of your translation" (VBA 3, 8/10/84). The masculine, phallic imagery of the gun being knocked out her doubters' hands—but only if she worked with a man (albeit, of course, Stoppard)—unconsciously recalls the world in which she was working.

When Papp refused to take the play in her translation, it was Stoppard who translated the play in England (from an uncredited "literal" translation). In fact, all of the next three plays of Havel's that were translated into English and published: *Largo Desolato*, *Temptation*, and *Redevelopment* were translated by men: Stoppard, George Theiner, and James Saunders (Havel, Selected Plays 1984–87: 137). Marie Winn in America had translated all three, and *Largo Desolato* and *Temptation* were performed at the Public (in not hugely successful productions—not as a result of her excellent translations); her translation of *Asanace/Slum Clearance* was adapted, without authorization by James Saunders and renamed *Redevelopment* (she is at least credited with the "literal translation" in the Faber edition). Havel's next plays (The *Beggar's Opera* and *Leaving*) were translated by Paul Wilson (who is a Czech-speaker, and a member of the Czech rock band, the *Plastic People of the Universe*, whose banning had led Havel to coauthor Charter 77).

While I don't want to suggest that this was some conspiracy to masculinize the experience of Havel's plays, it did speak to the hurdles of opportunity and power for women in the theatre, unless they were prepared to be "only" the "literal" translator. As Havel pointed out to Blackwell, it was actually not her translations that were the problem in terms of quality, skill, or ability, but it was the "tension" she caused surrounding the translation and production process. The fact that she was an "anti-Oblomov" person, a "demanding lady" was her downfall: she did not live up to the expectations—in the English-speaking world—of the translator. The continuing constraints placed on her as the years went on spoke to the attempts to make her understand the limitations of her role. Overtly censored by the Czechoslovak Communist regime—banned, silenced, and deported—who used her gender to slander her and render her suspect, Blackwell faced other forms of constraint in the West at a time when women and translators were not given their due.

Luise von Flotow, quoting Beate Thill about the "modesty" of translators arising from "problems of identity," argues that these problems are exacerbated for women due to the fact that "Translators live between two cultures, and women live between at least three, patriarchy (public life) being the omnipresent third" (von Flotow 1997: 36). Von Flotow adds that women are socialized into a private sphere "where empathy, submissiveness and industry are valued [. . .] This partially underlies their self-evaluation as 'sherpas' or 'coolies of the literary market' " (p. 36).

Blackwell, who was "demanding," feisty and a little thin-skinned, resisted these norms somewhat unconsciously at first, perhaps because of the respect for the profession in her native culture, but also because of an innate sense of being equal to those around her, despite being a woman, "foreign" and a translator. Blackwell's translations are now being consigned to the past as, rightly, newer translations are being made for a different era, but it would be wrong to assume that she was a "bad" translator and responsible for the resistance to Havel's work in the English-speaking sphere. In fact, she provides a model for the activist translator, having asserted herself as an important element of the translated work, as an hermeneutic advisor, and as a promoter of the work and the culture from which it sprang. Her active defense against the insularism of British and American culture toward translations makes her a role model for translators and readers as she fought against reductive readings of the translations, knowing that Havel's work explored this kind of censorship in ourselves: the language, the cuts, the delusions, and distortions of our everyday life.

3

Market censorship

You know what the theater's all about? Money,
money, money, money, money.

JOE PAPP

"I gave a speech in Paris for the representatives of the largest multinational corporations, the actual rulers of our current global world," Havel writes in 2005:

I wrote a pointed speech that was highly critical of the behavior of global corporations, of their unscrupulousness, of the growing uniformity of the world, of the omnipresent dictatorship of advertisements, of profit, and so on. I was extremely nervous of the speech, which I read in English, because I was afraid that they would boo me off the stage or walk out in protest. Just the opposite happened: they listened to me very attentively, and when the speech was over I was given an enormous round of applause that ended with a standing ovation. There are three ways to explain this: 1) they weren't applauding what I said but me personally, or more precisely the "icon" that Mr Hvizdala is talking about, that is, my "story," with its touch of the fairy tale about it and the remarkable happy ending; 2) they were applauding themselves, that is, their limitless power and their broad-mindedness in hiring such a sharp critic of their own activities to whom they could, at the same time, pay their respects and thus, in fact, in the most elegant way imaginable, undermine his ideas; 3) I don't discount the possibility that they simply agreed with me and were glad that someone had said it for them. Many of them, in what they do, may not be expressing their true feelings about the world and about how it ought to flourish but are merely being dragged along by the gigantic "automatism" of modern civilization, which they dare not say anything against, because in doing so they might risk their own livelihoods, the ambivalence of which they are very well aware. (Havel 2007a: 36–7)

Accustomed to giving controversial speeches or writing seditious open letters under Communism, Havel sees no difference in his role post-Communism in the West. His protest against "the omnipresent dictatorship of advertisements, of profit," however, leads to no persecution or arrest, but, instead, "a standing ovation." This, of course, is a vindication of free speech, a key difference between conditions of censorship in Communist Czechoslovakia and conditions in the free-market majority of Europe post-1989.

But Havel's typically legalistic analysis of the magnanimous reaction by "the actual rulers of our current global world" to his critique is both wry and suggestive. He does not think that they necessarily believe he is right or even that they are applauding his ideas. Even if they do agree, they "dare not say anything." There is more, he suggests, to this culture of axiomatic free speech than meets the eye. Havel is legally able—even invited—to say what he thinks, and applauded for it. But his critique is absorbed into the culture of the high financiers because they have "limitless power" and, thus, they can, "in the most elegant way imaginable, undermine his ideas" by applauding them, knowing that these ideas will not change anything. In essence, he thinks, they are applauding themselves for their own "broadmindedness" in allowing the critique while fundamentally aware that it can be safely contained or ignored. Worse, he thinks that his actual ideas, and the critique they contain, are completely irrelevant; the sole relevance Havel, the "icon," has is as a symbol of the fall of Communism, for many years the oppositional force to free market capitalism, and all that matters is the performance of this iconicity: it consolidates what is going on in the room. Havel is also an icon of free speech, but what that free speech says can be safely nullified by its very iconicity and ignored. Even if the audience members are agreeing with the message, then, in Havel's eyes, they cannot live in truth because "in doing so they might risk their own livelihoods." As a result of market forces, in the very act of applauding this icon of free speech, they "dare not say anything"; they have to censor, or at least, constrain themselves.

Provocative and palatable

Havel's surprise that, when he offers a social critique "in English" he is applauded rather than booed, offers some insight to the rewriting of Havel's persona and plays in English. Havel's fame as an "icon" of free speech served to imprison his plays in a kind of ideological straightjacket, as Cold War artifacts that were worthy, at times, to be performed because of their provocative nature in their homeland. But, in domesticating the plays, whether via textual changes for speakability or playability, or through reviews and explanations, the plays were made palatable to the target English-language audience. The plays were political critiques that applied to *over there*, and perhaps, maybe, possibly to here; the plays had to be relevant to the target audience and if they were not, they had to be made relevant. Cold War politics was a means of marketing Havel; dissidents were "news. Good news! They generate[d] healthy sales profiles and superb ideology. They offer[ed] compelling testaments of the genuine dangers inherent in all systems of statist control" (Jansen 1991: 17).

Garnering publicity and finally getting Havel's plays on the English-language stage were, on the other hand, vitally helpful to him. Translation was a lifeline for his work, especially after the blanket ban on his plays in Czechoslovakia in 1970. Keeping Havel in the public eye in the United States and the United Kingdom, was also, Blackwell felt, key to his safety, as he was being followed, interrogated, and then arrested in Czechoslovakia. She toned down the political side of Havel's endeavor, partly because Western publicity about Havel as a dissident could have severe ramifications back at home, but also, largely, to establish Havel as a writer rather than a political figure. But Havel seemed only to warrant national coverage when conceived of in political terms; in 1969, Blackwell offered *Time* magazine an article about Havel as a writer, to coincide with the opening of his play, *The Increased Difficulty of Concentration*, at the new Lincoln Center. "I've just had a note from TIME, saying they won't publish the piece on Havel *until* he's arrested!!" she wrote to her agent, adding, "Hard logic of hard news!" (VBA 9:1, 10/11/69).

But, unlike many other playwrights, Havel's plays were performed in translation on the professional stage, notably in the late 1960s in America and in the late 1970s in England, at times when Czechoslovakia and Havel were in the news (during the Prague Spring, after the Soviet invasion and following Havel's involvement with Charter 77). As a result, theatres and reviewers tended to conflate his plays with contemporary political reality, which made them understandable to the target audience; the plays had a reason for being in the target culture, that is, to shed light on life behind the Iron Curtain and, in doing so, to reinforce the rightness and freedoms of the target audience. Thus, Havel's provocative plays became, in translation, quite the opposite; they served to uphold the Cold War ideological framework of the West (as an opposition to the Communist East) by proving it right.

The emphasis on politics was thus, a form of acculturation, but it also led to a neutralization of Havel's poetics—the actual provocative element of his plays. Havel's investigations of language, how it's used and it uses us, the funny but somewhat traumatic use of recursive words and tropes, demanded of the audience some recognition of their own complicity in shaping the world whether through apathy, or "automatism"—what George Orwell called surrendering to words—or through an active misuse of words to construct false worlds. This central element of Havel's play was consistently the sticking point for artistic directors and reviewers; the repetitions and apparent overuse of language were seen as aesthetically faulty, boring, and redundant. English-language audiences were more used to realism on stage. The resistance to Havel's poetics, however, revealed expectations of his message—such recursiveness and repetitiveness made no sense if the central aspect of his work was political satire or irony. "We know!" one reviewer cried, fed up with the long speeches and endless language, because they had got the point that this was political satire of "a thinly-disguised Czechoslovakia." The decoding of the plays for political nuance rendered the aesthetics bad, wrongheaded and ultimately, for Western uses, pointless.

André Lefevere argues that societies—democratic, totalitarian, or otherwise—support "control factors" on literature, the first of which are the literary professionals ("critics, reviewers, teachers, translators"), the second is the system of patronage, "the powers (persons, institutions) that can further or hinder the reading, writing, and rewriting of literature" (Lefevere 1992: 14–15). According to Lefevere, literary professionals:

> will occasionally repress certain works of literature that are all too blatantly opposed to the dominant concept of what literature should (be allowed to) be—its poetics—and of what society should (be allowed to) be—ideology. But they will much more frequently rewrite works of literature until they are deemed acceptable to the poetics and the ideology of a certain time and place. (p. 14)

This rewriting, for Lefevere, can actually involve a network of rewriters: translator, editor, reviewer, biographer, educator, and so on, who acculturate and contemporize a given work for their domestic readership or audience (and this may change through time). Patrons, too, are agents of rewriting, acting as a "constraint on the choice and development of both form and subject matter" (p. 16) and in choosing who to finance or support (in terms of status or money). In return, some loyalty is demanded from the author: "Acceptance of patronage implies that writers and rewriters work within the parameters set by their patrons and that they should be willing and able to legitimize both the status and the power of those patrons" (p. 18). Patrons, he argues, are more interested in ideology and finance, than poetics (the controls of which are left to professionals).

The notion of these "external constraints" (Tymoczko 2007: 38) or what Denise Merkle calls "covert censorship" (Merkle 2002: 9) in free societies may seem overly cynical or Cassandra-like, especially in comparison to extreme totalitarian forms of censorship that can end in imprisonment or death, but nonetheless, this should not preclude us from examining how the various gatekeepers of culture function in relation to translations, how such networks shape translations and shape their own domestic cultures as they do so. As literature has increasingly become a "commodified artifact" and "the text or writer accumulates symbolic capital—recognition, prestige and, occasionally, celebrity—through a cumulative process of legitimation," the question of market demands on what literature is, and how it might legitimate or delegitimate certain forms of writing, needs to be explored (Huggan 2001: 158, 212). For if translation can open views onto other cultures, it is vital to understand how that view has been mediated—beyond the translator-author dyad—and to what ends.

Havel was only viewed in the West as having commercial viability as a writer when he was associated with newsworthy political events—after 1968 and 1977—but he did offer symbolic viability as an "iconic" dissident. Both *The Conspirators* and *Protest* would have been, or were, textually altered after the translation process in order to make them more political and directly relevant to Havel's political reality, more "authentic" as dissident documents. As Graham Huggan argues, in terms of postcolonial literatures, "the paradox remains that authenticity is valued for its attachment to the material contexts of lived experience even as it is so palpably the *decontextualization* of the commodified artifact that enables it to become marketably authentic" (p. 158). What Huggan dubs the "otherness industry" (p. xii) appears to promote work and authors from marginal cultures, but instead "banks its profits on exotic myths" (p. xii), "preferably in accordance with those tales and images of otherness already possessed" (p. 159), thus, in fact, making them ideologically familiar.

Sue Curry Jansen argues that the selling of East European dissidents as products served to uphold the tenets of "political capitalism" in the domestic sphere, a sphere subject to "market censorship" (Jansen 1991: 153–4). "Market censorship," she writes:

> points to practices that routinely filter or restrict the production and distribution of selected ideas, perspectives, genres or cultural forms within mainstream media of communication based upon their anticipated profits and/or support for corporate values and consumerism. Such practices are reified, naturalized and integrated into the organizational structures and routine practices of media organizations and re-presented to the public as outcomes of consumer choices within a rational market system rather than as the result of calculated managerial responses to profit imperatives. (Jansen 2010: 13)

The assumed post-Enlightenment curtailment of state censorship for Jansen masks the beginning of actual control of ideas by elites via the market: "[M]arket censors decide what ideas will gain entry into "the marketplace of ideas" and what ideas will not [. . .] *they decide what cultural products are likely to ensure a healthy profit margin*" (Jansen 1991: 16, her italics). The "oligopoly" of multinational corporations and what she dubs the "Consciousness Industry—press, advertising, public relations, mass entertainment, and organized leisure"—serve as gatekeepers for knowledge, which is not free but a commodity to be sold (Jansen 1991: 136, 164).

John Keane agrees with Jansen that "Market competition produces market censorship" adding that:

> there is a structural contradiction between freedom of communication and unlimited freedom of the market [. . .] market liberal ideology of freedom of individual choice in the marketplace of opinions is in fact

a justification of the privileging of corporate speech and of giving more choice to investors than to citizens. It is an apology for the power of king-sized business to organize and determine and therefore to *censor* individuals' choices concerning what they listen to or read and watch. (Keane 1991: 89–90, his italics)

But Keane also warns that this market censorship "is not an underhanded conspiracy to swindle or brainwash gullible publics for the sake of profit [. . .] It results from the fact that commercial publishers of opinion are little interested in the non-market preferences of readers, listeners and viewers" (p. 91). Keane rightly decries the notion of a faceless corporate conspiracy to impose censorship on a passive and "gullible" consumer; both notions presume a marked super-agency on the part of corporations and a complete lack of agency on the part of the consumer and also presume a division between the two groups. Citizens are also investors and active consumers; corporations are made up of citizens and investors. But Keane's point that media corporations do provide choice but that it is "always within the framework of *commercially viable* alternatives" (his italics), is important in terms of literature, theatre, and translation, because of the suspected commercial unviability of translations (p. 91).

"Among the decisive factors in the current marginality of translation," Lawrence Venuti writes, "is its tenuous economic value" (Venuti 1998: 124). Venuti argues that publishers are uninterested in publishing translations because they are "financially risky" and "inevitable losses"; the small amount of translations that are published "possess only cultural capital." But, he argues, publishers base their decisions on whether to publish translations largely on whether the foreign-language book has been a bestseller domestically and whether it will appeal to the norms and taste of the target audience. Thus, their approach is:

primarily commercial, even imperialistic, an exploitation governed by an estimate of the market at home, whereas the approach of the domestic reader is primarily self-referential, even narcissistic, insofar as the translation is expected to reinforce literary, moral, religious, or political values already held by that reader. (p. 124)

These commercial decisions and expectations of the target culture readers lead to an effect on sales and reviews—because the "foreign text has been made to serve domestic interests," neither the sales projections nor the reviews "can be seen as true and objective assessments of its value" (p. 125). In addition, publishers taking risks on translations often seek work that suits the prevailing aesthetic norms of the target culture, in the English-language case, Venuti argues, this means seeking work of the "realism typical of the popular aesthetic" and translations of that realist work that "produce the illusory effect of transparency" (p. 126). These kinds of translations "eschew unidiomatic constructions, polysemy, archaism, jargon, any linguistic effect that calls attentions to the words as words and therefore preempts or interrupts the reader's identification" (pp. 126–7).

The problem, then, is not an oligarchical or state-instituted attempt to censor foreign literature because it is politically or morally suspect, but a prevailing market sense that translations are not worthwhile economically. When the risk is taken to publish translations, work has to be done to make them economically successful during the translation process, the editorial process, and the marketing and publicity surrounding them. This, Venuti suggests, involves deliberate remolding of the texts for profit rather than aesthetic reasons. Acts of acculturation and domestication are often presented as altruistic attempts to make texts more comprehensible to the target audience, or as value judgements about aesthetic choices that seem strange to the target culture, which must be fixed. But the question of whether this constitutes censorship lies in the true motive behind these changes. While some acculturation is inevitable in translation because of the cultural differences underpinning languages, some deliberate changes are more suspect, especially if they are made to pander to the assumed public taste or given norms of a culture at a given time mainly for profit. The problem, of course, is that the true motivation of these demands and changes are often obscured and rarely clear-cut. An editor or a director can believe that they are improving a work aesthetically and in good faith while also making it marketable (and perhaps they are).

In Havel's case, a few champions of his work in the United States and England did choose to produce his plays despite the fact that they were, at the time, translations of an obscure writer from a relatively obscure place. Carol Rocamora rightly praises Joseph Papp of the Public Theater in New York and Sam Walters of the Orange Tree Theatre for doing so, writing: "They had convictions, both artistic and ethical ones; they had loyalty; they took risks"; "they were putting themselves at risk, to sustain Havel's life in the theater" (Rocamora 2004: 365–6). Rocamora's seemingly hyperbolic language, "*they* took risks", "*they* were putting *themselves* at risk,*" is suggestive of the constraints at work faced by producers of translations. While Havel's work would be banned by the Communist regime, the redemptive narrative of his plays finding a free platform in the West was complicated by the cultural and economic resistance to actually staging his plays. The Public and the Orange Tree could take risks because both theatres were, at the time, small, nascent off-Broadway or off-West End theatres. But they were both subject to artistic and financial risks, and the severity of these, what it might mean for a nascent theatre, speaks to the "risk" that Rocamora underlines. It also speaks to Tynan's comment, when he traveled to Prague during the Prague Spring, that the flowering of Czech theatre and cinema was related to a certain freedom not only from "ideological pressures" but "economic" ones; for Tynan, this small historical window afforded a glimpse into a more utopian theatre scene where, "the performing arts have had time to consider why they exist and what human purpose they should serve" (Tynan 1967: 102).

But something else is at work in Rocamora's insistence that *"they* took risks," *"they* were putting *themselves* at risk" and it relates to the marketability and meaning of putting Havel's play on in New York and London. Papp and Walters were clearly not putting "themselves at risk" by staging Havel's plays in the way that Havel and Czech theatre practitioners would have been after 1970 in Czechoslovakia (Andrej Krob's famous 1975 private staging of Havel's *The Beggar's Opera* near Prague, for instance, led to arrests, interrogations, and the loss of jobs for those involved and those in the audience) (Kriseová 1993: 92–5; Rocamora 2004: 130–7). Nevertheless, an equation is being made; in staging seditious literature by a playwright actually at risk (of imprisonment and worse), some form of ethical *nous* is being conferred. The hint of danger and political urgency, the risks of theatre that has social impact, belies the actual concrete risks at play—the risk of losing commercial and cultural capital in staging obscure translations. The evocation of risk itself also confers meaning within these parameters, making the play relevant politically within the domestic sphere and, thus, making it commercially viable. This is not to suggest in any way that Papp or Walters chose to stage Havel for financial reasons—quite the opposite, as they knew it would be a financial risk—but that the altruism attendant in staging dissident or seditious plays carries within it a perhaps unconscious self-serving element, whether that is a search for theatre that actually matters (beyond the bottom-line) or whether it is a more ideologically inflected search to consolidate ways of being in the domestic culture.

Either way, censored theatre, seditious elsewhere, is sexy and it sells. The danger is that the reason the plays are performed in the domestic sphere—politics and newsworthiness—tends to strangle the potential aesthetic impact of the translations. Walters' excitement about the political impact of what his theatre was doing when it first performed Havel's work in 1977 (Havel had just been arrested for his involvement in the Charter 77 petition), is infectious and, to a large extent, right—The Orange Tree did help Havel, in terms of political visibility, income, and simply having his plays performed. "We were involved in the politics of the moment," he said, "and making a positive contribution [. . .] Not often does it fall to theater to feel so much a part of history" (Rocamora 2004: 365). But it also meant that Havel's plays were politicized in order to make them relevant and to serve a more metaphysical use in showing that theatre actually mattered in an increasingly commercial sphere. It reflects a certain anxiety about the use of theatre in a society that judges value in economic terms; censored foreign theatre can provide a vicarious thrill of theatre not subject to the bottom-line, while at the same time and for the very same reason, becoming economically viable.

So, for instance, Ben Brantley, writing recently about the Belarus Free Theatre (who are currently in political exile), noted the "harrowing intensity and commitment" of their play *Being Harold Pinter*; it "is a startling and shaming presence in these United States, where the only work of theater regularly making headlines is a delay-plagued $65 million musical about a comic-book character" (Brantley 2011). The domestic effect of the Belarus Free Theatre is not simply to convey the newness of their wonderful experimental and physical theatre but to act as "a shaming presence" in the face of the economic excesses of the troubled *Spiderman: Turn off the Dark*, to prove that theatre matters beyond economic value. The Belarus Free Theatre gained huge publicity and support from the theatre and cultural communities in London and New York. But the international attention was generated by and focused on the Free Theatre's political plight—on receiving a prize for their theatre, Natalia Koliada expressed regret that it "was given not for artistic choice. It was given for our position against the Belarusian regime" (Gener 2009). If there had been a democracy in Belarus, in other words, what would be the likelihood that this innovative company would have received international coverage or been produced on the English-language stage? The impetus to stage the Free Theatre's productions was worthy and worthwhile, but what about Bulgarian, Slovenian, Montenegran plays—and that's just Europe—staged in English? And what about experimental theatre even at home? "I mentioned a friend's joke that if a dictator wanted to neutralize the subversive effects of experimental theatre in Belarus," [Randy Gener] writes, "he should do what we do in the States: Ignore it" (Gener 2009).

The interest in the Belarus Free Theatre, or in Havel, does not suggest a rabid openness to foreign-language theatre, unless it reflects on social anxieties or political and economic concerns of the domestic culture. In this sense, there are real constraints on choosing, translating, and performing translated work and what does get performed is often adapted—beyond the actual translation—for local rather than aesthetic concerns.

Yet, there is no theatre censor or censorship body (since the 1960s) in England or in the United States and professional theatres are free to perform what they want. With new technologies comes the repositioning of constraints, boundaries, and gatekeepers for theatre and literature: e-publishing, digital cameras, YouTube, and so on mean that the potential for publishing and performing translations (at least on film) are putatively democratized, as are the means for publicizing and reviewing translations (for instance, websites such as Three Percent which focus on and publish translated literature). One central problem is making a living doing so—for the translator, the theatre, the actors, and so on.

Another central problem is indifference to translations, especially in the English-speaking sphere, due to the primacy of English as a world language. Blackwell's worry about the "insularism" of the British is true of English-speakers now; despite increased access to writing from other languages and culture via the web, the tools to read it have been devalued, whether through the lack of emphasis on learning foreign languages or through a lack of education about other forms and styles of writing that may not hew to the

English-language commercial norm: "realistic narratives driven by strong plot and peopled by well-rounded characters struggling with serious ethical issues, conveyed in language anybody can understand" (Moore 2010: 3). There is nothing essentially wrong with this norm except for its hegemonic tendencies—look at how, in general, translated fiction (Orhan Pamuk) or plays (Yasmin Reza) mirror this style—and lack of platforms for, or understanding of, other styles.

Michael Cronin calls this a "censorship of indifference" toward translators and translations, "a pervasive censorship of a neo-liberal monoglossia" (Cronin 2003: 100). Cronin places this "insidious aggression of unconcern" (p. 95) in a social frame, a general sense of disinterest in the actual work of the translator or acceptance of works as having been translated. "Customers and readers want product," he writes, "they are bored by process" (p. 94). Cronin's rather dystopian critique of the homogenizing practices of globalization—what he dubs "clonialism" (p. 127), however, carries the seed of resistance in it. If there is such a censorship of indifference, then the question of agency of not only the translator (as advocated by theorists such as Maria Tymoczko) but also of the reader- or audience-consumer needs to be brought into focus. If the market has traditionally devalued translations (because of their low economic value) and translators, the element that can change that devaluation is the consumer. The responsibility for dealing with this "censorship of indifference" ends up being personal, and related to our own fears of existential discomfort, of difference or newness and of changes in habit. Shouldering such responsibility may not even require learning another language, immersing yourself in another culture, or actively going to see translated plays, but essentially requires an active awareness of what cultural products are before us, who has chosen them and why, where they come from, from what context they arise, and why they might challenge us, or seem obscure or complex or not necessarily immediately relevant to our cultural needs or expectations. We have to realize that censorship, or abdication to constraints, begins with us and our own fears.

The power of the powerless

Havel wryly beknights "the representatives of the largest multinational corporations" as "the actual rulers of our current global world" in his speech, above, suggesting that they have control not only of the markets but of epistemology. But Havel's response is more savvy than that—he both warns of their presence as potential constrainers or subsumers of knowledge; at the same time he is literally performing free speech in front of them, a report of which—satirical and self-satirical—is published by a prominent American publishing house. Havel does not, didactically, print his criticism of the corporate culture, but enacts his resistance in front of us—his analysis of why this act doesn't work is self-satirical but even in his perceived failure to elicit the reaction he wants, his analysis of their reaction is revealing of himself and them, and of censure as a personal act or evasion of responsibility.

Havel's prognosis of the "automatism" of modern life—the abdication of personal responsibility—speaks to the question of censure and censorship, in that it might suggest an existential basis for the impulse rather than a political or ideological one. Havel wants us—via his plays and philosophical essays—to confront ourselves in terms of what we deny and what powers we abdicate via language or silence. We may bemoan the power of that multinational organizations, transnational media, and so on have in controlling our lives and information but we also have to ask to what extent we are complicit in the process (and to what extent the humans involved in the multinational organizations are "victims" as well as enablers of the system)—the apportioning of blame sometimes acting as a safety valve for our own failures to question constraints in both our personal and civic lives.

In his seminal 1978 essay, "The Power of the Powerless," Havel revealed the "mutual totality" of the "post-totalitarian" system (Havel 1989: 52). He analyzed the role of the individual in upholding power, offering the example of a greengrocer who posts ideological signs up in his shop window, not because he believes in the messages therein but because it gives him an easy life. Havel argues that the minute that greengrocer refuses to put up the sign, he begins to "live in truth" and exposes the emptiness of the ideology:

> the crust presented by the life of lies is made of strange stuff. As long as it seals off hermetically the entire society, it appears to be made of stone. But the moment someone breaks through in one place, when one person cries out, "The emperor is naked!"—when a single person breaks the rules of the game, thus exposing it as a game—everything suddenly appears in another light and the whole crust seems then to be made of tissue on the point of tearing and disintegrating uncontrollably. (p. 59)

The abdication of civic responsibility, the playing of the game, makes individuals both victims and supporters of the regime, and Havel specifically indicates that this is not only true of "post-totalitarian" Czechoslovakia, but "a general inability of modern humanity to be the master of its own situation" (p. 115). Havel is unconvinced about the kind of freedoms promised by Western democracies, writing that "People are manipulated in ways that are infinitely more subtle and refined than the brutal methods used in the post-totalitarian societies" including via "the omnipresent dictatorship of consumption" (p. 116).

Havel calls for an "existential revolution"—not a political one—suggesting that power resides in the rejection of ideology and social manipulation of which we constitute the pillars (p. 117). The poetics of his plays, that investigate and reinvestigate our surrendering to language, speak absolutely to this tenet. His notion of "appellative theatre" in which the play and the audience are in a thinking, dialogic relationship is also centrally connected to this philosophy of personal responsibility. To requote Jan Grossman:

> A great theatre reveals not only itself and its story: it also reveals the viewer's story, and with it his urgent need to confront his own experience with the theme presented on stage. Such a play does not end with the performance; the curtain is only the beginning. (Grossman 1967: 118)

Money, money, money

"You know what the theater's all about?" Joseph Papp said in 1974, "Money, money, money, money, money" (Turan and Papp 2010: 228). It might seem an odd statement, given that Papp became famous for putting on free Shakespeare in New York, but even free cost money; he knew that "one of the main things that the arts entrepreneur has to do in the modern world is to get the money in" (Clive Barnes in Turan and Papp 2010: 299). Papp, a self-made man who grew up as Joseph Papirofsky in Brooklyn slums and who became politicized after seeing families evicted in the Depression (joining the Communist Party), was something of a theatre impresario, "the greatest money-maker in New York"; "his social conscience has a great way of inflicting guilt on wealthy people" (Epstein 1996: 38; Michael Moriarty in Turan and Papp 2010: 229).

Papp produced free Shakespeare in New York parks beginning in 1956; at the time he was a stage manager at the American television station, CBS, and was also being followed by the FBI, which was gathering evidence of his Communist beliefs for the HUAC, a committee he was brought before in 1958. He pleaded the Fifth and named no names. The Committee implied that he had injected Communist propaganda into his plays; when Papp replied that what they did was Shakespeare: "I cannot control the writings of Shakespeare. He wrote plays five hundred years ago," the Committee chairman said, "there is no suggestion here by this chairman or anyone else that Shakespeare was a Communist. That is ludicrous and absurd. That is the Commie lie" (Epstein 1996: 127–8). CBS fired Papp the same day, though he sued and was reinstated briefly.

But Papp, fundamentally, did see theatre as political, certainly in terms of social justice and full access to culture. He wanted to bring theatre to those who might not necessarily be able to afford it. "The most radical thing I'd ever done," he said in 1990, "was Free Shakespeare" (p. 121). In 1964, Papp traveled to Eastern Europe and compared what he saw there with American society in the McCarthy Era—it persuaded him that he should find a permanent home for his company and produce East European playwrights (p. 182). He bought the derelict Astor Library in lower Manhattan which had most recently been used by the Hebrew Immigrant Aid Society to house Holocaust survivors when they first arrived in the United States and put on his first season in 1967–68.

Havel's play, *The Memorandum*, was produced in that first season. "All the plays Papp chose [in the first season] reflected his fascination with poetic language, his attraction to plays with political themes that sidestepped accepted doctrines and his indifference to traditional form" (p. 208). Alongside *The Memorandum*, in that first season, was a theatrical version of the Holocaust survivor, Jakov Lind's satirical novel, *Ergo*, Charles Gordone's *No Place to Be Somebody*—the first off-Broadway play to receive a Pultizer and the first Pulitzer won by an African American—and an experimental antiwar musical called *Hair*.

"I had great contempt for Broadway," Papp said, "I felt it was just a commercial marketplace that had nothing to do with art" (Turan and Papp 2010: 195). Papp sold the rights to *Hair* to Michael Butler, "scion of a Chicago tribe of millionaires, involved with paper, aviation and real estate" who tightened up the script and added full-frontal nudity (Bender 1968). "Opening night, wow!" one of the actors told a journalist, "there'll be no clothes at all" (Bender 1968). That nudity was "promised" was part of the pre-Broadway hype (Sullivan 1968). In a *New York Times* article on nudity in the theatre, Dan Sullivan attributed the "barest season" on the New York stage to declining censorship, and film, with the stage starting "to claim a right to the extreme frankness now permitted its prime public competitor, the cinema" (Sullivan 1968). In other words, nudity was as commercial a decision as an artistic one.

Sullivan interviewed the Licensing Commissioner and a police lieutenant about "declining censorship"; the Licensing Commissioner had been told in 1966 that "censorship of theater or cabaret entertainment was no longer legally with the power of the Licenses Department" and that the Department and the police could only act once a play was legally declared obscene in the courts under Article 245 (Sullivan 1968). But it seemed uncertain what could be defined as obscene in the theatre and authorities were not enthusiastic about a "test case." The police were waiting for the reviews of *Hair* before they would make a decision. In the play itself, two police officers try to break up the nude "be-in" but they would only be "actors" (Sullivan 1968).

Clive Barnes, in his review of *Hair*, noted that the "totally new, all lit-up, gas-fired, speed-marketed Broadway version" was "a great deal franker" than the Public Theater version and, in response to letters from readers, he gives some warning of what the show contains (four-letter words, nudity, drugs, homosexuality, "arcane sexual practices," disrespect for "Christian rituals," and enthusiasm for "miscegenation"; Barnes 1968a).

Yet, ultimately, despite the play pushing these boundaries thematically, Barnes reassures his readership of its safeness. The pop-rock of its musical numbers had "strong soothing overtones of Broadway . . . its noisy and cheerful conservatism is just right for an audience that might wince at "Sergeant Pepper's Lonely Hearts Club Band" (Barnes 1968a). The "essential likeability" of the show meant that you didn't have to be "a supporter of Eugene McCarthy to love it," that is, left-wing, "but I wouldn't give much chance among the adherents of Governor Reagan" (later, of course, President Reagan) (Barnes 1968a). He connects the central message of dropping out to the American tradition of Thoreau.

Like Kenneth Tynan's *Oh! Calcutta!* the veneer of revolution coated a somewhat conservative musical that used its scandalousness to sell itself, with the commercial market co-opting the so-called countercultural movement for commercial ends. Although Papp had sold the rights to *Hair*, he retained a small royalty rate and the resulting couple of million dollars became "a very important subsidy" for the Public, allowing for experimentation (Turan and Papp 2010: 196). But, "[a]fter the success of *Hair*," Gerald Freedman said, "something happened in terms of play choices. There began to be one eye on 'Will this get to Broadway?' or 'Will this be picked up?' . . . there wasn't the same freedom of choice as there had been" (Turan and Papp 2010: 197). Papp also learnt his lesson; when *A Chorus Line* became a hit musical at the Public 7 years later, he did not sell rights and raised investment money to bring it to Broadway; for its time, it became "the longest-running show in Broadway history" running until 1990. It made the Public Theater an estimated $30 million (Turan and Papp 2010: 392).

The question of overt censorship had become, in the 1960s in America, a gray area focused on obscenity rather than the political or ideological repression of the HUAC era. Changes in what was permissible were often connected to what was permissible, even advantageous, to the market (in theatre, film, and TV). Censorship—or the threat of it—was sexy and sellable. Of the nudity, one journalist asked, "is it just a gimmick to drag in the Broadway bourgeoisie so they can be épaté-ed?" (Bender 1968). What of plays already censored? Was this a selling point? Was the market interested? For what reasons?

After the fall: 1968

Papp took on *The Memorandum*, after Vera Blackwell handed him the translation at a PEN meeting in 1966 and wrote to him, then, that given Havel's political situation, a New York production could be a "life-saving endeavor" (Rocamora 2004: 88). "That was enough for Papp," Carol Rocamora writes, adding that Papp immediately wrote to Havel, offering to put the play on in the Public Theater's first season (p. 88). Papp's wife, Gail Papp, said that Papp had already identified with the play because of his own experiences with political repression: "Having lived through the McCarthy era, Joe responded to the play very well" (p. 88).

The production—the first English-language production of Havel's plays—was a success, winning two Obies (for "Best Foreign Play" and "Distinguished Performance" for Mari Gorman) and garnering good reviews for the play and for Papp's theatre. Clive Barnes at *The New York Times*, reviewing *The Memorandum*, saw it as further indication of the quality of the new Public Theater which "in this one season has proved itself the most lively and vital theater organization in New York," partly because of "its superior choice of plays" (Barnes 1968b). "[I]t has added interest in the fact that it comes from Czechoslovakia," he wrote, indicating the appeal of hearing from a place that was undergoing its "Prague Spring," but he told his readers that it was not only an "anti-Communistic" play but one emanating from "the Eastern Bloc's ideological thaw" that "contains social criticism that at one time would not have been tolerated, let alone welcomed." He added that it worked "on more than one level" because it could also be viewed as a social critique of American capitalist society:

> Also we must not forget that "The Memorandum" has a message for us as well as for Eastern Europe, because the concept that the human being is more valuable than any bureaucratic organization controlling him is not irrelevant to our own paternalistic corporation-structured society. (Barnes 1968b)

Havel's play spoke not only to the apparent changing tide in Eastern Europe, and its attendant hopes, but also to the rise of countercultural critique in late 1960s New York, of which the repertoire of the Public had some input.

Yet the very success of the play led to questions of profit, and 9 months later—after the Soviet invasion of Czechoslovakia in August 1968, when Czechoslovakia was front-page news—Havel's plays suddenly acquired cultural—and possible commercial—capital. In February 1969, Ron Bernstein, Blackwell's American agent at the Robert Lantz Agency, wrote to Peggy Ramsay, her London agent:

> Vera Blackwell sent us her translation of the new Havel play [*The Increased Difficulty of Concentration*] recently. Have you read it? What do you think of it? I am particularly keen on this play and think it can attract top flight talent and be a very big commercial success. Even before her translation was in, one of Broadway's major producers, Irene Selznick, asked to have a look at it in German. So you can see that there has been a great deal of interest in it. We are certain that there will be a major Broadway producer who will want to do it. Kermit Bloomgarden, for example, is quite anxious to see the script. (VBA 9:1, 2/17/69)

For all the critical success of Papp's production of *The Memorandum*, Bernstein was angry at Blackwell for sending Papp her translation of the new script:

> I don't understand why you sent it to him directly [. . .] This is not in any way intended as a criticism of Joe Papp and his production, but it is just

that his theatre is small and does not attract the level of talent we think possible. I would also like to point out to you that with a Broadway production there would be considerably more money coming in. (VBA 9:1, 2/17/69)

Blackwell felt that her sending Papp the script did not constitute an offer and said that "It would be marvellous if it could be done on Broadway!" adding that she was sending Bernstein's letter to Havel "to cheer him up" (VBA 9:1, 3/1/69). At this point, Blackwell knew that a Broadway production would give Havel important visibility at a difficult and uncertain time for him in Czechoslovakia—after 6 years of trying to get him on a major English-language stage—and, importantly, would give him a revenue stream, when it was becoming impossible for him to earn a living on the Czech stage because of increasingly tight informal censorship.

Ramsay, however, was more skeptical about the possibilities, or even desirability, of producing Havel on Broadway. "Like you," she wrote to Bernstein, "I greatly admire the new Havel play. I think it is witty, amusing, wise, and is quite excellent technically":

> However, when you say it will be a big success commercially, I wish I could believe that a play written by a brilliant intellectual would be a commercial success, either in America or in England.

> The real trouble with the successful plays at the moment, is their emptiness and lack of any intellectual content [i.e. *Hair, The Boys in the Bad, Mame,* your own thing] . . . Havel, on the other hand, is both witty and profound, and above all, the play would need a brilliant and witty director and cast.

> I am often in touch with Bloomgarden on the phone, and I never think his taste interesting, whereas I think Papp extremely intelligent and clever, and he has already done Havel very well indeed.

> On the other hand, Vera tells me that he only has a small theatre, which runs plays for a limited season. It could transfer though, I take it. (VBA 9:1 2/21/69)

She suggested Eli Wallach for the main role, and Mike Nichols as a director, but Bernstein wrote back with objections: "Surely you realize that neither Mike Nichols nor Eli Wallach would consider working off Broadway in a two hundred and ninety nine seat house." He noted that Papp had never transferred a show to Broadway and was worried that if Papp produced the show, "this brilliant, witty play will not be done with talent equal to the writing" (VBA 9:1, 2/25/69).

Despite the sudden interest in Havel, the "Broadway Managers" did not bite: "I'm sorry the Broadway Managers didn't respond to this play, but we ourselves never expected them to do so," Ramsay wrote to Bernstein, adding that "the Broadway Managers are quite right, as they agree with us that it's not a 'commercial' play." In Ramsay's terms, this was a positive attribute; there was a division between commercial and artistic theatre that, in her letters, comes across initially as slightly snobbish. Havel's play, she wrote:

> needs the kind of "special" audience which supports Beckett, Ionesco and other "intellectual" writers. My own opinion is that Havel is too good for the Broadway commercial theatre, which I despise for its banal taste, so I'm delighted that you now want to try Papp and theatres of this genre. (VBA 9:1, 5/15/69)

The British actor, Simon Callow, in his memoir about Ramsay, wrote that, "It was immediately evident that she judged her clients, and herself, by direct comparison with the great dead" (or the great living—it was rumored that both Ionesco and Beckett were her lovers) and that she "had a characteristic method of phrasing which bore some resemblance to Queen's Victoria's epistolary manner" (Callow 2000: 5–7). But at the heart of Ramsay's dismissal of commercial theatre was a fear that Havel's play would be understood only in terms of its commercial viability—the newsworthiness of his dissident appeal—rather than in terms of its artistic newness.

The capriciousness of that interest, though, was apparent in trying to get publicity for the play. Blackwell offered *Time* magazine an article about Havel and his theatre to coincide with the opening of *The Increased Difficulty of Concentration* at the new Lincoln Center in the fall of 1969. "I've just had a note from TIME, saying they won't publish the piece on Havel *until* he's arrested!! Hard logic of hard news!" she wrote to Bernstein (VBA 9:1, 10/11/69). The "hard logic of hard news" dictated that Havel the playwright was only of interest once he fit into a political identity, that of the embattled and imprisoned dissident. Only then could his plays warrant national coverage.

Blackwell told Bernstein that "we should try to publish as much news as we can about the play and Havel and his work etc." and that this publicity might "*prevent* his arrest," but that it was important that any articles *not* be "about his political involvement and his present precarious situation" because any direct reference to it in the foreign press might lead to imprisonment for Havel (VBA 9:1, 10/11/69). She also protested the initial Lincoln Center press release for the *The Increased Difficulty of Concentration* which emphasized that Havel was in prison (something that was rumored but not true). "Havel's play is good enough not to need this kind of irresponsible publicity!" she wrote, "They should also realize that for the sake of a cheap sensation they're putting Havel's liberty in jeopardy!!!" (VBA 9:1, 11/23/69).

The problem was in selling Havel; part of the acculturation process was making Havel relevant to the domestic American audience and that relevancy, rather than being in the aesthetic sphere, was in the political one.

To make a Czechoslovak play viable, it seemed it had to fit into a narrative about the Eastern Bloc and about America itself. The program for the Lincoln Center production still emphasized the political side of Havel's biography:

> Recently, Mr Havel's passport was revoked because of his outspoken resistance to the Communist invasion and the popularity of his plays abroad. At present, Havel is living in the Sudeten Mountains where he is at work on a play about Stalinism. The security police visit him three or four times a week and stay for as much as six hours at a time. (VBA 9:3)

This part of the program was referenced in a number of reviews, implying that Havel's precarious position in postinvasion Czechoslovakia was the *raison d'etre* of the production or at least for audience interest in a translated Czechoslovak play. *The Increased Difficulty of Concentration* played in the Forum series at a theatre under the Vivien Beaumont theatre at Lincoln Center for "younger writers" who "think of it as a haven for experiment and exposure of their works" (Funke 1969). The Forum also offered rush student tickets in order to attract a younger audience, something it mentions in the advertisement for Havel's play, under the title "Discover the Underground." The rest of the Havel biography seems to speak to this youth audience, with similar hints of the counterculture, including a quote from a drama critic who had just visited Havel at his country cottage to find "*Hair* pounding away as you drive through the mud. There are message buttons all over the place and psychedelic posters; and even his outside privy has got a Flower Power sticker" (VBA 9:3). The cottage, the critic adds jokily, winking to a young audience, is "a Yankee imperialist stronghold" (VBA 9:3).

The representation of Havel as a political dissenter not only feeds into a Cold War narrative—one man standing against repressive Communism—but also into the American "underground" zeitgeist. He is both one of them and one of us; what connects the two ideas is the political dissent. And yet, it is also a commercialized version of political dissent (the *Hair* record, message buttons, psychedelic posters, Flower Power sticker), one apparent in the selling of the theatre scene at the time. The advertisement for *The Increased Difficulty of Concentration* in *The New York Times* is surrounded by ads for other plays and musicals that sell their counterculture status with strong nods to *Hair*: "The Original Nude Production of *CHE!*"; "The New Smash Hit Rock Musical: *Salvation*: Funny, Naughty, Zany, Bouncy and Zippy!"; "*The Way it Is!!!*: *The* Adult Musical, No One Under 18 Admitted" (this latter one, with a naked cartoon man chasing a naked cartoon woman, whose left nipple is deliberately obscured by one of the exclamation marks).

The exuberant sense of barriers being broken—nudity and zaniness—is somewhat mitigated by the commercialism (spinning-off from the hit, *Hair*, and the realization that nudity meant money), but also by the conservatism of form. These musicals were not promising anything avant-garde or revolutionary in epistemological terms; the content, youthful zaniness, and nudity, constituted a co-opting and commercial neutralizing of any dangerous or socially critical element. Havel, who had been entranced by the "be-ins in Central Park," "the huge antiwar demonstrations," and the premiere of *Hair* on Broadway that he attended on his trip to New York in 1968 noted that when he went back to America the next time, 22 years later, he was President and the "former hippies were no doubt respected senators or bosses of multinational corporations" (Havel 2007a: 7).

The banality of Huml

The problem with *The Increased Difficulty of Concentration* was that it did not give the impression, to an American audience, of pushing boundaries, of defying social constraints either in Czechoslovakia or in America. *Women's Wear Daily*'s vitriolic condemnation of "these naïve, middle European anti-conformity plays" as "cockroaches" that needed to be sprayed and eradicated, argued that they "ironically, conformed remarkably to each other" and of Havel's play wrote:

> Again we are in a thinly disguised Czechoslovakia; again we are given a bureaucratic state trying to eliminate individuality with pseudo-science; again we find human personality indestructible because of its sheer confusion; and again the message is the equivalent of the Boy Scout oath . . . Such predictability of attitude is not particularly interesting, nor is the predictability of style. In their own way, these plays suggest that the Communist superstates have succeeded in molding the thoughts and styles of the very artists who are complaining about molding in the first place. Or else, as anywhere else, the non-conformists are conformists too. (VBA 9:3, 12/5/69)

The "predictability of attitude" and the "predictability of style" lies, of course, in the assumptions and predictions of the reviewer who, despite the abstract and never defined setting of the play, insists it's a "thinly disguised Czechoslovakia" (the equivalent of saying *Godot* is a "thinly disguised Ireland"). What the reviewer expects and reads is a tale of the individual against the "bureaucratic state," that is, Professor Huml as an earnest portrayal of an earnest hero. The *Newsday* critic, too, dismisses the "trite and unworthy" message of "the gratuitous speech near the play's end, of what sounds cloyingly like a moral. Huml tells one of the researchers, 'The key to man is not in his brain but in his heart.' We know" (VBA 9:3, Seligsohn, 5/12/69).

The excessively literal readings of what Huml says, as opposed to *how* he says what he says, reveal something of how the American critics approached the play, that is, expecting a message play, one pointed in political or sociopolitical satire. Huml's "gratuitous speech" to Miss Balcar, giving evidence as to why he cannot continue participating in the experiment with the robot Puzuk, is a long speech redolent of Huml's manner in his dictation of his lecture on human happiness:

> For example, it should be enough to point out the rather obvious fact that things which from one angle appear as predictable may from another angle appear as coincidental, and vice versa; because predictability and coincidence are no absolute categories, nor are they any objectively existing and differentiated spheres of reality—their extent depends merely on the chosen viewpoint, or angle. It can't be helped, from the scientific point of view everything is always to some extent predictable, while science itself is but a gradual disclosing of this predictability; what we call coincidental is either that which lies beyond the radius of predictability, or simply that which so far we've been unable to establish as predictable [. . .] I'm afraid the key to real knowledge of the human individual does not lie in some greater or lesser understanding of the complexity of man as an object of scientific knowledge [. . .] Such values as love, friendship, compassion, sympathy and the unique and irreplaceable mutual understanding—or even mutual conflict—are the only tools which this human approach has at its disposal. By any other means we may perhaps be able more or less to explain man, but we shall never understand him—not even a little—and therefore we shall never arrive at a basic knowledge of him. Hence, the fundamental key to man does not lie in his brain, but in his heart. (Havel 1993: 179–80)

After the rousing end of this monologue, moving from his long, clause-ridden sentences to the final declarative statement, Miss Balcar bursts into tears and Huml, aghast, says "Just forget everything I said!" The speech is written for comedic effect, with the verbose professor substantiating his claim that Puzuk is worthless with rhetoric that at a closer reading is utterly banal. The weight of Huml's scientific refutation of Puzuk's computational ability to distinguish human individuality is not balanced on what he says, but the fact that it is conveyed in a seemingly scientific register. Huml's conclusions *are* trite and unworthy, because the phrases he utters are hollow and subordinate to how he says them. Puzuk the computer emits random sentences and, in the guise of *über*-rational discourse, so does Huml. The recursive syntax reveals the rhetorical blindness of Huml's speech—the repetition of "predictability" reverberates in the actual predictability of Huml's rhetoric, stance, and conclusion.

Marketa Goetz-Stankiewicz argues that in drawing us into "the social scientist's 'reasonable' arguments," Havel critiques our unquestioning adherence to the form of rational argument (Goetz-Stankiewicz 1999: 235). His characters "talk well, indeed convincingly, if we do not listen too closely" but when we do, "their web of words becomes transparent and another reality appears behind it"; Huml's language "is reduced to a burbling sound counter-pointing the predictable patterns of events" (pp. 235 and 236). Its meaninglessness demands us to question language as a tool and to question our respect for the structure of rhetoric that blinds us to its sometime vacuousness. We can become craven to it, and imprisoned by it; language, or how we use it, dictates how we think. As George Orwell wrote, "the slovenliness of our language makes it easier for us to have foolish thoughts" (Orwell 1954: 163).

"Predictability" is, of course, a key word. Huml's take on humanity, predicated on post-Heisenberg view of the world and scientific inquiry, posits predictability as a relative judgement, "science itself is but a gradual disclosing of this predictability; what we call coincidental is either that which lies beyond the radius of predictability, or simply that which so far we've been unable to establish as predictable," and therefore scientific inquiry cannot determine what the human is. Only humans can do so, through the "heart." Havel, through Huml's rational exegesis, pointedly reveals a sentimentality at the heart of such relativist thinking and the weakness of relying entirely on automized identity as the vanishing point of metaphysics. The plays do not investigate the mechanization of man, but his "automatism," the predictability of the human, finding a common world through using a common language, that becomes so used, so usual, that it becomes debased. We think that we express our individuality through language, but if we do so unthinkingly, with "slovenliness," than there is little individual about us at all.

How language works in this way, the infectiousness of it as an unthinking tool, is evident in how the *Women's Wear Daily* reviewer critiques Havel's play using the same language and style of language as Huml, without any sense of pastiche. The reviewer uses the same recursive language and the repetition of "predictability": "Again we . . . again we . . . again we . . . again the message is"; "Such predictability of language . . . the predictability of style; "molding the thoughts . . . molding in the first place." The reviewer's accusation that Havel is as "conformist" as the next person, is steeped in linguistic conformity generated by the play, serving to elucidate Havel's inquiry in the play. Havel does not claim to be "nonconformist"; his play suggests that we are all conformists and is interested in how we are so, how we imprison ourselves into such "automatism." The *Women's Wear Daily* reviewer was right to be scared about infestations and infection from the roaches, but not in the way she or he thought. The performative effect of the play's consideration of language and interpretive censorship, despite the scandalously xenophobic review, can be seen.

The market in Havel's plays

In 1983, the Public Theater staged Havel's three one-act plays, *Audience*, *Private View*, and *Protest* to great acclaim. Several reviewers specifically mentioned and liked the set design: "the proscenium framing the action is covered with slogans in Cyrillic," Sy Syna wrote, adding: "This constantly reminds us that everything we see is taking place within a Communist regime in which all lives serve the state" (*New York Tribune*, VBA 6:2, 11/24/83). The literal framing of the plays by "a mural with hammers and tanks" that "surrounds the stage" (*USA Today*, VBA 6:2, 11/21/83), "a marvelous piece of agitprop, which puts the whole thing in perspective" (*Women's Wear Daily*, VBA 6:2, 11/22/83), is redolent of a figurative framing of the play into a commodified, falsely transparent, and comforting window into the "East."

Havel's one-act, or "Vaněk" plays (they all share the same "dissident" character Vaněk), were his breakthrough plays in England and America. In contrast to his previous work, these three plays seemed to be realist dramas rather than absurdist or experimental ones. They also seemed more directly political and autobiographical. They were short and, with either two or three actors, relatively economical in tone and price. Most of all, their author was no longer an obscure experimental playwright but was an internationally famous dissident who had made headlines in 1977 because of his involvement with Charter 77. His imprisonment in 1977 and 1979 also made international headlines, with vociferous support from theatre figures, notably Tom Stoppard. Finally Havel was "hard news"; the plays appeared to be messages from the front line. They made sense.

What struck the reviewers was their "authenticity." "Czechoslovakia, one of the most repressive Communist dictatorships outside the Soviet Union, is the scene of three short, chillingly authentic plays" wrote the *Christian Science Monitor* (6:2, 11/30/83); "The plays are authentically Eastern European," *WINS* radio broadcast (6:2, November 1983); "Theatrically speaking, there's nothing startling" about the plays, Peter Wynne wrote in *The Record*: "What makes the plays fascinating—and they truly are—is their authenticity. Havel was writing about repression up close" (6:2, 11/22/83). Wynne's comment reveals the apportioning of cultural capital onto the plays that are "fascinating" because of their "authenticity" but "there's nothing startling" about their aesthetics, except their perceived realism and documentary value.

As Graham Huggan argues, "with regard to indigenous postcolonial artifacts and writing, '*authenticity itself*,' can be made to circulate as a commodity" (Huggan 2001: 158, his italics). The choices of texts, and marketing of "indigenous" texts turns the sense of authenticity into a marketable attribute, even though it is constructed through the market. In the Western commodification of postcolonial literatures (quoting Sonia Kurtzer), "authenticity" is "part of a wider exoticist representational mechanism through which images of the indigenous other are created, manipulated, and controlled by the dominant culture" (p. 159). The West, in other words, decides what is authentic and the outcome often serves to consolidate Western images of other cultures and its image of itself. The postcolonial paradigm can be applied to the "East" of Europe and certainly in this case, where the authenticity of Havel's plays fit into a preconceived and politicized Cold War notion of the East, framed as it was by agitprop and tanks. The realist form, too, is important to a notion of authenticity, because—even though it is fiction—it appeared to provide a documentary, transparent vehicle for representation. It also fit into the dominant stylistic norm on the commercial Anglo-American stage.

Of course, there was agitprop and there were tanks. But not in Havel's plays. None of the three plays was specifically set in Czechoslovakia or referred to the political or historical context there (though there are references to real Czech writers and actors). Havel acknowledged that the plays arose "out of my own experiences"—he did, for instance, work briefly in a brewery, the setting of *Audience*. Vaněk, read in the reviews as directly autobiographical, was to Havel "a dramatic principle," a device through which to reveal the other characters and their unraveling of their own selves. He was not, Havel wrote, "Havel" (Goetz-Stankiewicz 1987: 238). Though conceptually simple, the three plays are not straightforwardly realistic. Vaněk's interactions with the Malster in *Audience*, with the materialistic couple Věra and Michal in *Private View*, and with Staněk in *Protest*, are, like Havel's earlier plays, meditations on language and how we use it to imprison ourselves and to censor our experiences. The plays were written just before and just after Havel wrote "The Power of the Powerless" and we see Havel exploring the notion of living in truth in the plays, in thinking nondidactically about virtue, morality, and personal responsibility (Pontuso 2004: 73). Vaněk's interlocutors are all living a lie, something that is a semiotic as much as a moral experience in that language is the performative construction of their worldviews and experience. The plays consider the mechanisms of this performativity and so the language in them is carefully calibrated to reveal the characters at the very moments they attempt to conceal and censor themselves.

In *Private View* Vaněk visits his friends, a couple, Věra and Michal, who spend the evening trying to get him to admire the life and goods they enjoy because of their acquiescence to the society they live in. One of the first things that Vaněk sees when he sits down in their living room is a baroque "confessional" the couple bought from a church that was "liquidated" (Havel in Goetz-Stankiewicz 1979: 33). Vaněk asks: "What are you going to do with it?" (p. 33), a shocking question to Michal and Věra who don't understand how he doesn't understand that, in their home, it is just decorative. A reference on one level, to the Communist regime's suppression of the Church, it also sets the scene for the play which is a confessional. Věra and Michal want Vaněk to validate their lifestyle by acceding to it but, in the face of his embarrassed pauses, they reveal themselves, and unwittingly confess: the confessional emptied of moral significance in this setting but still pregnant with it, reflects the emptiness of their words, the weight underneath that emptiness, and the aridity of their materialistic lives. The linguistic and semantic repetitions in their language reflect the rhythmic rote nature of acquisitiveness.

If *Private View* is read simply as a realist play—a transparent view into Havel's world—then it seems to be a critique of materialism and consumerism in a Communist society. Peter Steiner argues that, perhaps surprisingly to the West, consumerism was on the minds of Czechoslovaks under Communism; "state property was pilfered with abandon" and "Western products" desired (p. xxv). "The result was a socialist East," Paulina Bren writes, "that differed quantitatively but not qualitatively from the capitalist West" (Bren 2010: 190). For reviewers in America and in England this critique gave the play some appeal in the domestic market; audiences in the "capitalist West" could identify with this self-absorbed materialistic couple. "What's astonishing is how recognizable these people and their lives are," *The Village Voice* wrote, "Havel has bypassed the huge differences between our systems" (*Village Voice*, 12/6/83, VBA 6:2). Both the *New York Times* and *Associated Press* noted that Michal and Vera seemed *almost* American; they "would be leisurely at home in an affluent American suburb" and their "shallow conversation is hilarious, partly because it sounds like American cocktail parties" (VBA 6:2). Rather than being "exotic messages from terra incognita" (*Village Voice*, 12/6/83, VBA 6:2) or "literary travelogues about an utterly foreign society" (*The Rebel*, undated, VBA 6:2) the plays spoke to American audiences as a critique of consumerism, but it was a superficial universality. As James Pontuso points out, Havel was not interested in satirizing greed but in questioning "a world in which everyday moral and ethical behavior is absent" (Pontuso 2004: 109).

Private View and *Audience* were performed in England on primetime television in 1978 with one of the most famous television sitcom actors of the time, Michael Crawford. It was the first time any foreign play was part of the popular "Play for Today" series on the BBC. As in America, *Private View* seemed to speak to domestic conditions. "The first play, *Private View*," *Stage and Television Today* wrote, "had a more universal target [than *Audience*]. Pseuds are not, apparently, confined to London N1; it seems they exist even in Communist Czechoslovakia, with their trendy pads and their records and bourbon brought back from the States" (VBA 6:6, 11/30/78). The conservative *Daily Mail* chimed in, with a swipe at the Callaghan government, writing that *Private View* "reveals some truths of the 'classless society' with Ian Richardson and Zena Walker looking as if they have stepped out of *The Good Life*—a kind of Marx and mink-coated Margo and Jerry" (VBA 6:6, 11/21/78). The deliberate and particular references to English class markers (London N1), politicians (Callaghan and his classless society), or television (*The Good Life* sitcom), gave viewers the license to comprehend the plays domestically and to consider their own potential relationships to the market economy, especially at a time of political and economic crisis in Britain. Indeed, one left-wing paper expressly made a link: *The Morning Star* wrote that the plays were: "testaments to the tragic situation in Czechoslovakia and to the need to fight any repressive system, such as the one which exists in Britain, for example" (VBA 6:6, 3/4/77). From the other end of the spectrum, the more conservative *Financial Times* wrote: "They not only reflect the sad political condition of Czechoslovakia. They stand, too, as a personal and beautifully achieved theatrical statement on the place, however small, of Big Brother in the loves of everyone even in seemingly democratic countries" (VBA 6:6, 2/22/77).

The domestic readings seemed a positive step in the interpretation of Havel's plays because this critique of materialism resonated in both West and East. Yet, the jokey tones of the comparisons with cocktails and suburbs, bourbon, and Marxist mink coats neutralized any impact such a critique might have in the West. Western audiences might recognize themselves in *Private View* but they could also distance themselves from it because it, after all, was from another world. *Private View* and *Audience* were "satires on *his* society" (VBA 6:6, 11/19/78, my italics). They were "semi-autobiographical satires about People's Democracy" (VBA 6:6, 11/21/78). Mary Kenny in the *Evening News* wrote about these "two rather boring Czech plays" and could not see the point of them: "They were all about a dissident writer, Vaněk (Crawford), who is obliged to take a job in a brewery . . . It really was very boring and terribly pretentious" (VBA 6:6, 11/22/78). Worse, in her mind, the plays were in fact not authentic because they were imitative of a British writer:

> Havel's dialogue has frequently been called Pinteresque. This is a great mistake for any writer. Harold Pinter is *sui generis*. It is fatal for other people to imitate him since it never quite works. (VBA 6:6 11/22/78)

It is a convoluted formulation of nonauthenticity—some identified British critics have dubbed Havel's dialogue "Pinteresque" and therefore Havel is guilty of imitation, rather than the critics being guilty of framing him as derivative of an English playwright. Another critic dismissed the "dissident" content of *Audience* as being derivative of Tom Stoppard; it was an unnecessary play because "we know all about that situation," she writes, "from Stoppard's *Professional Foul*" (VBA 6:6, 11/30/78). She seemed unaware that *Professional Foul* was written in homage to Havel's plays (and was dedicated to Havel) or that an English writer might possibly be influenced by a Czech one. The anxiety of theatrical miscegenation was reflected onto the Czech playwright.

The neutralizing readings of the plays as a realist portrayal of life in Czechoslovakia, which were "more interesting for their origin than their content" (VBA 6:6, 11/19/78) ossified them into timely curiosities distanced from the audience. The audience was not required to react to (in terms of analyzing their own interpretation and lives), but instead to *consume*, a portrait of the terrifying "East." Their content, beyond this political window, and aesthetics were generally dismissed as subpar and derivative. As seen above, the aesthetic origins were read as imitative of British playwrights and therefore also impure, mixed origins.

The only critic, either side of the Atlantic, to suggest that there was something interesting happening on the aesthetic level was the experimental British screenwriter, Dennis Potter, writing a review of the TV versions in *The Sunday Times*. Initially, the repetitions drove Potter mad: "the irritating structure of the play, in which passages of dialogue were repeated again and again in an apparently trivial liturgy of the deliberately mundane" but at the end he realized that there was a point to it; that these repetitions "suddenly tightened into pain and pity" (VBA 6:6 11/26/78). The visceral frustration, anger, and then compassion was a deliberate effect of Havel's calibration of language that allowed audiences to judge the characters and then question their own judgement.

In the Public Theater production, all three plays were performed as one play and this required substantial cuts to each play. Blackwell wrote that though these cuts did not utterly "disrupt" the characters, she warned that they did affect the portrayal of them. The prolix language, she argued, should allow the viewer to "extract the breadth" of the characters, looked at from a variety of angles (through the language) so that eventually characters that initially seemed "unsympathetic" became fully human (VBA 6:2, February 1984: 16). Rather than a realist portrayal of the "good dissident" versus the "bad" collaborators, the plays let us into the mechanisms by which people deceive themselves. We are not supposed to sympathize with Vaněk and condemn the others; he functions as an active uncensor, letting the other characters unpeel their justifications and their very human fears. We see ourselves in all of them. The plays were not "an inspiring statement about life in communist Czechoslovakia" (6:2 *WVOX*, 11/23/83), but an interrogation of us.

The director, Lee Grant, who made the cuts was given due praise in the reviews and it was felt that her experience on McCarthy's blacklist made her an apt reader of the plays. She "*knew* these people" Helen Dudar wrote in the *New York Times*; "director Lee Grant's experience on a McCarthy blacklist has enabled her to bring an urgency and relevance to this forceful production" *WINS* radio reported (VBA 6:2). It was these political credentials of being oppressed and censored that gave her authority to present the plays authentically and give them "relevance." The nod to historical American censorship also historicizes that censorship—the American past compared to the Czech present. But in making the cuts and framing the play (literally and metaphorically) in a political light Grant was placing her own political constraints on the play. That John Simon read "Vanek-Havel" as annoyingly martyr-like, "so patient, brave, and incorruptible" made him think of Havel as a "decent" writer not in the league of compatriots Milan Kundera and Bohumil Hrabal. Havel's portrayals were too black and white and also "overlong" (VBA 6:2 *New York*, 12/5/83) but in fact Simon was reading Grant's reading of the oppressed artist as a beacon of truth; the "overlong" language made no sense in this realist presentation, framed by agitprop. For Simon, the production was simply "an act of justice" for plays that had been banned in their homeland.

In some ways this is the crux of the problem; viewing productions of the plays as just "acts of justice" for an oppressed and imprisoned playwright devalued the artistic worth and real newness of the plays. At the same time, the goodwill and support from both the American and English theatre communities helped keep Havel's plight in the news, helped get him released, and finally brought his plays to the English stage and back again to the American one. After 13 years of trying to get Havel produced on the British stage, he finally was an overnight *cause célèbre*. Sam Walters, who decided to produce *Private View* and *Audience*, at the Orange Tree Theatre in London, before Havel's arrest, expanded the program when Havel was arrested. He saw the Havel plays as a platform to bring attention to Havel's political plight, setting up a petition calling for Havel's release that garnered 1,200 signatures. He produced a "docudrama" called "A Faraway Place," compiled by Vera Blackwell, which

> provided background information on Prague Spring and the Russian invasion in August 1968. It also sought to explain why Havel's works were banned and described events leading up to his imprisonment as the leading signer of Charter 77. (Rocamora 2004: 357)

Following Havel's arrest, Walters added *The Memorandum* to the bill: "One got caught up in what was happening in Czechoslovakia," he said, "In our own little way, we became supporters and champions" (Rocamora 2004: 356). The one-acts received good reviews and the opening night of *The Memorandum* was full of critics, including Kenneth Tynan. Nearly one hundred people were turned away that first night (p. 356).

Walters's "championing" of Havel's plays was utterly commendable and the Orange Tree went on to be the main London home for Havel's later work. Havel was immensely grateful for the exposure and the fact that his plays were finding success on the English-language stage; he wrote to Blackwell thanking her for her work in promoting his plays while he was in prison ("I don't need to underline how grateful I am to you" (VBA 3, 6/18/77)) and to Tom Stoppard, who had launched a very public campaign to keep his plight in the news. "Solidarity from abroad was certainly instrumental in my being released," he wrote to Stoppard:

> and it has a deeper meaning as well: it curbs the wantonness of power and it protects all the others who would—if this solidarity did not exist as a phenomenon—doubtless also become victims of that wantonness. I'm personally very happy that it was precisely you who stood up for me, because I've long respected you as a writer. (VBA 2:1, 10/4/77)

But after *Private View* and *Audience* were performed in Vienna and "were successful," Havel wrote to Blackwell:

> I have to confess that I'm not as happy about it as I expected. I realized that these two miniatures, written really on the side, basically only for the

pleasure of my friends, are the only texts of mine since 1968 that have been taken up abroad—and that seems to me a little bit off-kilter. I would have preferred if perhaps *The Beggar's Opera* would have been taken up, but no one wants it. (VBA 3, 10/24/76)

The Beggar's Opera, written in 1972, was not the right kind of play for the West, even though it was an intertextual rewriting of two Western plays: John Gay's 1728 ballad opera of the same name and, at least in reference to, Brecht's *The Threepenny Opera*. Gay's characters populate Havel's work "on Gay's theme": Macheath, Peachum, Polly, Lockit retain their names; and, as with *Private View*, he explores the idea of collusion and materialism in this transplanted London underworld. Yet, like the one-act, he posits a more profound question about why:

> people act as if they believe in nothing [. . .] Havel does not argue that people must follow moral codes. He is quite aware that people often behave badly [. . .] Rather, Havel attempts to lay the groundwork for the possibility of responsible behavior. (Pontuso 2004: 115)

The thieves all speak in the rhetoric of philosophers and social scientists, again justifying their positions through the empty fortifications of language; they require us to react in recognition, distaste, laughter, and finally compassion.

Havel was right: no one wanted it. It took 30 years for *The Beggar's Opera* to be translated (by Paul Wilson in 2001) into English and it was performed to celebrate the culmination of his political career (by the Orange Tree in 2003). Ironically, the play was performed in Communist Czechoslovakia, for one night in 1975, thanks to censorship: the functionary who signed the permission for it to be staged did not recognize Havel's name because of the government's official erasure of Havel and his work. The play was suffused with textual deliberations on censorship: as with the one-acts, the characters censor themselves and their actions. There were also metatextual and inter-textual issues of censorship: Havel was commissioned by a Prague theatre to adapt an English play that had ignited stricter censorship laws in Augustan England (Winton 1992), because it was a means to get his own work—via a pseudotranslation onto the Czech stage (Havel 1999: 4; Steiner 2001). But Havel did not choose Brecht's didactic route with his adaptation, leaving the play to its own ambiguities and open-endedness, its dialogue with the other *Operas* and its dialogic presentation of the situation from the views of various characters, mutable and fallible.

In both East and West the one-night performance on the outskirts of Prague was seen as a political act and the play as a political satire. Havel protested openly to the Czech regime:

> In the text of my play, you will find nothing that is directed against our State, its foundations or its morals. Of that, any interested agent could

easily work out for himself: I would be happy, if he is interested, to lend him a copy of the play to judge. (Havel 1999:4: 116)

Havel was not being fatuous or disingenuous (though he was likely trying to protect those involved); he did not just adapt *The Beggar's Opera* as a "political allegory" or a "political parable" for "a Czech audience who readily understood it" (Rocamora 2004: 137, 140). For Havel, the criminals were not allegories of the regime, or an Aesopian take on it, they were us. His challenge to the regime to read the play for itself is a direct call for responsible and interactive, rather than reductive, interpretation. Havel castigated the regime for believing the *Der Spiegel* journalist who had been at the performance and judged it as a political satire. He asked why they would believe the "biased interpretation of a foreign journalist" (Havel 1999:4: 119) who "connected the performance with things that it wasn't connected to, and attributed some demonstrative oppositional sense that it didn't have" (Havel 1999:4: 118).

Havel was clearly frustrated with the reductive political readings of his plays abroad; after reading the German reviews of his 1971 play *The Conspirators*, he wrote to Blackwell that the critics "did not understand the play much," concentrating instead on the political context: "half of [one] article was about how I and Pavel Kohout suffer, the other half is some babble about Dubček" and "the critics waste time on whether the play is political or not, and whether the only reason I say in my notes that it's not political is for some kind of tactical reason" (VBA 3, 12/2/74). If he denied his work was political, Westerners assumed he was doing so only to protect himself from the regime.

What was accessing him the Western stage—at a crucial time personally for him as he was being harassed, arrested, and imprisoned—was politics because it gave the plays "relevance"; it made them "acts of justice." But the political framing of the plays that gave them a market in the West via their "authenticity" also resulted in an attenuation of or disregard for their aesthetics, making them appear less artistically worthy. Havel's inquiry into language and (self)censorship made no sense if the plays were interpreted, through Western tastes and preferences, as realist political portraits of the "East" and yet it was the essential core of the plays.

The marketable translator

EDWARD: Some hero.

SUZANA: Some hero.

BERTRAM: Some hero.

LUCY: Some hero.

Largo Desolato. Translated and inserted text by TOM STOPPARD

Tom Stoppard visited Havel in Czechoslovakia in 1977. "He was glad to see me," Mr Stoppard remembered of his visit to Mr Havel, "but he also made it clear it was a little bit of a drag to see another Western sympathizer wheeled in. He felt a bit like a tourist attraction, like the Taj Mahal" (VBA 2:4, *New York Times* 1986). Havel's commodification into a "tourist attraction" indicated his unease with the "dissident" mantle, sensing it spoke to Western simplification of both his role and métier. But he respected Stoppard as a writer and Stoppard had "always felt a real affinity with Havel's point of view" and had felt, from the time he first "came across" Havel's plays in the late 1960s that "They were plays which I would have liked to write. They are very playful plays" (Shulman 1994: 110). Stoppard, who had emigrated from Czechoslovakia as a child (born Tomáš Straüssler), had expressed interest in translating one of Havel's plays, but spoke limited Czech. His name, as "one of two or three most prosperous and ubiquitously adulated playwrights at present bearing an English passport" (Tynan 1979: 46), however, ensured interest in any translation with which he might be involved.

In 1986, he "translated" Havel's *Largo Desolato* (the "literal" translator is unidentified). It opened at the Bristol Old Vic, and was well received. The same year, Marie Winn (also a child émigré from Prague, albeit one who grew up speaking Czech at home) translated the play for the Public Theater in New York, but Stoppard's version is the one published in a 1994 Faber edition, alongside English playwright, James Saunder's "English version" of another Havel play, *Asanace/Redevelopment*—Marie Winn is listed here as the "literal translator" although she was not contacted for permission to rework a translation she regarded to be a "real" translation (Winn, personal communication). Both Winn's and Stoppard's are good translations, although Stoppard includes some textual omissions and additions.

Michael Billington, writing about Stoppard's "faithful adaptation" (1987: 179) of *Largo Desolato*, noted how close in style the playwrights were: "Verbally elegant and ironically repetitive, the play may seem in some ways like an expression of a highly Stoppardian viewpoint" (p. 179). In Havel, Ken Tynan wrote, Stoppard had found "his mirror image [. . .] his *Doppelgänger*" (Tynan 1979: 120).

If Havel's plays had become innately associated with his political life, and read reductively as a result, Stoppard's political interest in Czechoslovakia from 1977 onwards and his interest in Havel was seen as a politicization of Stoppard as a playwright. Prior to this, Stoppard's plays were read as "apolitical" (Billington 1987: 180), going against the political engagement of his English theatrical contemporaries: "he put more trust in questioning than in attempts to create a fixed ideological position" (Bull 2001: 137). Like Havel's plays, his plays provided no answers or any didactic political stance, and the use of language to define and misdefine the human was central to his work (and particularly successful in his 1972 play, *Jumpers,* which, like *Largo Desolato* centered on a moral philosopher).

To British critics, 1977 was a turning point in Stoppard's career, from an apolitical absurdist to a politicized one: "When he met Czech playwright, Václav Havel, in 1977, two strands of his literary heritage—the British absurdist (ahistorical) strand and the Eastern European (politicized) strand—merged in his writing" (Kelly 2001: 17). Though his 1977 plays, *Every Good Boy Deserves Favour* and *Professional Foul* (dedicated to Havel) shared the humor of his earlier plays, they were seen as "bleaker" because of their political settings (in the Soviet Union and Czechoslovakia) and thus were connected to the perceived political absurdist tradition of Havel, a tradition "that had a directly political intent, albeit one usually and necessarily disguised" (Bull 2001: 144). Among critics, there was a sense that this new Stoppard, for the first time publicly outspoken about politics (in his protests against the Czechoslovak government's mistreatment of Havel and others), had gained a more vital perspective in his plays, no longer just ludic entertainments. As Billington wrote, Stoppard had:

> gradually moved from stylish, apolitical disengagement towards an active involvement with current issues [. . .] I believe this has made him a richer, better writer in that his wit, intelligence and ingenuity are now enlisted on the side of the preservation of basic freedoms, a profound hatred of tyranny and a belief in the dignity of the individual. (1987: 180)

Tynan, in a *New Yorker* profile of Stoppard in 1978, presented the meeting with Havel as a damascene moment: that Havel was the "mirror image" of Stoppard, living a life that Stoppard might have had to, if his parents had stayed in Czechoslovakia; "history has lately been forcing Stoppard into the area of commitment" (Tynan 1979: 56). For Tynan, who advocated committed theatre, this was an improvement—he is quietly arch about the uses or purpose of Stoppard's prepolitical plays in the article. Havel differed from the early Stoppard in that he "gave Absurdism a human face, together with a socially critical purpose" (p. 76)—Tynan paraphrasing Aleksandr Dubček's famous aphorism about "Socialism with a human face."

In an interview in 1974, Stoppard said he had no "revolutionary designs" and if you wanted to change society, "you could hardly do worse than write a play about it" (Gussow 1994: 75), but he would undoubtedly write plays from the late 1970s onwards that directly dealt with dissent and revolution, including some directly involving the Czech situation—*Cahoot's Macbeth* and, more recently, the critical and commercial hit, *Rock n'Roll*—a play based quite largely on Havel's experience and his plays (with noticeable riffs on Havel's Vaněk plays). But, in talking about Havel, he stressed that he was not just concerned with Havel "the Chartist but with the author of *The Garden Party, The Memorandum, The Audience* and other plays" (Stoppard 1978: 9). He denied that it was the political events surrounding Havel that led to his interest and emphasized the stylistic kinship: "In fact I've had a feeling of kinship with Havel for a hell of a long time," he said, "When I read *The Garden Party* about twelve years ago [1969], I just thought he was somebody who wrote like I would like to write (Gollob and Roper 1994: 155).

Striking about the criticism on what could be called the "Havel effect" on Stoppard is the assumption that Havel's theatre (and East European absurdism) was political and this is what drove Stoppard to become more political or committed a playwright (and a more meaningful one). In this context, his translation of *Largo Desolato*, a play ostensibly about a dissident, made sense, given both his vociferous public support of the Chartists and his own "dissident" plays. But it also meant that Havel's play would likely be read in the same narrow vein: "This is totalitarianism in sonata form," one critic wrote, "The Czechs arguably know more about tyranny than other civilized people" (Rocamora 2004: 361); another critic sat in his hotel after the play "cheering Havel on to take his next prison sentence on the chin" (p. 255).

As the title of the play suggests, *Largo Desolato* has musical foundations that come through in the structure and use of recapitulation, linguistic repetitions, and variations (it is the title of the sixth movement of Alban Berg's *Lyric Suite*, written about his illicit love for Hanna Fuchs, the Czech novelist Franz Werfel's sister). It suggests the gradual descent into personal crisis, made up of the larger issues in life—here, he is the dissident Leopold Kopřiva's obsessive fear of being arrested for "intellectual hooliganism"—but also the mundane and often self-imposed fears and injuries building up, through repetition. Kopřiva is in trouble with the police because of his essay, *Ontology of the Human Self*, but it is precisely his inability to figure out the ontological basis of his real life that becomes problematic and funny. Those around him want him to be a certain thing: the dissident hero and philosopher but in his daily life, he is neither—he wants food, sex, to be able to pee properly. Two unnamed men—shades of Kafka—finally arrive:

FELLOW 1:   In short if you sign us a brief declaration saying that you aren't Doctor Leopold Kopřiva, the author of the composition in question, the whole thing will be considered invalid and all previous charges will be dropped—

LEOPOLD: If I understand you correctly, you want me to declare that I am not I —

FELLOW 1:   That may be a suitable interpretation for a philosopher; still it's legally absurd. It's not, for goodness sake, a matter of you declaring that you aren't you, but a matter of you declaring that you're not identical to the author of the thing— (Havel 1986a, translation by Winn, 47–8)

As in Kafka, this is a world of interpretation and interpretation is what Kopřiva, as a moral philosopher, does as a living. The problem is, as with

Kafka's protagonists, the hermeneutic barriers in the world around him keep shifting. By the end of the play, the men arrive once more and tell him there has been a "postponement" because, Kopřiva guesses, he is no longer himself, aping the language of his friends, and his friends and those around him aping the language of each other. Although he can write about love, metaphysically, he cannot talk about it in person because language he does not want to speak "kitschily"; the language of love so overused that it can no longer be genuine. Kopřiva unearths a truth, but at the same time uses it as an excuse not to talk about love, so he can just sleep with his lover. At a crescendo, at the end of the penultimate scene, he imagines all those who've visited him in the apartment, accusing him with the language they've used earlier, wittily and scarily, repeating excerpts of what they've said and others have said at increasing speed (contrapuntally to the almost redemption in the last scene): everyone accuses him of not being who they think he is or who they want him to be, an accusation he levels at himself all the time, knowing his personal fallibilities fail to sync with his public persona. It is literally his guilt speaking:

ZUZANA:	You're a chicken!
OLBRAM:	It's the opinion of ordinary people—
OLDA:	Did you sign anything?
LADA:	You're sick and tired of me and now you want to get rid of me in some clever way—
LADA II:	You're a chicken!
LUCY:	It's the opinion of ordinary people
ZUZANA:	Were you scared?
OLBRAM:	You're sick and tired of me and now you want to get rid of me in some clever way—
OLDA:	You're a chicken!
ZUZANA:	It's the opinion of ordinary people—
LADA II:	Did you sign anything?

(*The pace of these retorts is progressively faster; Leopold keeps turning in confusion from one to another, then he cries out:*)

LEOPOLD:	Enough!

At least, that is about a third of it (the rest is in Marie Winn's translation); once again, Havel uses an almost unbearable repetitive structure, but the pace and confusion of it replicate the workings of Kopřiva's mind, as it bends under the pressure from friends and strangers who want something from him. The slapstick element—not only of the sound and pace—but also of characters, such as the paper mill workers, Lada I and II, articulating the words of Kopřiva's wife and lover, carries the darker more tragic sense of the emptiness of phrases we think define us, or others.

Havel, in author's notes smuggled out of Czechoslovakia (as the script was), pled for two things from producers of the play: not to omit or add anything from the script and secondly, not to concretely set the play in Communist Czechoslovakia or tie it closely with Havel's own experiences. The two elements were linked: Havel felt that in the past theatres had cut or added material in the plays to get to a political message, the prolixity of the plays seemed to get in the way. What Havel wanted to be understood was that the prolixity and boredom were part of the music of the play:

> Everything there has its own purpose—from the viewpoint of structure, rhythm, atmospheric variety, timing, intricacies and gradations of meaning [. . .] I always try to put together a play as a coherent time-space entity (in the manner of a musical composition) and it is my experience that any disturbance in this composition however well-intended (provoked, for example, by a desire to shorten or speed up a boring passage), will effectively turn against the musical ebb and flow of the whole. (Havel 1986b)

Havel conceived of the play as a "sort of 'musical reflection' on the burden of human existence" and the way in which he used language was meant to reflect that, in its banality as well as excitement, and certainly in its humor. The "irony" and "mysterious poetry" of the language, he believed lay in the "curious tension between 'high-class' "educated" even some sort of descriptive-analytic language on the one hand, and the triviality, or banality of the themes, situations and problems discussed by means of this language on the other hand." He felt the "entire existential ambiguity, tension and comedy often stands or falls precisely on the use of this manner of speaking and the imbalance between it and what's really going on." So, both the language itself—its register and use—and they way in which it is counterpointed via the characters, in terms of pace and repetitions—show the mystifications and paradoxes of language and its inability or/and perhaps overability to encapsulate the human.

The linguistic motifs of the characters, repeated in variations through the play open up the ambiguities of the characters themselves, giving the play its "paradoxical quality and ambiguity of meaning." For Havel, it means none of the characters are heroes or villains; he is decidedly not portraying a brave, broken-down dissident versus the evil secret police and warned potential producers that if they made "moral judgements" about the characters it would make them "one-dimensional stereotypes" and the play "a moralistic bore." The protagonist, "Leopold—is in his way a hero and at the same time a coward; he is ever honest, and at the same time he is ever cheating just a bit"; his potential jailers are in a sense "Devil's Envoys, but at the same time they are basically decent, unaggressive, polite, 'normal' people"; Leopold's friend, Olbram is both his "conscience" and a "pain in the ass"—"after all, isn't our conscience often that very thing we would most like to kick in the ass?" All of the characters were "tragic and at the same time, in their own way, comical" (Havel 1986b).

From the notes, it is evident that Havel worried about his plays being produced as "mere documents of a certain special environment or social system"; if they were seen as such, "I would consider it as my failure as a writer." If a translator, director, or dramaturg read the play as purely auto-biographical, about a given context, the ambiguities would be lost and it would turn into a "moralistic bore" and he spelled it out clearly:

> I believe that any attempts by the play's producers to localize it more clearly in the environment from which it originated, and any reminders or emphases on any sort of Czech, Communist, or even "dissident" realities or aspects would greatly harm the play. This would drag it down to the level of being a document about something, albeit interesting, that simply does not affect those playgoers coming out of a different environment. (Havel 1986b)

Havel spoke from experience; the problem was not that foreign producers wanted to domesticate and localize the plays into their own cultural context or idiom, but that they were intent on keeping it in the perceived context of Eastern Europe: a place of the heroic dissident and the evil secret police. Not that there wasn't heroism and villainy, but that that was not the whole story; for Havel, making heroes and villains was the easy way out. Leopold Kopřiva was the embodiment of the corrosive effects of such expectations, not only on the "dissident" but also on people wanting him to be their voice, rather than facing up to their own human mixture of heroism and villainy. The play, he wrote, "both understands and accuses us all. It is not an animated thesis, but an attempt to paint a picture that makes no claims but simply wants to unsettle the playgoer's soul":

> Therefore I beg those putting on the play to avoid as much as possible all concretizing references in this direction: not for tactical or safety reasons (it can't hurt me any more), but for artistic reasons and reasons of principle. Anything that might allow the playgoer to hope that the play does not refer to him personally would go directly counter to its meaning. (Havel 1986b)

Havel, stuck in Czechoslovakia and under surveillance by the police, could only intervene on paper via suggestion and pleas to potential Western producers, but his worry was clear: that any reductive and purely political readings of the play by those choosing to produce it would inherently hobble the effect of the play. In some ways, Stoppard was a guarantee, as he clearly felt an affinity to Havel's "playful plays" rather than their political value. His "translation" is sensitive to the poetics of the play, does not wildly differ from the language style, and largely retains the structure, style and punctuation of Havel's text, although the names are anglicized ("Kopřiva" is literally translated into "Nettles").

The one major rewriting in the play occurs at the end of the penultimate scene. The confused chorus of all the characters, who embody each other by repeating each other's phrases (mentioned above), is substantially cut. In addition, rather than all of them speaking each other's phrases, only some change phrases—it is a much more subtle and less blatant confusion. Stoppard adds some new material (the "Some hero" repetition), and it does not follow Havel's text:

SUZANA:	What is there to consider, for goodness sake.
BERTRAM:	And how are things between you and Suzana?
LUCY:	You've had enough of me and now you want to get shot of me—
EDWARD:	Did you sign anything?
FIRST SIDNEY:	We've only taken the liberty of giving you our opinion—
SECOND SIDNEY:	The opinion of ordinary people—
FIRST SIDNEY:	Lots of ordinary people—
EDWARD:	Some hero.
SUZANA:	Some hero.
BERTRAM:	Some hero.
LUCY:	Some hero.
FIRST SIDNEY:	You've had enough of me and now you want to get shot of me.
SECOND SIDNEY:	Some hero.
FIRST SIDNEY:	Did you sign anything?
LEOPOLD:	(Shouting) GET OUT!

(Havel 1994: 50)

ZUZANA:	Jsi bačkora!
OLBRAM:	Je to názor obyčejných lidí -
OLDA:	Podepsals jim něco?
LADA:	Nabažil ses mě, a teď se mě chceš nějak šikovně zbavit —
LADA II:	Jsi bačkora!
LUCY:	Je to názor obyčejných lidí—
ZUZANA:	Bylo ti úzko?
OLBRAM:	Nabažil ses mě, a teď se mě chceš nějak šikovně zbavit —

OLDA: Jsi bačkora!

ZUZANA: Je to názor obyčejných lidí—

LADA II: Podepsals jim něco?

(*Sled těchto replik se postupně zrychloval; Leopold se stále zmateněji obracel z jednoho na druhého, teď náhle vykřikne*)

LEOPOLD: Dost!

(Havel 1999:2: 746)

Stoppard's shortening of this section (it is about two-thirds longer in the Czech) and his recalibration of the repetitions dilutes the effect of the section; it is not as fast-paced (and the stage direction is mostly deleted which states that the replies should quicken and he should turn from one to another) and fails to replicate the confusion of identities and the clear humor and slight terror of the characters articulating each other's lines. His addition of the repeated line "Some hero" makes sense within the play but it is a much more direct articulation of what the scene and the play is about, that is, Leopold does not see himself as a hero and is constrained by that identity. Rather than letting the audience work that out and having the effect *affect* them, it directly tells them.

Catastrophe

Havel described Leopold as a "real caricature" of his situation (Havel 1990: 65) as a dissident. Ten years earlier, he had written to Blackwell saying he was thankful for some manual employment because "the idle life of a prominent dissident or prominent enemy of the state or whatever I am, is getting on my nerves a bit [. . .] I have an urge to be among normal people and live a normal life again for a moment" (VBA 3, 1/27/74). When Marie Winn interviewed Havel in 1987, he told her that he did not "like the word 'dissident' [. . .] It makes it seem like a special profession. I'm simply a playwright." He also spoke about waking up depressed in the mornings burdened by the pressure of both identities: "I'll despair that I can't write [. . .] I'll keep feeling wretchedly oppressed by all the expectations people heap on me" (Winn 1987). But he insisted that he was not the "deranged Dr. Kopřiva"; "if I was as badly off as Kopřiva, I couldn't have written a thing, certainly not with any ironic distance, so in fact the very existence of this play argues against it being autobiographical" (Havel 1990: 65). Afraid, though, that it would be read autobiographically, he had second thoughts about writing it, but felt he could not "censor" his experiences to avoid reductive readings (p. 64), even if it meant people would assume Leopold was him and feel "sorry that I'm in such terrible shape" (p. 65). Despite being out of prison when he wrote it, having "had a bad case of nerves" (p. 63), and writing it in "a feverish haste, in a bit of a trance" (p. 64), worried about a police search that might take the manuscript from him, Havel's first question to Winn when she arrived at his bugged apartment, even before he said hello, was about the New York production of *Largo Desolato*. "Did they laugh?" he asked (Winn, personal communication).

Winn did not tell Havel how serious the production had been, with "pauses as forbidding as Soviet tanks" (Rich 1986). Hindered by a director, Richard Foreman, who "wasn't crazy about the play" and was bored in rehearsals (Schechner and Foreman 1987: 130), the Public Theater production conveyed a concrete perception of Havel as a dissident, even commodified him as one. Despite his warning in his author's note that the play should not be seen as a "political document" because this would estrange the audience from the play and attenuate the effect it would have on them, it inevitably was.

Samuel Beckett wrote a play, *Catastrophe*, for Havel in 1982 (who was still, then, imprisoned) in which a "Director" enforces his will on the "Protagonist" standing on a plinth. The Director is accompanied by his Assistant who notes down exactly what should happen to the Protagonist, undressing him as required. The short play ends with the lights going down and the Protagonist, silent throughout the play, raising his head. Canned applause suddenly dies down. In *Catastrophe*, Beckett "fused the tyrannies of theatre and state" (Abbott 1988: 87); the connection between the two, H. Porter Abbott argues, "is rooted with the aesthetic will that seeks to dominate the human through formal representation" (p. 87). Rather than being a superficial tale of political repression it posits a connection between the "discursive violence" of the imposition of interpretation with that of the imposition of political doxa (Hill 1997: 910). The canned applause, Craig Owens argues, "exposes the spectators' performance as a performance that helps constitute the text of the play and the experience of theater-going" (Owens 2003: 78); reminding the audience of their responsibility and collusion engages with Havel's own dramatic aims.

The image of the Protagonist on the plinth being molded and moved for the performance is suggestive of the absolutist readings being imposed on Havel and his plays and thus the silencing and censorship of his aesthetics. *Catastrophe* displays quite an affinity with Havelian ideas on theatre, Beckett initiating a real dialogue with Havel's work that attempts to release it from the political bind. When the Assistant, looking at the shivering Protagonist, asks, "What about a little . . . little . . . gag?" the Director snaps back at her, "For God's sake! This craze for explication! Every i dotted to death! Little gag! For God's sake!" (Beckett 1990: 459). The Director's repetition of "God" and his use of exclamation marks underline his denial of "explications" other than his own. The use of the lower case "i" conveys his sense of the inferiority of his Assistant's and others' identity. The Assistant's speech is literally (as a text) "dotted to death" in her use of Vaněkian ellipses, and the request for the "little . . . gag" a sense of his/her fear of putting forward a different interpretation. "Gag" carries a double meaning here, both of a "gag" to silence the Protagonist and as a joke; one oppressive, the other subversive—the Director rejects both but the "gag" has been introduced, indicatory of Beckett's bleak humor. Havel had written an essay in 1963 entitled "Anatomy of a Gag"/"Anatomie gagu" in which, using the films of Charlie Chaplin and formalist theory, he argued that the "gag," a meeting of the comic and the absurd, was a method by which we could "defamiliarize" ourselves from the "automatism" of human existence (Havel 1999:4: 594). Such gags make us laugh, but they should also shake us from torpor. Beckett's dark take on this, the idea that a gag has a place in a world that potentially gags us, at least suggests the possibility of a gag's power in a discursive world of censorship. Finally, the Protagonist who has been the Director's object looks up and at the audience at the end of the play, "*Praises his head, fixes the audience. The applause falters, dies*" (Beckett 1990: 451). His gaze challenges them to *see* him as something other than the object he has become.[1]

---

[1] Havel wrote a play for Beckett, *Chyba/Mistake*, after coming out of prison in 1983, with another silent protagonist, Xiboj, who is being ordered about by King and his prisoner associates, but won't answer. He only looks at them with a "confused smile"; finally one of them wonders if he simply does not understand them because he speaks another language, that he is "some Hungarian or something . . ." (Havel 1999:2: 684). "His mistake," King says; the curtain falls as they beat him up. Replete with prison slang and the claustrophobic sense of Havel's recent prison, the play, at its heart, is still about language and effect on the prisoners' mentality, itself a reflection of the society outside. Xiboj's difference, his otherness and foreignness, and the lack of translation, makes him a victim, albeit a smiling one.

Conclusion: *Leaving*

Use your head, can't you, use your head, you're
on earth, there's no cure for that!
SAMUEL BECKETT, Endgame

Havel's most recent, and last, play, *Odcházení/Leaving* (2007) was his first post-Presidential one, though he had written a version of it in 1989 before the Velvet Revolution, called *King Lear* (Keane 2000: 147). It follows the post-Presidential life of Vilém Reiger whose sanctity in the Presidential villa is being threatened by his arch-rival, Vlastík Klein. An intertextual reading of three plays written under or subject to conditions of censorship at different times and in different places: Shakespeare's *King Lear*, Chekhov's *The Cherry Orchard*, and Beckett's *Endgame* (facing censorship conditions in Ireland and England), *Leaving* contends with the censorship of the market economy. Rieger's interview with the tabloid, *Fuj*, full of sociopolitical blather is turned into a scandalous expose of his sex life; further articles come out before events have even happened. In the Czech version, the hack journalist and photographer for *Fuj* have the English-language names of two Kennedys: Jack and Bob (Jack is changed to "Dick" in Wilson's translation, a reference perhaps to a trickier American president and *Fuj*, the Czech for "yuk" or "ugh" to *The Keyhole*).

Reiger, like his Cold War counterparts Huml and Leopold, censors himself, able only to speak in the bland rhetoric of the globalized politician, something that Klein, too, has adopted and which superficially conceals his corrupted regime of bribes and brothels. At one point, when the two are in dialogue, the "Voice" of the author chimes in (the recorded "Voice" was played by Havel, in English, in the English production at the Orange Tree and by F. Murray Abraham at the Wilma Theater, Philadelphia):

I have the feeling that this dialogue, as important as it is to the play, might also be somewhat boring. But it's not entirely my fault. Of course, I have an influence on my own play, undeniably, but the main thing is that, when I write, I try to serve the logic of the thing itself, which seems more important than my own feelings. (Havel 2008: 31)

With humor and modesty, the Voice announces its authorial presence and authority but sees the limits of it too; the Voice knows the language is neither poetic nor interesting but it is true to the logic of the characters. The language these politicians use is deliberately bland and vapid because of what it hides; it becomes an empty semiosis of applied power. The Voice speaks to an audience, especially abroad, who might just think, as Charles Isherwood did that the "high toned rhetoric [. . .] followed by more generic sloganeering" makes it a "mostly leaden satire of contemporary politics" (Isherwood 2010), without thinking about how the Voice self-reflexively questions the authorial use of that language in order to make the audience think about the mechanisms of its use.

Isherwood snorted at the "Voice" in his review, writing that the play was "tricked out with a meta-theatrical conceit that might not have been fresh even when Mr. Havel put down his playwriting pen in 1989 to become a leader of the Velvet Revolution" (Isherwood 2010). Yet, the introduction of the Voice is clearly a response from Havel to the misreadings of his plays as just political satires; but it is not a demagogic or even censoring Voice, but a questioning of the authorial voice and its ability to control meaning. At the same time, the authorial voice does have an epistemological inside track on the language and aims of the play and of Havel's dramatic aesthetics. Though always undercutting its own authority—"I'm always forgetting who's on stage . . ." (Havel 2008: 34)—it is a direct voice to the audience, and directly engages them. At one point, when the busy stage, deliberately full of "the entrances and the exits and the re-entrances" (that are suggestive of life and death), empties, the Voice waits to see what the audience will do. "I also love an empty stage," the Voice finally says:

> The question is, how long can it remain empty? In my observation, nothing much happens at first: the audience is simply waiting. Next they start to become restless because they don't know what's going on. Then they begin muttering and mumbling, because they're starting to suspect that something has gone wrong [. . .] Finally, people start leaving, or they laugh. But the main point is that an empty stage has its own special content, its own message. It is the emptiness of the world, concentrated into a few minutes. An emptiness so empty that it remains silent, even about itself. (Havel 2008: 56–7)

Havel deliberately asks the audience to think about the stage and its meaning, one that they personally have to interpret, because although the "message" of the stage is, for the Voice, "the emptiness of the world" that emptiness "remains silent, even about itself." In the production I saw twice (at the Wilma Theater), the audience did start to murmur quietly and fidget, before the Voice came on, clearly wondering whether something had gone wrong, and then began to laugh as the Voice spoke. The lack of action, the lack of words, created a dialogue.

And he retains that dialogue even as the "real" author: in an "Author's Note" for the UK Faber & Faber edition of the play, Havel directly addresses potential producers and actors. He asks them to act it out in "a civil manner" without tricks or exaggerations; it "should not be tarted up" (Havel 2008). He also "suggests that not a lot of cuts be made to the text, especially not random cuts," reiterating his private instructions to translators and theatres for *Largo Desolato*. Havel writes that he asks for this not because of any:

> blind attachment to his own words, but from practical experience: cuts can easily tear the web of meaning that holds the play together, or can disrupt the play's own rhythm, usually resulting—paradoxically—in greater boredom than might be the case if the text were left as it is. (Havel 2008)

The emphasis on boredom is central because of the lack of patience, in English translation, for the expansiveness and length of his language, and the misapprehension about its function. Havel's call to the potential producers of the play is complemented by the Voice within the play which is not a postmodern "trick" but one that emphasizes the complexity of the linguistic aesthetic in order to retain a heteroglossic element that enables the audience to interpret the language as they will. The Voice's comment about the "empty stage" is itself intricately wrought, with Havel using repeated phrases, words, alliteration, and assonance to sound out and euphonize the thoughts within:

> **Prázdnou scénu** mám taky rád. Otázka je, jak dlouho může být **prázdná.** Pozoroval jsem, že **v první fázi** se obvykle neděje nic. **Lidé** čekají. **V druhé fázi** zneklidní, protože nevědí, co se stalo. **V třetí fázi začnou** lehce hučet, protože v tom spatřují jakousi bezradnost divadla . . . No a **ve čtvrté fázi začnou lidé odcházet** nebo se smát. Hlavně však: **prázdná scéna** má svůj zvláštní obsah. Své **poselství.** Je to do několika minut zhuštěná **prázdnota** světa. **Prázdnota** do té míry **prázdná,** že mlčí i o sobě samé. (Havel 2007b: 746)

> **An empty stage,** I also love. The question is, how long can it be **empty?** I have noticed that **in the first phase** usually nothing much happens. **People** wait. **In the second phase,** they become restless because they don't know what's happening. **In the third phase,** they **start** to quietly murmur, because they see some sort of mishap by the theatre [. . .] Well and **in the fourth phase, people start** to leave or laugh. The main thing is: **an empty stage** has its own special content. Its message. It in those several minutes that the **emptiness** of the world is condensed. An **emptiness** so **empty** that it keeps silent, even about itself (my translation).

My translation is deliberately unpolished to give some sense of word order in the Czech, but it shows Havel's use of repeated motifs and phrases—he does not only speak about emptiness but it rings through the passage (questioning whether emptiness is empty and what kind of emptiness might be or whether that sense of emptiness is mutable); he adopts a pseudoscientific voice in the structured repetition of "phase," deliberately mixing it with the colloquial "No a" when introducing "the fourth phase." He does not speak of the "audience" or "they," but of "people," thus emphasizing the individuality and humanness of the entity he addresses. The punctuation is important too: in placing "People wait" in its own sentence, he retains the significant pause, imitating that wait; similarly, he emphasizes "Its message" by keeping it in its own sentence. Some elements are untranslatable; the long vowels in four of the five words in the first sentence lend it a deliberative and ruminative tone as does the repeated use of the plosive "p": "prázdná," "pozorval," "první," "poselství," "prázdnota." The sonic effect of the passage scaffolds the "message"; the emphasis on certain repeated words and sounds suggesting meaning, its mutability, and ambiguities.

"Sadly," Isherwood wrote, "the uncertainty voiced by this fictionalized authorial ego is reflected in the play's meandering construction and lack of trenchant point" (Isherwood 2010), but the uncertainty is the trenchant point and the tight construction of the language enables that uncertainty and heteroglossia to remain. Havel is, thus, not telling the "people" what to think but inciting them to think for themselves, to discover what that emptiness is in their own terms. Speakability is important—*Leaving*'s translator, Paul Wilson, emphasizes the collaborative effort in rendering the play into speakable English in his "Translator's Acknowledgement" in the Faber edition, working with the Orange Tree in rehearsals and acknowledging Tom Stoppard's advice and his "many helpful suggestions, particularly in places where I was still clinging too tightly to the original" (Havel 2008). However, the original language does have its own inner coherence that opens it out to multivalency and dialogue, while openly revealing its mechanism in doing so. Collaborators, unable to speak the source language, may know what sounds best domestically, but this may also diminish or attenuate the very careful intricacy of the play's linguistic and epistemological aims.

"[I]s it not the primordial undecidability of language as such, the heteroglossia feared by censors," Michael Holquist asks, "that is also the source of the translator's anxiety? (Holquist 1994: 18). The fear of ambiguity in meaning, of having to interpret the text hermeneutically can be at the heart of translation, but it can also be the strength of the translator. Translators are the first readers and the initial hermeneutic interpreters of translated texts and, as such, provide a model for an active dialogue with a play or text, often being self-aware of the way in which they read as they open and close avenues in the ambiguities of the play. In working so closely with it, they can come to intimate understanding with the aesthetics and form of the play, which are central to the meaning of it. This style may not fit domestic norms, but that could, and perhaps should, be viewed as a valuable thing: we should be challenged by our expectations.

We, the audience and the readers, are the upholders of cultural norms; although such norms may be enforced at given points even in free, democratic cultures by various institutions (in the McCarthy era, for instance, or under the Lord Chamberlain's aegis), ultimately norms are upheld and agreed to by individuals. Havel's figure of the greengrocer taking down the Marxist sign in his shop window reflects our own responsibilities in questioning the doxa of those norms. Translations help because, as Ken Tynan suggested, they are "infusions" of difference: different aesthetics, worldviews, and ways of speaking. If the "foreign often attracts the censor's hostility" (Ní Chuilleanáin, Ó Cuilleanáin, and Parris 2008 13), it can also attract ours; our rejection or repackaging of texts that seem faulty, strange, or uncomfortable often conceals an anxiety about our own worldview. Being aware of our own agendas in reading and recognizing our own propensity to want to fully understand and fully interpret foreign texts without allowing ambiguity or mystery, is central to reading actively and responsibly.

Havel's theory that the play is an event that should disquiet the soul, something that will "tantalize and irritate us" (Havel 170–1) and demand that we not "leave with this, or any other, exclusive conceptually clarified awareness of its "meaning" (pp. 170–1) forces us to question the act of interpretation itself. We should not come out of the theatre applauding ourselves for seeing a worthy play by a dissident about life over there; in doing so, we censor our own experiences and our own responsibilities. Havel's plays demand of us to think about censorship as it emanates from us and present the possibilities, even in this fallible, human world, of interrogating our denials, collaborations, and propensity for the unquestioning life.

The ossification of notions of censorship into the "crude axiology" of "an absolute choice between prohibition and freedom" (Holquist 1994: 16) in the end serves to deflect those responsibilities and our actions as readers and thinkers. For Holquist, as for Coetzee, the effective antidote to censorship lies in us as readers of fiction and reality who do not demand or consume absolutist interpretations that satisfy rather than provoke. Holquist argues that the traditional model of censorship, what Coetzee called the "David-and-Goliath" model, does not serve the "complexity of censorship, in which relations between censors and victims appear dynamic and multidirectional" (p. 16); an understanding of the importance of individual human actions at given times and given places (that are often mutable), reveals different, often concurrent, methods of censorship. "Censorship *is*," Michael Holquist writes, "One can only discriminate among its more and less repressive effects" (Holquist 1994: 16).

"When the play ends," the Voice in *Leaving* says, "it's all over. The play's world ends when the play ends, and all that remains is our impression, our interpretation, our memories, our joy, or our boredom" (Havel 2008: 78). For Havel, the act of being in the theatre is a dialogic one: the play is not just the playwright's, or the director's, or the translator's, or the actors', it is also ours. The ephemeral nature of the experience, its lack of a posteriori tangibility, is suggestive of life and our attempts to find signification. Our constant constructions and reconstructions of meaning shape reality, ours and others. The Voice refuses to definitively end the play because it hasn't made up its mind about how it will do so; ultimately that knowledge of final, absolute meaning—the currency of the censor—is ineffable, an escape artist. "I don't want to hold things up while I make up my mind," the Voice says, "So, I'll leave the matter open. I won't be the first author, nor the last, who left things open-ended, not because he intended to, but simply because he didn't know what else to do" (Havel 2008: 78).

BIBLIOGRAPHY

Aaltonen, Sirkuu. 2000. *Time Sharing on Stage. Drama Translation in Theatre and Society*. Clevedon: Multilingual Matters.

Abbott, H. Porter. 1988. "Tyranny and Theatricality: The Example of Samuel Beckett." *Theatre Journal*, 40.1: 77–87.

Baer, Brian James. 2011. "Translating Queer Texts in Soviet Russia: A Case Study in Productive Censorship." *Translation Studies*, 4.1: 21–40.

Barnes, Clive. 1968a. "Theater: 'Hair'—It's Fresh and Frank." *New York Times*, April 30, 40.

—. 1968b. "Public Theater Presents Memorandum." *New York Times*, May 6. http://query.nytimes.com/mem/archive/pdf?res=F00616F73F5F127A93C4A917 8ED85F4C8685F9.

Bassnett, Susan. 1998. "Still Trapped in the Labyrinth: Further Reflections on Theatre and Translation." In *Constructing Cultures: Essays on Literary Translation*, edited by Susan Bassnett and André Lefevere, 90–108. Clevedon: Multilingual Matters.

Beckett, Samuel. 1990. *The Complete Dramatic Works*. London: Faber and Faber.

Bender, Marilyn. 1968. "Topless—And no Bottoms Either." *New York Times*, April 28, D1.

Beneš, Hana. 1972. "Czech Literature in the 1968 Crisis." *The Bulletin of the Midwest Modern Language Association*, 5.2: 97–114.

Billiani, Francesca. 2007. "Accessing Boundaries—Censorship and Translation. An Introduction." In *Modes of Censorship and Translation: National Contexts and Diverse Media*, edited by Francesca Billiani, 1–25. Manchester: St. Jerome.

Billington, Michael. 1987. *Stoppard. The Playwright*. London and New York: Methuen.

Blackwell, Vera. *Archive. Bakhmeteff Collection*. New York: Columbia University.

Bogic, Anna. 2011. "Why Philosophy Went Missing: Understanding the English Version of Simone de Beauvoir's *Le deuxième sexe*." In *Translating Women*, edited by Luise von Flotow, 151–66. Ottawa: University of Ottawa Press.

Boswell, Laurence. 1996. "The Director as Translator." In *Stages of Translation: Translators on Translating for the Stage*, edited by David Johnston, 145–52. Bath: Absolute Classics.

Brantley, Ben. 2011. "Political Theater, Brought to you by the Politically Powerless." *New York Times*, January 7, C5.

Bren, Paulina. 2010. *The Greengrocer and His TV: The Culture of Communism after the 1968 Prague Spring*. Ithaca: Cornell University Press.

Brodsky, Joseph. 1987. *Less than One. Selected Essays*. Harmondsworth: Penguin.

Bull, John. 2001. "Tom Stoppard and Politics." In *The Cambridge Companion to Tom Stoppard*, edited by Katherine E. Kelly, 136–53. Cambridge: Cambridge University Press.

Burian, Jarka M. 1992. "Review: *The Garden Party, The Memorandum, The Beggar's Opera, Largo Desolato, Slum Clearance.*" *Theatre Journal*, 44.3: 407–10.

—. 2000. *Modern Czech Theatre: Reflector and Conscience of a Nation*. Iowa City: University of Iowa Press.

—. 2002. *Leading Creators of Twentieth-Century Czech Theatre*. New York: Routledge.

Burt, Richard. 1994. "Introduction: The 'New' Censorship." In *Administration of Aesthetics: Censorship, Political Criticism, and the Public Sphere*, edited by Richard Burt, xi–xxix. Minneapolis: University of Minnesota Press.

Calder, John. 2002. "Martin Esslin: Illuminating Writer and Radio Drama Producer." *The Guardian*, February 7. www.guardian.co.uk/news/2002/feb/27/guardianobituaries.booksobituaries.

Callow, Simon. 2000. *Love Is Where It Falls: An Account of a Passionate Friendship*. London: Penguin.

Chamberlain, Lori. 1992. "Gender and the Metaphorics of Translation." *Rethinking Translation: Discourse, Subjectivity, Ideology*, edited by Lawrence Venuti, 57–74. London and New York: Routledge.

Clark, Noel. 1996. "Translating for the Love of It." In *Stages of Translation: Translators on Translating for the Stage*, edited by David Johnston, 23–34. Bath: Absolute Classics.

Coetzee, J. M. 1996. *Giving Offense. Essays on Censorship*. Chicago and London: University of Chicago Press.

Cronin, Michael. 2000. *Across the Lines. Travel, Language, Translation*. Cork: Cork University Press.

—. 2003. *Translation and Globalization*. New York: Routledge.

Donellan, Declan. 1996. "The Translatable and the Untranslatable: In Conversation with David Johnston." In *Stages of Translation: Translators on Translating for the Stage*, edited by David Johnston, 75–80. Bath: Absolute Classics.

Epstein, Helen. 1996. *Joe Papp. An American Life*. New York: Da Capo Press.

Espasa, Eva. 2000. "Performability in Translation: Speakability? Playability? Or just Saleability?" In *Moving Target. Theatre Translation and Cultural Relocation*, edited by Terry Hale and Carole-Anne Upton, 49–62. Manchester: St Jerome.

Esslin, Martin. 2004. *The Theatre of the Absurd*, 3rd edn. New York: Vintage.

Farrel, Joseph. 1996. "Servant of Many Masters." In *Stages of Translation: Translators on Translating for the Stage*, edited by David Johnston, 45–55. Bath: Absolute Classics.

Friel, Brian. 1999. *Brian Friel. Essays, Diaries, Interviews: 1964–1999*, edited by Christopher Murray. London: Faber and Faber.

Funke, Lewis. 1969. "Lincoln Repertory: Busy and Collected." *New York Times*, December 9, 66.

Gelb, Arthur. 1956. "Wanted Intellects. Producer Myerberg Seeks 70,000 of Them to Support Plotless Play." *New York Times*. April 15. http://select.nytimes.com/gst/abstract.html?res=F10B10F63459137A93C7A8178FD85F428585F9&scp=1&sq=gelb%20wanted%20intellects&st=cse

Gener, Randy. 2009. "Fomenting a Denim Revolution." *American Theatre*, 26.5. http://www.tcg.org/publications/at/mayjune09/belarus.cfm

Gentzler, Edwin and Tymoczko, Maria. 2002. "Introduction." In *Translation and Power*, edited by Maria Tymoczko and Edwin Gentzler, xi–xxviii. Amherst: University of Massachusetts Press.

Gibbels, Elisabeth. 2008. "Translators, the Tacit Censors." In *Translation and Censorship: Patterns of Communication and Interference,* edited by Eiléan Ní Chuilleanáin, Cormac Ó Cuilleanáin and David Parris, 57–75. Dublin: Four Courts Press.

Gooch, Steve. 1996. "Fatal Attraction." In *Stages of Translation: Translators on Translating for the Stage*, edited by David Johnston, 13–21. Bath: Absolute Classics.

Goetz-Stankiewicz, Marketa. 1979. *The Silenced Theatre: Czech Playwrights without a Stage*. Toronto, Buffalo, London: University of Toronto Press.

—. 1987. "Introduction." *The Vaněk Plays. Four Authors, One Character*, edited by Marketa Goetz-Stankiewicz, xv–xxix. Vancouver: University of British Columbia Press.

—. 1992. *Good-bye Samizdat. Twenty Years of Czechoslovak Underground Writing*, edited by Marketa Goetz-Stankiewicz. Evanston: Northwestern University Press.

—. 1999. "Variations of Temptation—Václav Havel's Politics of Language." In *Critical Essays on Václav Havel*, edited by Marketa Goetz-Stankiewicz and Phyllis Carey, 228–40. New York: G.K. Hall.

Gollob, David and Roper, David. 1994. "Trad Tom Pops In." In *Tom Stoppard in Conversation*, edited by Paul Delaney, 150–66. Ann Arbor: University of Michigan.

Grossman, Jan. 1967. "A Preface to Havel." *The Tulane Drama Review*, 11.3: 117–20.

Gussow, Mel. 1994. "*Jumpers* Author is Verbal Gymnast." In *Tom Stoppard in Conversation*, edited by Paul Delaney, 73–6. Ann Arbor: University of Michigan.

Hare, David. 1996. "Pirandello and Brecht." In *Stages of Translation: Translators on Translating for the Stage*, edited by David Johnston, 137–43. Bath: Absolute Classics.

Havel, Václav. 1978. *Sorry . . .* Translated by Vera Blackwell. London: Eyre Methuen.

—. 1980. *The Memorandum*. Translated by Vera Blackwell. New York: Grove.

—. 1986a. *Largo Desolato*. Translated by Marie Winn. Unpublished script.

—. 1986b. "Author's Comments about the play *Largo Desolato*." Unpublished.

—. 1988. *Letters to Olga. June 1979–September 1982*. Translated by Paul Wilson. New York: Knopf.

—. 1989. *Living in Truth*, edited by Jan Vladislav. Translated by Paul Wilson and E. Kohák. London: Faber and Faber.

—. 1990. *Disturbing the Peace*. A Conversation with Karel Hvížd'ala. Translated by Paul Wilson. New York: Knopf.

—. 1993. *The Garden Party and Other Plays*. Translated by Vera Blackwell, Jan Novák and George Theiner. New York: Grove.

—. 1994. *Selected Plays 1984–1987*. Translated by Tom Stoppard, George Theiner and James Saunders with Marie Winn. London: Faber and Faber.

—. 1997. *The Art of the Impossible. Politics as Morality in Practice. Speeches and Writings 1990–1996*. Translated by Paul Wilson. New York: Knopf.

—. 1999:2. *Hry, Spisy 2*. Prague: Torst.

—. 1999:4. *Eseje a jiné texty z let 1970–1989, Spisy 4*. Prague: Torst.

—. 2001. *The Beggar's Opera*. Translated by Paul Wilson. Ithaca: Cornell University Press.

—. 2007a. *To the Castle and Back*. Translated by Paul Wilson. New York: Knopf.

—. 2007b. *Projevy a jiné texty 1999–2006. Prosím stručně. Odcházení, Spisy 8*. Prague: Torst.

—. 2008. *Leaving*. Translated by Paul Wilson. London: Faber and Faber.

Hale, Terry and Upton, Carole-Anne, eds. 2000. *Moving Target. Theatre Translation and Cultural Relocation*. Manchester: St Jerome.

Hamšík, Dušan. 1971. *Writers against Rulers*. Translated by D. Orpington. New York: Random House.

Heaney, Seamus. 2000. *Diary of One Who Vanished. A Song Cycle by Leoš Janáček of Poems by Ozef Kalda*. New York: Farrar, Strauss, Giroux.

—. 2002. "Through-Other Places, Through-Other Times." In *Finders Keepers. Selected Prose 1971–2002*, 364–82. London: Faber and Faber.

Heylen, Romy, 1993. *Translation, Poetics, and the Stage. Six French Hamlets*. London and New York: Routledge.

Hill, Leslie. 1997. "Up the Republic!: Beckett, Writing, Politics." *MLN*, 112.5: 909–28.

Holquist, Michael. 1994. "Corrupt Originals. The Paradox of Censorship." *PMLA*, 109.1: 14–25.

Holý, Jiří. 2010. *Writers under Siege. Czech Literature since 1945*. Brighton, Portland, Toronto: Sussex Academic Press.

Houchin, John. 2003. *Censorship of the American Theater in the Twentieth Century*. Cambridge: Cambridge University Press.

—. 2000. "Hair: The Legal Legacy." *Journal of American Drama and Theater*, 12.2: 25–37.

Hubner, Zygmunt. 1992. *Theater and Politics*. Evanston: Northwestern University Press.

Huggan, Graham. 2001. *The Postcolonial Exotic. Marketing the Margins*. London and New York: Routledge.

Imison, Richard. 1991. "Radio and the Theater: A British Perspective." *Theatre Journal*, 43.3: 289–92.

Isherwood, Charles. 2010. "A Leader Waits to Learn When to Leave the Stage." *New York Times*. June 9. www.theater.nytimes.com/2010/06/09/theater/reviews/09leaving.html.

Jansen, Sue Curry. 1991. *Censorship. The Know that Binds Power and Knowledge*. Oxford: Oxford University Press.

—. 2010. "Ambiguities and Imperatives of Market Censorship: The Brief History of a Critical Concept." *Westminster Papers in Communication and Culture*, 7.2: 12–30.

Johnston, David. 1996. "Theatre Pragmatics." In *Stages of Translation: Translators on Translating for the Stage*, edited by David Johnston, 57–66. Bath: Absolute Classics.

Kafka, Franz. 1998. *The Castle*. Translated by Mark Harman. New York: Schocken.

Keane, John. 1991. *The Media and Democracy*. Cambridge: Polity.

—. 2000. *Václav Havel. A Political Tragedy in Six Acts*. London: Bloomsbury.

Kelly, Katherine E. "Introduction: Tom Stoppard in Transformation." In *The Cambridge Companion to Tom Stoppard*, edited by Katherine E. Kelly, 10–22. Cambridge: Cambridge University Press.

Klaidman, Stephen. 1968. "Czech Writer, Here, Sees Opportunity for Liberals." *New York Times*, May 5. http://select.nytimes.com/gst/abstract.html?res=FA0 C13FD3F5E1A7B93C7A9178ED85F4C8685F9&scp=2&sq=klaidman%20 czech%20writer&st=cse

Krebs, Katja. 2007. "Anticipating Blue Lines: Translational Choices as Sites of (Self)-Censorship. Translating for the British Stage under the Lord Chamberlain." In *Modes of Censorship and Translation: National Contexts and Diverse Media*, edited by Francesca Billiani, 167–86. Manchester: St Jerome.

Kriseová, Edá. 1993. *Václav Havel. The Authorized Biography*. Translated by Caleb Crain. New York: St Martin's Press.

Kundera, Milan. 1985. *The Unbearable Lightness of Being*. Translated by Michael Henry Heim. London: Faber and Faber.

—. 1990. "A Life Like a Work of Art." *New Republic*, January 29, 16–17.

—. 1996. *Testaments Betrayed*. Translated by Linda Asher. London: Faber and Faber.

Laufe, Abe. 1978. *The Wicked Stage. A History of Theater Censorship and Harassment in the United States*. New York: Frederick Ungar.

Lefevere, André. 1992. *Translation, Rewriting and the Manipulation of Literary Fame*. London and New York: Routledge.

—. 1998. "Acculturating Bertolt Brecht." In *Constructing Cultures: Essays on Literary Translation*, edited by Susan Bassnett and André Lefevere, 109–22. Clevedon: Multilingual Matters.

Letts, Quentin, 2008. "Protest and Private View: Don't Give Up Your Day Job, Mr. President." *The Daily Mail*, November 13. www.dailymail.co.uk/tvshowbiz/reviews/article-1085525/Protest-Private-View-Dont-day-job-Mr-President.html.

Lyon, James K. 1980. *Bertolt Brecht in America*. Princeton: Princeton University Press.

Marranca, Bonnie, Rabkin, Gerald, and Birringer, Johannes. 1986. "The Controversial 1985–86 Theatre Season: A Politics of Reception." *Performing Arts Journal*, 10.1: 7–33.

Martinus, Eivor. 1996. "Translating Scandinavian Drama." In *Stages of Translation: Translators on Translating for the Stage*, edited by David Johnston, 109–21. Bath: Absolute Classics.

Merkle, Denise. 2002. "Presentation." *TTR: traduction, terminologie, redaction*, 15.2: 9–18.

Moore, Steven. 2010. *The Novel: An Alternative History. Beginnings to 1600*. New York and London: Continuum.

Mulvey, Laura. 2000. "Visual Pleasure and Narrative Cinema." In *Feminism and Film*, edited by E. Ann Kaplan, 34–47. Oxford and New York: Oxford University Press.

Neumann, Julek. 1994. "Shadows on the Stage: Indirect Theatre Censorship in Czechoslovakia, 1969–1989." *Comparative Criticism*, 16: 39–69.

Ní Chuilleanáin, Eiléan, Ó Cuilleanáin, Cormac, and Parris, David, eds. 2008. *Translation and Censorship: Patterns of Communication and Interference*. Dublin: Four Courts Press.

Orwell, George. 1954. "Politics and the English Language." In *A Collection of Essays*, edited by Sonia Brownell Orwell, 162–77. New York: Doubleday.

Owens, Craig N. 2003. "Applause and Hiss: Implicating the Audience in Samuel Beckett's 'Rockaby' and 'Catastrophe'." *The Journal of the Midwest Modern Language Association*, 36.1: 74–81.

Pavis, Patrice. 1989. "Problems of Translation for the Stage: Interculturalism and Post-Modern Theatre." Translated by Loren Kruger. In *The Play Out of Context: Transferring Plays from Culture to Culture*, edited by Hanna Scolnicov and Peter Holland, 25–44. Cambridge: Cambridge University Press.

Pontuso, James F. 2004. *Václav Havel. Civic Responsibility in the Postmodern Age*. Lanham, Boulder, New York, Toronto, Oxford: Rowman & Litttlefield.

Remnick, David. 2006. "Exit the Castle: Václav Havel." In *Reporting. Writing from the New Yorker*. New York: Vintage.

Reynolds, Matthew. 2007. "Semi-censorship in Dryden and Browning." In *Modes of Censorship and Translation: National Contexts and Diverse Media*, edited by Francesca Billiani, 187–204. Manchester: St Jerome.

Rich, Frank. 1986. "Largo Desolato, by Havel, at the Public." *New York Times*, March 26. www.theater.nytimes.com/mem/theater/treview.html?res=9A0DE2DE 123CF935A15750C0A960948260.

—. 1989. "The Asterisks of Oh! Calcutta!" *New York Times*, August 8, www.nytimes. com/1989/08/08/theater/critic-s-notebook-the-asterisks-of-oh-calcutta.html.

Rocamora, Carol. 2004. *Acts of Courage: Václav Havel's Life in the Theater*. Hanover: Smith and Kraus.

Sammells, Neil. 1992. "Introduction." In *Writing and Censorship in Britain*, edited by Paul Hyland and Neil Sammells, 1–14. London and New York: Routledge.

Sandbrook, Dominic. 2006. *Never Had it so Good. A History of Britain from Suez to the Beatles*. New York: Little, Brown.

Santaemilia, José, ed. 2005. *Gender, Sex and Translation. The Manipulation of Identities*. Manchester: St Jerome.

Schechner, Richard and Foreman, Richard. 1987. "Richard Foreman on Richard Foreman: An Interview." *The Drama Review: TDR*, 31.4: 125–35.

Shaked, Gershon. 1989. "The Play: Gateway to Cultural Dialogue." Translated by Jeffrey Green. In *The Play Out of Context: Transferring Plays from Culture to Culture*, edited by Hanna Scolnicov and Peter Holland, 7–24. Cambridge: Cambridge University Press.

Shellard, Dominic and Nicholson, Steve. 2004. *The Lord Chamberlain Regrets . . . A History of British Theatre Censorship*. London: The British Library.

Shulman, Milton. 1994. "The Politicizing of Tom Stoppard." In *Tom Stoppard in Conversation*, edited by Paul Delaney, 107–12. Ann Arbor, MI: University of Michigan Press.

Simon, Sherry. 1996. *Gender in Translation: Cultural Identity and the Politics of Transmission*. London and New York: Routledge, 1996.

Šmejkalová-Strickland, Jiřina. 1994. "Censoring Canons: Transitions and Prospects of Literary Institutions in Czechoslovakia." In *Administration of Aesthetics: Censorship, Political Criticism, and the Public Sphere*, edited by Richard Burt, 195–215. Minneapolis: University of Minnesota Press.

Špirk, Jaroslav. 2008. "Translation and Censorship in Communist Czechoslovakia." In *Translation and Censorship in Different Times and Landscapes*, edited by Teresa Seruya and Maria Lin Moniz, 215–28. Newcastle: Cambridge Scholars' Publishing.

Steiner, Peter. 2001. "Introduction." Translated by Paul Wilson. In *The Beggar's Opera*, ix–xxxi. Ithaca: Cornell University Press.

Stoppard, Tom. 1978. *Every Good Boy Deserves Favour and Professional Foul*. London: Faber and Faber.

Sturge, Kate. 2002. "Censorship of Translated Fiction in Nazi Germany." *TTR: traduction, terminologie, rédaction*, 15.2: 153–69.

Sullivan, Dan. 1968. "Nudity Moves into Center Stage." *New York Times*, April 25, 52.

Taban, Mandana and Woods, Michelle. 2006. "Analogy and Translatability: Iranian and Czech New Wave Film." In *Between and Betwixt: Place and*

Cultural Translation, edited by Ciaran Carson, David Johnston, and Stephen Kelly, 93–106. Newcastle: Cambridge Scholars' Publishing.

Trensky, Paul. 1978. *Czech Drama since World War II*. White Plains: Sharpe.

Turan, Kenneth and Papp, Joseph. 2010. *Free for All. Joe Papp, The Public and the Greatest Theater Story Ever Told*. New York: Anchor.

Tymoczko, Maria. 2007. *Enlarging Translation, Empowering Translators*. Manchester: St Jerome.

—. 2008. "Censorship and Self-Censorship in Translation: Ethics and Ideology, Resistance and Collusion." In *Translation and Censorship: Patterns of Communication and Interference*, edited by Eiléan Ní Chuilleanáin, Cormac Ó Cuilleanáin, and David Parris, 24–45. Dublin: Four Courts Press.

Tymoczko, Maria and Gentzler, Edwin, eds. 2002. *Translation and Power*. Amherst: University of Massachusetts Press.

Tynan, Kathleen. 1988. *The Life of Kenneth Tynan*. London: Methuen.

Tynan, Kenneth. 1967. "The Theatre Abroad: Prague." *The New Yorker*, April 1, 99–123.

—. 1979. *Show People. Profiles in Entertainment*. New York: Simon & Schuster.

—. 2008. *Theater Writings*. London: Nick Hern Books.

Venuti, Lawrence. 1998. *The Scandals of Translation. Towards an Ethics of Difference*. New York: Routledge.

—. 2008. *The Translator's Invisibility. A History of Translation*, 2nd edn. New York: Routledge.

Vivis, Anthony. 1996. "The Stages of a Translation." In *Stages of Translation: Translators on Translating for the Stage*, edited by David Johnston, 35–44. Bath: Absolute Classics.

Von Flotow, Luise. 1997. *Translation and Gender: Translating in the "Era of Feminism."* Manchester: St Jerome.

—. 2011. "Preface." *Translating Women*, edited by Luise von Flotow, 1–10. Ottawa: University of Ottawa Press.

Walton, Michael J. 2007. "Good Manners, Decorum and the Public Peace. Greek Drama and the Censor." In *Modes of Censorship and Translation: National Contexts and Diverse Media*, edited by Francesca Billiani, 143–66. Manchester: St Jerome.

Winn, Marie. 1987. "The Czechs' Defiant Playwright." *New York Times*. October 25. www.nytimes.com/1987/10/25/magazine/the-czechs-defiant-playwright.html.

—. 2011. Interview with Michelle Woods, 27 July.

Winton, Calhoun. 1992. "John Gay: Censoring the Censors." In *Writing and Censorship in Britain*, edited by Paul Hyland and Neil Sammells, 81–90. London and New York: Routledge.

Wolf, Michaela. 2002. "Censorship as Cultural Blockage: Banned Literature in the Late Habsburg Monarchy." *TTR: traduction, terminologie, rédaction*, 15:2: 45–61, Web.

Woods, Michelle. 2006. *Translating Milan Kundera*. Clevedon: Multilingual Matters.

Yagoda, Ben. 2001. *About Town. The New Yorker and the World it Made*. New York: Da Capo Press.

Zaitlin, Phyllis. 2005. *Theatrical Translation and Film Adaptation: A Practitioner's View*. Clevedon: Multilingual Matters.

—. 2007. "Robin Midgely." *The Times*. www.timesonline.co.uk/tol/comment/obituaries/article1842434.ece.

INDEX